A FIELD GUIDE TO
AUCKLAND

A FIELD GUIDE TO
AUCKLAND

Exploring the Region's
Natural and Historic Heritage

Ewen Cameron • Bruce Hayward
Graeme Murdoch

Acknowledgements

The authors thank their supportive families for their patience, sacrifices and support during the extended process of compiling and writing this book. We thank Jane Connor of Godwit for the original idea and for all her guidance and advice during its preparation.

All the photographs are taken by the authors with the following exceptions: Auckland War Memorial Museum Library, 69, 76 (top), 79, 90, 93, 153, 173, 179; Auckland Public Library, 80, 81, 82, 83, 86, 87, 91 (top); Auckland Regional Council, 109, 235, 259, 272; Chris Gaskin, 29; Roger Grace, 104; Jack Hobbs, 232; Tim Lovegrove, 48, 49; Brett McKay, 39, 42 (top), 52 (right), 97, 147, 261, 263; Grant Sheehan, 185

Maps and diagrams: Bill and Jonathan Paynter/Chris Gaskin, 10, 13, 15, 19, 27, 33, 36, 246; Jonette Surridge, 21, 98, 111, 126, 145, 163, 186, 195, 199, 234, 262. Painting on page 75 by Chris Gaskin, courtesy Nigel Prickett, Archaeologist, Auckland War Memorial Museum.

Published with the support of:
Auckland Regional Council
North Shore City Council

First published 1997 by
Godwit Publishing Ltd
15 Rawene Road, P.O. Box 34-683
Birkenhead, Auckland, New Zealand

ISBN 1 86962 014 3

Front cover photographs (clockwise from top left): Mangere Mountain; The Pumphouse, Takapuna; gannet colony, Muriwai Regional Park; pohutukawa in flower.
Back cover photograph: Waharau Stream.
Opposite title page: Pakiri Beach.

Design and production: Jane Connor and Sarah Bowden
Colour separation and film output: Spectra Graphics
Printed in Singapore

Contents

About this Book

The first part of this book contains introductory essays on the region's natural and historic heritage. These are intended to provide the background to help readers better understand the specific detail on various sites given in the second part.

The main part of the book is a selection of 140 publicly accessible localities that contain the best examples of the region's rich natural and historic heritage.These places have been grouped into six geographic areas and are presented under the headings: North, North Shore, West, Central, South and Islands.

A map of each area shows the location of sites. Each location has been given a unique number and this is used to refer to it throughout the book.

Site entries contain a brief description of how to get there and list the main facilities available. For further information, contact the administering agency or owners:

Auckland Regional Parks. All 16 are included. These are administered by the Auckland Regional Council Parks Dept. Dogs are prohibited from most parks as many run farm stock or protect sensitive wildlife populations. Information can be obtained by telephoning 303 1530, or by visiting their information centres in Regional House, Pitt St or at Arataki (**49**) on the Scenic Drive.

Walkways. All those in the region are included. Some cross sections of privately owned land that may be closed in spring during lambing. Dogs are prohibited from all walkways. Walkways are administered by the Department of Conservation. A leaflet describing them is available from their information centre in the Ferry Building, at the foot of Queen St (**76**).

Hauraki Gulf Maritime Park. This includes most of the islands mentioned (except Waiheke). These reserves are administered by the Department of Conservation. Additional information can be obtained by telephoning 379 6476, or from their information centre in the Ferry Building (**76**).

Local body reserves. A number of the sites described are administered by the Parks and Reserves department of the local council. Many have information pamphlets available. Contact details are:

Rodney District Council, Centreway Rd, Orewa, ph. 426 5169
North Shore City Council, The Strand, Takapuna, ph. 486 8400
Waitakere City Council, 6 Waipareira Ave, Henderson, ph. 836 8000
Auckland City Council, 16 Wellesley St, ph. 379 2020
Manukau City Council, 31 Wiri Station Rd, Manukau, ph. 263 7100
Papakura District Council, 35 Coles Cres, Papakura, ph. 299 8870
Franklin District Council, 82 Manukau Rd, Pukekohe, ph. 09 237 1300

Historic buildings and museums. These are administered by a wide range of local bodies, historical societies or are privately owned. The New Zealand Historic Places Trust Office administers several (Auckland Regional Office, ph. 307 1538).

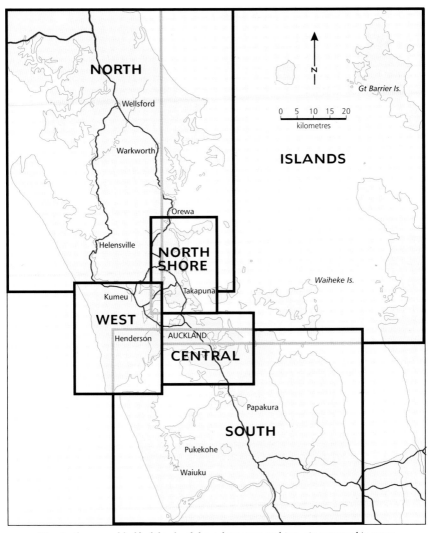

Sites in the second half of this book have been grouped into six geographic areas.

Further Reading

Geology and Landforms

A Natural History of Auckland, J.E. Morton (ed.), David Bateman, 1993.

Ancient Undersea Volcanoes: A Guide to the Geological Formations at Muriwai, West Auckland, B.W. Hayward, Geological Society of NZ Guidebook, no. 3, 1979.

City of Volcanoes, E.J. Searle, Longman Paul, 1964 & 1981.

Fountains of Fire: The Story of Auckland's Volcanoes, G.J. Cox, Collins, 1989.

Geology of the Auckland Urban Area, L.O. Kermode, Institute of Geological & Nuclear Sciences, 1992.

Volcanoes and Giants, B.W. Hayward and B.J. Gill, Auckland Institute & Museum, 1994.

Walks through Auckland's Geological Past: A Guide to the Geological Formations of Rangitoto, Motutapu and Motuihe Islands, P.F. Ballance & I.E.M. Smith, Geological Society of NZ Guidebook, no. 5, 1982.

Plants and Animals

A Guide to the New Zealand Seashore, D. Gunson, Viking Pacific, 1983.

A Natural History of Auckland, J.E. Morton (ed.), Bateman, 1993.

Between the Tides: New Zealand Seashore and Estuary Life, M. Bradstock, Reed Methuen, 1985.

Common Insects in New Zealand, D. Miller & A.K. Walker, Reed, 1984.

Common Names of Plants in New Zealand, E.R. Nicol, Manaaki Whenua Press, 1997.

Field Guide to the Birds of New Zealand, B.H. & H. Robertson, Viking, 1996.

Margins of the Sea: Exploring New Zealand's Coastline, R. Cometti & J.E. Morton, Hodder & Stoughton, 1985.

New Zealand Ferns and Allied Plants, P.J. Brownsey & J.C. Smith-Dodsworth, Bateman, 1989.

New Zealand Frogs & Reptiles, B.J. Gill & A.H. Whitaker, Bateman, 1996.

Seaweeds of New Zealand: An Illustrated Guide, N.M. Adams, Canterbury University Press, 1994.

The Botany of Auckland: A Book for all Seasons, L.M. Cranwell, Auckland Institute & Museum, 1981.

The Native Trees of New Zealand, J.T. Salmon, Reed, 1990.

The New Zealand Sea Shore, J.E. Morton & M.C. Miller, Collins, 1978.

Trees and Shrubs of New Zealand, L. Poole & N. Adams, DSIR Publishing, 1990.

History

Auckland City Life: A Celebration of Yesteryear, D. Johnson, David Bateman Ltd, 1991.

Auckland's South Eastern Bulwark: A History of the Hunua Ranges, I. Barton, Published by the author, 1978.

Digging up the Past: New Zealand's Archaeological History, B. McCulloch & M. Trotter, Viking, 1997.

Early Days in Franklin, N. Morris & Percy Salmon, Wills & Grainger Ltd, 1965.

Maori Auckland, D.R. Simmons, The Bush Press, 1987.

Old Manukau, A.E. Tonson, Tonson Publishing House, 1966.

Once the Wilderness, J.T. Diamond, The Lodestar Press, 1977.

The History of Howick and Pakuranga, A. La Roche, Howick & Districts Historical Society, 1991.

The Rock and The Sky: The Story of Rodney County, H. Mabbett, Wilson & Horton, 1977.

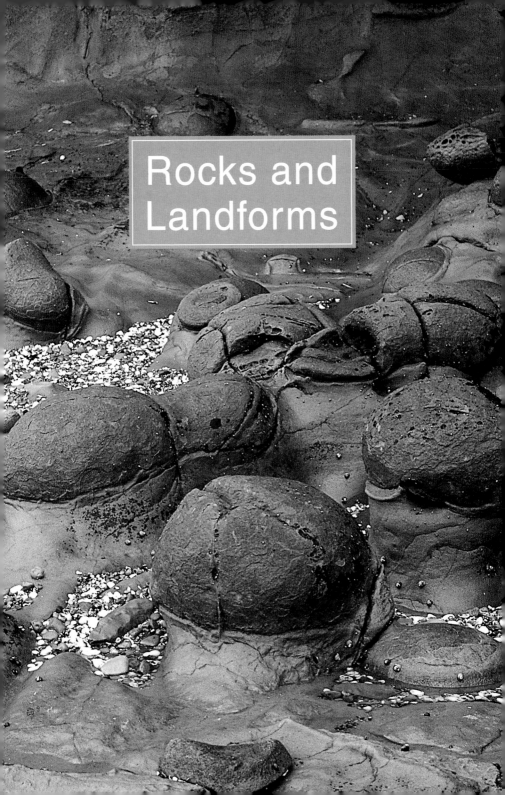

Rocks and Landforms

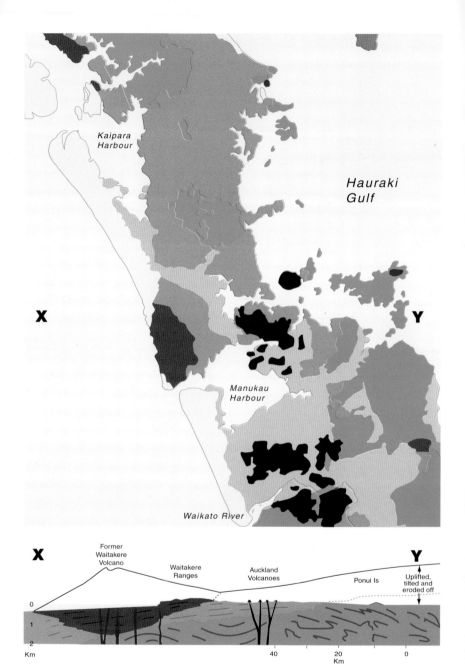

Geological map of the Auckland region showing where the various types of rocks occur at the surface today. Cross-section shows their relationship at depth.

Time line for the Auckland region

Years ago		Geological periods
6500	Present coastline formed	

Million years ago		
0–0.15	Auckland volcanoes erupted	
0.5–1.5	Franklin volcanoes erupted	
0–2	Yo-yo sea levels of the Ice Ages with young coastal sand dunes deposited and young river plain, swamp & mudflat sediments deposited	**Quaternary**
1.5–3	Little Barrier strato-volcano erupted	
2–3	Hauraki Gulf & Firth of Thames subside	**Pliocene**
3–5	Auckland region uplifted & tilted to the west	
5–16	Auckland region eroded to a low-lying plain	
8–15	Basalt, andesite & rhyolite volcanoes erupted at Leigh, Waiheke & Great Barrier	
15–16	Auckland region uplifted out of sea	
15–22	Waitakere & Kaipara volcanoes' andesite erupted (flows, intrusions, conglomerate)	**Miocene**
18–22	Waitemata Sandstones deposited (in Waitemata Basin)	
20	Sub-seafloor failure of displaced older rocks on northern slopes of Waitemata Basin	
22–25	Ocean floor rocks displaced onto Northland (Northland Allochthon)	
30–100	Auckland region eroded to a low-lying plain	**Oligocene**
55–80	Tasman Sea opened and New Zealand formed	
100–140	Uplift forms mountains on coast of Gondwanaland	**Cretaceous**
140–250	Ancient greywacke rocks accumulate in sea off coast of Gondwanaland	**Jurassic–Triassic**

*Page 9: Concretions in early Miocene Waitemata Sandstone on the coast of Musick Point (**105**).*

Rocks and Landforms

The long and complicated history of Auckland's origins is stored in the landforms and rocks of the region and can be easily read and enjoyed once it is pointed out. While the story of the underlying rocks stretches back 250 million years to the early part of the Age of Dinosaurs, the shape and landforms of our region were formed in just the last few million years and are still being modified today.

The Young Volcanoes of Auckland and Franklin (0–1.5 million years ago)

Auckland is not only the city of sails but also the city of volcanoes. Many of the landforms and soils of Auckland, North Shore and Manukau Cities are the product of volcanism in just the last 150,000 years. Much of the Franklin District, to the south of Auckland, was shaped by similar volcanic activity 0.5–1.5 million years ago.

The magma that fed Auckland's and Franklin's volcanoes originated some 100 km below the surface. Periodically a large 'bubble' of molten magma rose up through the denser overlying rocks to erupt at the earth's surface as a volcano.

Each volcano was formed during a single eruption, or short sequence of eruptions, generally lasting no longer than a year or two, although it is possible for a scoria cone or tuff ring to form in a matter of days. Once eruptions had ceased, the magma in the subsurface plumbing solidified so the volcano never erupted again. Franklin's volcanic field is extinct, but a new volcano in the Auckland field is likely sometime in the future.

Pukaki Lagoon explosion crater, near the airport, is surrounded by a low tuff ring.

Styles of eruption

Three styles of eruption built the small basalt volcanoes of Auckland and Franklin. Each style produced a different type of rock and a different kind of landform. While some volcanoes were created by only one style of eruption, many were built by a combination of all three. The style of eruption at any particular time depends on how much gas is dissolved in the magma, the rate of magma upwelling, and whether it comes in contact with water.

Most volcanoes started life with a series of explosive eruptions. These occur when rising magma encounters ground or surface water, which produces superheated steam. Gases dissolved in the magma are released explosively with the steam, and a mushroom-shaped cloud of ash and shattered rock from the volcano's throat is thrown hundreds of metres into the air. A shallow explosion crater, up to 2 km across and 100 m deep, is formed, and debris from the collapsing cloud builds up a low, circular rim of bedded ash and debris, known as a tuff ring.

Lava-fountaining eruptions occur when gas-rich magma reaches the surface without coming into contact with water. The gas is released quickly, creating frothy lava that is sprayed from the vent as a near-continuous stream of brightly glowing fragments. As they fly, the fragments cool to form red-brown scoria, which accumulates around the vent and builds up a steep-sided scoria cone, often with a deep central crater.

Lava flows develop when degassed magma rises in the vent and bursts out from the base of the cone or breaches the crater rim. Rivers of lava initially flow off down

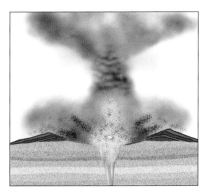

Three styles of eruption formed the volcanic landforms of the Auckland and Franklin fields. Top: Explosive eruptions produced wide explosion craters with surrounding tuff rings. Middle: Fire-fountaining produced steep-sided scoria cones. Bottom: The quiet extrusion of lava flows.

existing valleys, but if the outpouring continues, a sequence of overlapping flows may be erupted, building up a cone, called a shield volcano, that gently slopes away in all directions. When lava flows cool they solidify into a hard, dark, fine-grained rock, called basalt. This has been used extensively in Auckland for kerb stones and many older buildings.

There are only two shield volcanoes in the Auckland field — One Tree Hill (**85**) and Rangitoto (**132**) — and both are capped by steep-sided scoria cones. Far more lava flows were erupted in the Franklin field, with at least 16 shield volcanoes developing. Typical examples are the twin-peaked Bombay shield volcano and the large, gently sloping Pukekohe volcano (**124**).

Thick basalt lava flows cool slowly and as they solidify they contract, producing vertical shrinkage cracks with characteristic polygonal columns. This exceptional example in an old quarry face behind Mt Eden jail is now the training ground for Auckland's rock climbers.

Auckland Volcanoes

Auckland is built on an active field of 48 small volcanoes, all of which have erupted in the last 150,000 years. Five of the volcanoes, including Lake Pupuke (**33**) and the Domain (**80**), are believed to have erupted prior to 50,000 years ago, but the majority erupted 10,000–50,000 years ago. The two youngest are Mt Wellington (**92**) at about 9000 years old and Rangitoto (**132**), which erupted in the middle of the Waitemata Harbour just 600 years ago.

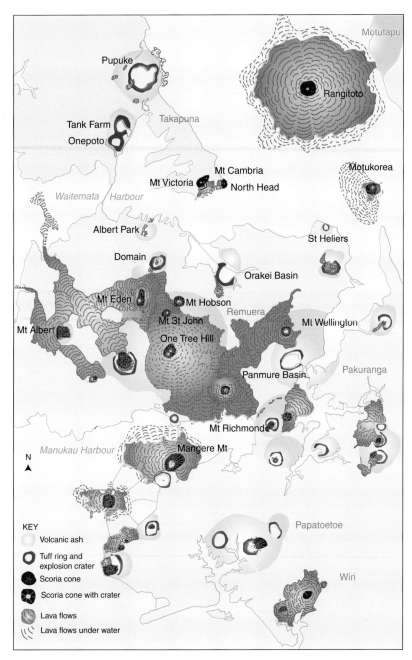

Map of Auckland volcanic field, active during the last 150,000 years.

KEY

- Volcanic ash
- Tuff ring and explosion crater
- Scoria cone
- Scoria cone with crater
- Lava flows
- Lava flows under water

Pupuke
Tank Farm
Onepoto
Takapuna
Motutapu
Rangitoto
Mt Cambria
Mt Victoria
North Head
Motukorea
Waitemata Harbour
Albert Park
Domain
St Heliers
Orakei Basin
Mt Eden
Mt Hobson
Remuera
Mt St John
One Tree Hill
Mt Wellington
Mt Albert
Panmure Basin
Pakuranga
Mt Richmond
Mangere Mt
Manukau Harbour
Papatoetoe
Wiri

N

View from the top of One Tree Hill over some of Auckland's young volcanoes, including Mt Hobson (left), North Head (centre) and the youngest, Rangitoto Island (right).

Auckland's volcanoes erupted onto a landscape of lush kauri and broadleaf forest. In the vicinity of each volcano, this forest was stripped, flattened, burned or buried. In several places today, fossilised remains of these forests tell the story of their destruction (**34**, **101**).

When the first humans arrived in Auckland, most of the lava-flow fields were covered in scattered, rubbly basalt blocks sticking out of the young volcanic soils beneath a dense forest cover (**82**). The forests were burned and the rocks cleared into heaps and rows as prehistoric gardens were created. Later in early European times, the rocks on the lava-flow fields were further cleared and used to build drystone walls between farm paddocks. The pasture has long since been subdivided into suburban housing, but in many places remnants of these stone walls still form boundary fences or have been transformed into retaining walls for gardens.

The scoria cones and lava flows provided the only source of hard rock within easy reach of the growing settlement of Auckland. Over the years dozens of quarries have actively nibbled, bitten and gulped at our volcanic heritage to satisfy the city's endless demand for building aggregate, road metal and solid fill. Dense basalt rock is obtained from Auckland's lava flows and its removal has generally had less impact on our landscape than the quarrying of scoria, which is only available from our volcanic cones. The solid basalt was used in most of our early stone buildings, such as the Melanesian

Mission House (**88**), St Pauls and St Andrews in Symonds Street (**75**), and Mt Eden Prison. Prisoners quarried basalt lava from a Mt Eden flow to make the basalt kerb stones seen throughout Auckland.

Quarrying of scoria from Auckland's cones has been going on since early European times. It is cheap to extract, needing no blasting or crushing. Being frothy and light, it is also much cheaper to transport than denser rock. Thus scoria has been used as the cheapest source of road metal and clean fill throughout the city. NZ Railways quarried away Mt Smart and large portions of Wiri Mountain and Mt Albert to obtain scoria for railway-line ballast throughout the northern North Island.

*The remnants of a broadleaf–podocarp forest, devastated by the explosive eruption of Maungataketake Volcano, are exposed near Auckland Airport (**101**). Here the base of a tree still stands where it was buried by volcanic ash c. 30,000 years ago and is now being exposed by erosion of the cliffs.*

*Below: Layers of volcanic ash exposed in the eroding cliffs of North Head's tuff ring (**39**). They were thrown out by the volcano's early explosive eruptions. Small blocks of dark basalt rock and light-coloured Waitemata Sandstone, ripped from the walls of the volcano's throat, are clearly visible.*

Franklin Volcanoes

The Franklin field contains 80 identified volcanoes, which erupted 0.5–1.5 million years ago. This volcanic field stretches from Papakura (**120**) in the north to Pukekawa on the south side of the Waikato River, and from the Hunua Falls (**121**) in the east almost to Waiuku in the west. The bulk of onions, cabbages and other vegetables that Aucklanders consume are grown in the rich, red volcanic soils that have developed in the weathered volcanic ash and lava flows from these volcanoes, particularly in the Bombay and Pukekohe areas (**124**).

Because they are much older than Auckland's volcanoes, the Franklin examples are more eroded and weathered and a little more difficult to recognise. The scoria of the cones is deeply weathered, the cones themselves are more rounded than those in Auckland city, and their craters are generally partly filled and less distinct. The soft ash forming many of the tuff rings in Franklin has been partly eroded away, leaving numerous incomplete arc-shaped ridges behind. At Hunua Falls (**121**), erosion has removed most of the volcano and the solid basalt plug that fills the throat is virtually all that remains.

The gently sloping 1-million-year-old Bombay shield volcano viewed from the north. Its weathered rocks provide rich red soils for horticulture.

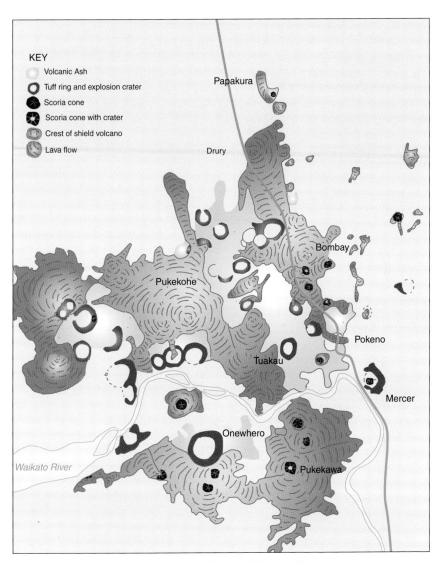

KEY

- Volcanic Ash
- Tuff ring and explosion crater
- Scoria cone
- Scoria cone with crater
- Crest of shield volcano
- Lava flow

Papakura

Drury

Pukekohe

Bombay

Pokeno

Tuakau

Mercer

Onewhero

Pukekawa

Waikato River

Map of Franklin volcanic field, active 0.5–1.5 million years ago.

Ice Ages and the Shape of the Coast
(0–2 million years ago)

The world has experienced alternating periods of cold and warm climate during the Ice Ages of the last few million years. These cyclical climate fluctuations have been driven by variations in the amount of solar energy reaching different parts of the earth's surface, due to the changing position of the earth's axis in its path around the sun.

There have been at least 30 of these cold-warm cycles in the last 2 million years. Each cycle lasted 40,000–100,000 years and included a warm period similar to the present day and a cold or glacial period when large ice caps formed on northern hemisphere continents. These ice caps froze large amounts of the world's water on land and resulted in major world-wide drops in sea level of 100-150 m during each Ice Age period. Sea level has only been up at around its present level during the peaks of the warmer periods, for about 10 percent of the time in the last 2 million years. It has probably never risen more than 5 m higher than what it is today.

During the coldest part of the Last Ice Age, just 18,000 years ago, sea level fell to 110–120 m lower than at present. At that time, glaciers and snowfields covered the mountains throughout the South Island and southern North Island, but here in the north the Auckland region was still covered in forest. Today's harbours were forested valleys with streams flowing seaward across the broad coastal plain. In Auckland, a small river flowed down the forested Waitemata Valley and straight out past the Motutapu hills

The Tamaki Estuary, bisecting Auckland's eastern suburbs, is a typical example of a river drowned by the rising sea level 6500–8000 years ago.

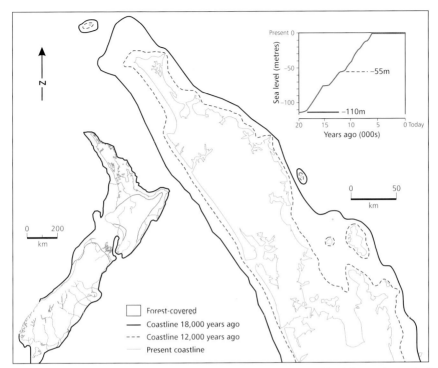

Map showing the location of the coastline around Northland and Auckland during the peak of the Last Ice Age (18,000 years ago), and as sea level rose with a warming climate until it reached its present height 6500 years ago.

through the area now occupied by Rangitoto. From there it still had 120 km to flow before reaching the coast out beyond Great Barrier Island.

Following the peak of the Last Ice Age, the world's climate began to warm, the ice caps slowly melted, and the world's sea level rose correspondingly. Sea level reached its present level about 6500 years ago, although a slightly warmer period about 5000 years ago resulted in a temporary rise to nearly 1 m above what it is now (**116, 117**).

The cycles of wildly fluctuating sea levels had a major impact on the shape of the world's coasts. During each of the Ice Age periods, erosion on land was greatly increased because of reduced forest cover. Sediment poured down the rivers and was spread along the coasts by longshore drift. In northern New Zealand large volumes of volcanic ash and sand were erupted and eroded from the Taupo and Bay of Plenty region. This sediment was carried down the Waikato River to the west coast and at times into the Hauraki Gulf via the Waikato's alternative route through the Hauraki Plains.

At the end of the Last Ice Age the rising sea encroached over the land and the sand that had built up along the coast was swept shoreward. Shallow valleys that flowed out across the former coastal plain were drowned and rapidly filled with sediment. For

Most of our coastal cliffs began forming only about 6500 years ago. Those in softer rocks, like these Waitemata Sandstones north of Waiwera (18), have eroded back as much as 100 m or more in that short time.

several thousand years after the sea reached its present level, vast quantities of sand were thrown up against the land to form beaches, barriers and dunes. Where there was a plentiful supply, whole valleys were filled or large sand barriers created, enclosing estuaries and shallow harbours, as at Mangawhai Heads, Omaha, Wenderholm (**17**), and Orewa sand spits.

Where there was less sand available, the river valleys were drowned to become our modern embayed coastline and harbours. The meandering and branching shape of these former river valleys is still recognisable in the extensive headwaters of places like the Mahurangi, Kaipara, Manukau and Waitemata Harbours, and Tamaki Estuary.

Most of the cliffs around our modern coast are very young and have been eroded out of the sloping hillsides in the last 6500 years. The Waitemata Sandstone cliffs around Auckland are eroding back at rates of 1–5 cm per year. The intertidal reefs in front of them, extending up to 100 m out to sea, are an indication of the amount of cliff retreat since sea level rose. Some of the higher cliffs in harder rocks, such as those along the Waitakere's west coast, would have been carved back during periods of higher sea level and became frittering inland bluffs during the intervening Ice Age intervals.

Today our youthful coast is still changing, in places eroding and elsewhere growing, as nature continues to respond to the post-Ice Age rise in sea level and to the variable patterns of winds, waves and currents.

Western Sand-dune Barriers
(0–2 million years ago)

The origins of the Manukau and Kaipara Harbours go back about 2 million years. Prior to this they were large embayments wide open to the Tasman Sea. But this was to change as the supply of sand off the west coast rapidly increased. Large quantities of white quartz and pumice sand were carried down the Waikato River from the earliest large volcanic eruptions in the centre of the North Island, and this was mixed with black titanomagnetite (magnetic iron oxide) sand swept up the west coast by longshore drift from erosion of ash layers from Mt Taranaki's volcanic ancestors around New Plymouth. The sand was thrown up on the beaches and blown inland as a series of coastal dunes, which gradually built up to form the Manukau and Kaipara barriers, creating the two harbours (**21, 23, 131**). Over time an almost straight western coastline of high coastal sand-dune barriers was formed, linking together the more erosion-resistant rocky promontories at Waipoua, Waitakere Ranges and south of Port Waikato.

Dark lignite and mud layers within the sand-dune sequences tell of the temporary presence of dune lakes and swamps, and the growth of forests over the older stabilised dunes. Occasionally we see logs and stumps of trees that were killed and buried by further advancing dunes.

Since the Manukau sand-dune barrier started forming, the bay in behind has largely filled with rhyolitic ash and alluvium brought down the Waikato River after huge ignimbritic eruptions in the Taupo-Rotorua areas. Low white cliffs of this rhyolitic sediment are present in many places around the Manukau Harbour and nearby Tamaki Estuary (**103**) today.

*Manukau South Head (**131**) is the northern end of a sand-dune barrier, which built up over the last 2 million years creating the harbour in behind.*

Uplift, Erosion and Local Eruptions
(2–16 million years ago)

Around 16 million years ago, forces deep within the earth pushed the Auckland region upwards out of the sea. The ancient Waitakere Volcano initially stood as a high sentinel out to the west, with somewhat lower hills over Auckland city (uplifted Waitemata Sandstones). By about 5 million years ago both had been eroded down to an extensive coastal and subtidal plain.

From 16 to about 3 million years ago, dry land extended right across to the Coromandel Peninsula and Great Barrier Island, where a line of large andesitic and rhyolitic volcanoes were periodically erupting. Eroded remnants of the westernmost of these andesitic volcanoes form the top of Stony Batter (**137**) at the far east end of Waiheke Island. Around 10 million years ago, there were also small eruptions of basalt lava flows in the north of the Auckland region. Their eroded remains form Ti Point and several other promontories near Leigh.

Around 3–5 million years ago, the Hauraki Gulf area was forced upwards, tilting the Coromandel region to the east and the Auckland region to the west. The eastern parts of Auckland were pushed up much further than those in the west and the resulting erosion has removed a greater thickness of rocks from the east. Indeed in places, such as around Leigh (**7**) and Omana (**110**), the entire 1.5 km thickness of the underlying Waitemata Sandstones (formed 15 million years previously) has been stripped off, exposing the older greywacke rocks beneath. Virtually all the sandstones have also been eroded off the top of the Hunua Ranges, which was pushed up higher than other parts of the region.

The westerly tilting of the Auckland region resulted in more runoff flowing west than east. This is still reflected in the drainage pattern around Wellsford, where west-flowing Hoteo River drains most of this sector of the peninsula, almost as far across as Pakiri.

*Little Barrier Island, seen here from Great Barrier (**140**), is an isolated andesite stratovolcano that erupted in the subsiding Hauraki Gulf graben between 1.5 and 3 million years ago. It still retains some of its volcanic shape, with a steep-sided central cone surrounded by gently sloping ring-plain remnants.*

From a distance the Waitakere Ranges appear to have a flat top that is gently tilted down to the north-west. This is the remains of the uplifted coastal plain, which here is underlain by more resistant volcanic rocks and therefore has not been completely eroded away. Its shape is still preserved in the flat tops of the higher ridges.

Following the up-doming of the Hauraki Gulf area, it dramatically subsided about 2–3 million years ago, to form the elongate, fault-bounded Gulf, Firth of Thames and Hauraki Plains.

The flat top of the Waitakere Ranges (skyline) is the eroded remains of a coastal plain that was uplifted and gently tilted to the west about 3–5 million years ago.

Submerged Beneath the Ocean
(16–22 million years ago)

The most common rocks in the region are layered sandstone and mudstone (known as Waitemata Sandstones). These accumulated on the floor of a deep marine depression (called the Waitemata Basin) that covered Auckland during the early Miocene period, 16–22 million years ago. The Waitemata Sandstones have since been uplifted and today form the cliffs around the shores of the northern Manukau Harbour (**96**), Waitemata Harbour (**89**), East Coast Bays (**35**), Whangaparaoa (**24**), Mahurangi Harbour (**13**) and up the coast to Pakiri (**5**). Inland the layered rocks can be seen in numerous road cuts from Whitford and Manurewa in the south to Dome Valley and Kaukapakapa in the north. In many parts of the region, these rocks have been exposed at the surface for many thousands of years and have weathered to clay-rich soils.

Basal Waitemata rocks

The Waitemata Basin began forming about 22 million years ago as the low-lying Auckland region subsided. The sea flooded the land, forming islands out of the low greywacke hills and ridges. Gravels and shelly sands were deposited on the beaches

and in shallow water around the rocky shore of these islands. These deposits, known as the basal Waitemata rocks, contain the fossilised remains of numerous shellfish, lampshells, sea eggs and corals. Today they can be seen draped over the ancient rocky shorelines along parts of the east coast, in places such as Mathesons Bay (**7**), Tawharanui (**9**), Kawau (**139**), Motutapu (**133**) and Motuihe (**135**) Islands, and Omana (**110**).

An early Miocene rocky coastline of sea stacks, cliffs and bays is buried beneath layers of shallow water, cobble and pebble conglomerate (basal Waitemata rocks), in the cliffs on the north-east side of Kawau Island.

Waitemata Basin

The region continued to subside, all the islands were submerged, and a marine basin, 1000–3000 m deep, was formed. This Waitemata Basin (which is unrelated to the modern Waitemata Harbour) became shallower to the north with the land beyond occupying most of the present-day Northland region. Erosion of this northern land produced sediment that was carried down rivers and streams to the coast, which lay in the vicinity of Wellsford. Large quantities of gravel, sand and mud that accumulated along the coastal shelf periodically became unstable and flowed in a slurry into the basin. This sediment was funnelled down submarine canyons and on reaching the gentler slopes of the basin floor, spread out to form undersea fans of sediment, rather like a delta at the mouth of a river.

Waitemata Sandstones

As the sediment flowed down into the basin, the larger clasts dropped out first, followed by progressively finer and finer grains. Thus these turbulent slurries, called turbidity currents, were responsible for depositing the 10 cm–3 m thick layers of sandstone.

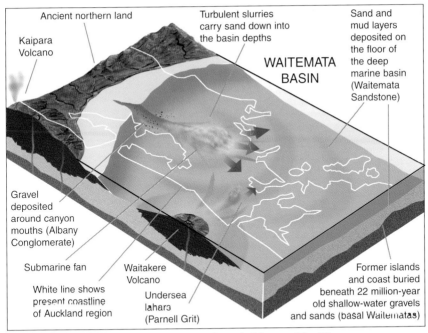

| Ancient northern land | Turbulent slurries carry sand down into the basin depths | Sand and mud layers deposited on the floor of the deep marine basin (Waitemata Sandstone) |

Kaipara Volcano

WAITEMATA BASIN

Gravel deposited around canyon mouths (Albany Conglomerate)

Submarine fan

White line shows present coastline of Auckland region

Waitakere Volcano

Undersea lahars (Parnell Grit)

Former islands and coast buried beneath 22 million-year old shallow-water gravels and sands (basal Waitematas)

Geography of the Auckland region in the early Miocene, 20 million years ago.

These layers grade upwards from coarse or medium sand at their base to fine sand or mud at the top. Between the sandstone layers there are usually 5–20 cm thick layers of soft, grey mudstone. These accumulated very slowly on the sea floor as mud settled out of suspension from the sea water overhead. Each sandstone was deposited in only a matter of hours, whereas the thinner mudstone layers accumulated during the periods of hundreds of years between each successive sediment flow.

During major floods on land, vast quantities of branches, twigs and leaves were swept down rivers into the Waitemata Basin. These became waterlogged and sank to the sea floor to form thin, black, woody layers, which can be seen in the cliffs in many places today.

Patterns like these are common in sandstones around Auckland (35, 59, 89, 105). They are the traces of animals that burrowed through the sediment soon after it was deposited on the floor of the Waitemata Basin, 20 million years ago.

Unusually thin beds of Waitemata sandstone and siltstone form cliffs at Orewa.

Close study of the Waitemata Sandstones often reveals numerous mud- or sand-filled meandering burrows (called trace fossils). These ancient burrows were made by worms or heart urchins that lived and fed in the sea-floor sediment.

During the 3–5 million years of the Waitemata Basin's existence, up to 1.5 km thickness of sand and mud accumulated on its floor. As the layers built up, they were compressed and hardened into the sandstone and mudstone we see today.

Albany Conglomerate

Cobbles and pebbles eroded from the northern land were also fed down the submarine canyons but were too heavy to be transported far out into the Waitemata Basin. They formed extensive sheets of gravel around the mouths of the canyons and at times choked and filled the canyons themselves. Today these ancient gravels (called Albany Conglomerate) can be seen in the Riverhead-Kaukapakapa area (**20**), where they are an important source of aggregate and road metal.

Parnell Grit

The western boundary of the Waitemata Basin was formed by the large and actively growing Waitakere Volcano, with a second large Kaipara Volcano near the top of the basin's north-western slopes. Occasionally volcano quakes loosened the sea floor high on the volcanoes' slopes, causing volcanic gravel and sand to slide eastwards down into the basin as undersea lahars. These deposited thick beds of darker-coloured volcanic sediment (called Parnell Grit) within the sequence of more normal Waitemata Sandstones. Examples can be seen today at Waiwera (**18**), Army Bay (**24**), Judges Bay (**77**), Waikowhai (**96**), Kaitarakihi (**59**), Motutapu (**133**) and Motuihe (**135**) Islands.

Folding and faulting

In many places, the layering we see in the Waitemata Sandstone cliffs is flat-lying or only gently tilted, but elsewhere the layers are broken, folded or crumpled. Much of the tight folding of layers seen within otherwise unfolded sequences was probably produced by minor sliding or slumping of the near-surface layers within a few thousand years of their deposition. An excellent example can be seen in Takapuna cliffs (**35**).

Giant sea-floor failure

Much of the deformation we see, however, is thought to have occurred when a huge volume of layered sediment (many kilometres across and hundreds of metres thick) on the northern slopes became unstable and slid up to 30 km southwards down into the Waitemata Basin as a giant sea-floor failure. Huge blocks of Waitemata Sandstones and underlying Northland Allochthon rocks piled up at the foot of the slope in the Silverdale-Orewa area and further sheets slid in behind them, partly riding up over the top of the ones in front.

Rocks displaced by this sea-floor failure form much of the inland area between Wellsford and Albany. This immense slide compressed and deformed the Waitemata Sandstones well beyond its limits and is thought to have produced the low-angle thrust faults and numerous zones of intense folding to be seen in places like the cliffs of Waiwera (**18**) and around Shakespear Regional Park (**24**).

*These contorted and folded strata of Waitemata Sandstone in the cliffs of Whangaparaoa Peninsula (**24**) are believed to have been deformed by a major sea-floor slide that slumped southwards down the northern slopes of the Waitemata Basin c.20 million years ago.*

Ancient Waitakere Volcano
(15–22 million years ago)

Forming the western boundary to the Waitemata Basin was an actively growing Waitakere Volcano, which was centred some 20 km offshore from the present west coast. It began erupting on the floor of the deep sea about the same time as the basin was subsiding, 22 million years ago. It eventually grew so big that its top pierced the waves and was capped by one or more volcanic islands. Over a period of 6–7 million years it built a 50-km-diameter, 3000-m-high volcano on the floor of the sea. It was similar in nature to our modern volcanoes of Ruapehu, Ngauruhoe and Tongariro, except that it grew to five or six times the size of all three of these volcanoes combined.

Eroded remnants

The modern Waitakere Ranges are the greatly eroded remnants of the eastern slopes of the huge Waitakere Volcano. Out to the west of the Waitakeres, beneath the continental shelf and slope, geophysicists have used seismic reflection profiling to detect and map the former extent of these old volcanic rocks. Now all that remains out there is the flattened-off footprint of a once majestic volcano, its former glory removed by millions of years of erosion by the incessantly pounding waves of the stormy Tasman.

Piha Conglomerate

Most of the west and central Waitakere Ranges today consist of weakly layered volcanic conglomerate and breccia (Piha Conglomerate) that had been swept down the sides of the growing volcano in undersea lahars of gravel, sand and water and came to rest on its submarine slopes. These rocks can be seen in the sea cliffs and inland bluffs from Whatipu to Te Henga along the Waitakeres' west coast (e.g. **47, 52, 53, 55, 56, 63**).

Weakly layered volcanic conglomerate (Piha Conglomerate) that accumulated on the upper submarine slopes of the Waitakere Volcano.

Nihotupu Sandstone

The eastern Waitakeres are made of beds of volcanic sandstone and mudstone (Nihotupu Sandstone) that interfinger with Piha Conglomerate beds. They accumulated around the lower eastern slopes of the volcano on the side of the Waitemata Basin. These rocks can be seen in road cuttings along parts of the Scenic Drive, in the Mokoroa (**42**), Waitakere (**48**) and Fairy Falls (**50**), and alongside the Upper Nihotupu Reservoir (**51**).

Submarine slides

Scattered throughout the Waitakeres are folded, contorted and mixed strata and blocks within the more consistently layered sequences. These record periodic rock slides down the volcano's submarine slopes. Examples can be seen in a road cutting near Arataki (**49**), and in cliffs at Whatipu (**63**) and Anawhata (**52**).

Pillow lava flows

Preserved within the sequences of Piha Conglomerate and Nihotupu Sandstone are a few, hard, dark grey, pillow lava flows formed by the cooling of lava that had spewed out into the sea on the volcano's slopes. When seen in cross-section in cliffs, these often appear to be composed of a pile of discrete pillow-like forms. As narrow lobes of hot lava are extruded into the cold sea water, their outsides are rapidly quenched, forming a black glassy skin around the flowing molten lava inside. The skin sometimes breaks and another lobe may branch off. Later, as the lava inside the lobe slowly cools to form rock, it contracts and distinctive radiating joints are formed. Examples of these pillow lava flows can be seen at Muriwai (**40**), Te Henga Beach (**47**) and Nihotupu Falls (**51**).

These narrow lobes of pillow lava were extruded onto the sea floor about 17 million years ago and are now exposed in the cliffs 1 km south of Muriwai (40).

Eruptions on the eastern flanks

As volcanic activity was drawing to a close about 16 million years ago, the Waitakere Volcano (and presumably also the Waitemata Basin) was pushed up out of the sea by enormous forces deep in the earth. Two lines of volcanic vents began erupting on the volcano's uplifted eastern flanks. The remnants of one line of vents now lie in the vicinity of the Scenic Drive, and remains of a second, more active line of vents can now be seen along the Waitakeres' west coast. Some of these are eroded volcanic necks, composed of scoria, volcanic bombs and lava flows that had collapsed back into its throat, like Lion Rock at Piha (**55**). Others are explosion craters filled with lava flows or

*This solidified andesite dike at Karekare (**56**) was once a lava conduit that fed flows on the eastern flanks of the ancient Waitakere Volcano.*

domes of extruded viscous lava, such as The Watchman at Karekare (**56**) or in the cliffs of Whites Beach (**53**) and O'Neill Bay (**47**).

These two lines of vents poured extensive lava flows over the surrounding land. Today these eroded and deeply weathered flows form a thin cap along the ridges of the central Waitakere Ranges and can be seen as the weathered red and purple clays in many of the cuttings on the Piha Road.

Kaipara Volcano

North of the Waitakere Volcano, extending in a line along Northland's west coast, were several more large volcanoes that were erupting during the same period of time, (c. 15–22 million years ago). Centred off the entrance to the Kaipara Harbour was the huge Kaipara Volcano, which erupted at the top of the Waitemata Basin's north-western slopes. Like the Waitakere Volcano, it was an andesite stratovolcano, erupted for a long time and grew to similar immense proportions. It too has been worn down by the Tasman Sea and has been mapped by geophysical prospecting methods as a flattened stump beneath the floor of the continental shelf and slope.

The Displaced Rocks
(22–25 million years ago)

About 25 million years ago, the modern boundary between the Pacific and Australian tectonic plates was formed through what is now New Zealand. The leading edge of the westward-moving Pacific Plate began sliding down beneath ancestral Northland, which sat on the eastern edge of the Australian Plate.

The Northland Allochthon

On top of the down-going Pacific Plate was a thick sequence of basalt lava flows and sedimentary rocks that had accumulated on the floor of the Pacific Ocean out to the east of New Zealand, 25–100 million years ago. As these rock layers collided with Northland, they were scraped off the top of the down-going plate and pushed upwards out of the sea. With further pushing from behind, huge slabs of these rocks (0.5–2 km thick and up to hundreds of square kilometres in area) peeled off and slid onto and over Northland from the northeast. These displaced rocks are collectively known as the Northland Allochthon (meaning the displaced land).

In front of the moving slabs ancestral Northland subsided and was flooded by the sea to depths of several thousand metres. This subsidence began in the north and moved

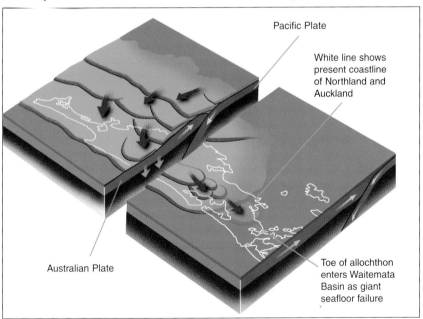

Pacific Plate

White line shows present coastline of Northland and Auckland

Australian Plate

Toe of allochthon enters Waitemata Basin as giant seafloor failure

Rocks that had formed on the floor of the ancient Pacific Ocean were pushed up and slid onto Northland from the north-east (as the Northland Allochthon) between 22 and 25 million years ago, as a result of the collision forces between the Pacific and Australian Plates.

*Large displaced blocks of muddy limestone around Wellsford, Warkworth (**10, 11**) and Redvale have been extensively quarried as a source of lime for cement, farm roads and topdressing. These rocks accumulated as an ooze of calcareous plankton shells on the ocean floor north-east of Northland, 25–35 million years ago (Oligocene period).*

southwards, allowing the displaced rocks to slide progressively further onto Northland under the pull of gravity. The further the slabs moved, the more they broke up into smaller blocks with mixed, sheared layers between them.

Deep-water mudstones among the displaced rocks were rich in clays which when mixed with water readily swelled and flowed. These helped lubricate the movement of the huge blocks of more coherent rocks as they were displaced up to 300 km across Northland, reaching almost as far south as Auckland city.

The wave of subsidence that moved southwards through Northland in front of the displaced rocks culminated in the rapid subsidence and formation of the Waitemata Basin. As the slabs moved in they filled much of the sea to form land in the vicinity of modern Northland. They advanced as far south as Wellsford, where they formed the northern slopes of the Waitemata Basin. About 20 million years ago, a large sub-seafloor failure on these slopes, possibly lubricated by the clay-rich mudstones, carried blocks of Northland Allochthon rocks into the Waitemata Basin to where they lie today around Dairy Flat, Orewa and Warkworth.

Farewell to Gondwanaland
(30–140 million years ago)

Most of the rocks that later became New Zealand were first pushed up out of the sea in the early Cretaceous period (100–140 million years ago) as two major crustal plates collided. These uplifted greywacke rocks became a mountainous strip along the coast of the giant southern hemisphere supercontinent of Gondwanaland, adjacent to ancestral Antarctica and south-east Australia. During this uplift episode the greywackes were crunched up and intensely deformed.

Between 80 and 55 million years ago a vast rift developed through the eastern part of Gondwanaland and a separate New Zealand landmass was split off as the Tasman Sea opened. The Auckland region was land throughout this time and gradually eroded down to a subdued, flat-lying landscape by about 30 million years ago (Oligocene period).

Our Oldest Rocks — Greywackes
(140–250 million years old)

The greywackes are the oldest rocks in the Auckland region. They can be seen in various places along the east coast such as Leigh (**6**), Tawharanui (**9**), Kawau (**139**), Tiritiri (**138**), Motutapu (**133**) and Waiheke (**136**) Islands, Duders (**111**), Tawhitokino (**113**), Tapapakanga (**114**) and Waharau (**115**) Regional Parks. Greywacke also forms the uplifted Hunua Ranges (**118**).

These hard grey rocks accumulated on the sea floor as sand and mud off the coast of Gondwanaland during the Age of Dinosaurs (Jurassic and Triassic periods, 140–250 million years ago). At this time, the coast of Gondwanaland lay along a boundary between two crustal plates. Here the leading edge of the ancient Pacific Ocean Plate was sliding down (subducting) beneath the edge of the Gondwanaland Plate. As the oceanic plate descended it dragged down the sea floor, creating a deep, elongate ocean trench parallel to the coast.

Chert and pillow lava

The crust of the ancient Pacific Plate consisted of basalt pillow lava flows that had been extruded onto the ocean floor at the spreading ridge far out to the east. As the plate moved slowly westwards towards Gondwanaland, these flows became mantled by thin deposits of silica-rich mud (called ooze). This was composed of the shells of dead microplankton that continually rained down on the floor of the Pacific Ocean. The ooze eventually hardened into splintery red and green chert beds. These can be seen in places like Motutapu (**133**) and in association with the underlying pillow lavas at Kawau and Waiheke Islands.

Trench sediments

As the ancient Pacific Plate moved down into the deep trench, the pillow lavas and cherts became buried by sand and mud derived by the erosion of adjacent Gondwanaland.

Folded layers of red chert occur within the greywacke sequence on the foreshore of Administration Bay, Motutapu Island (133).

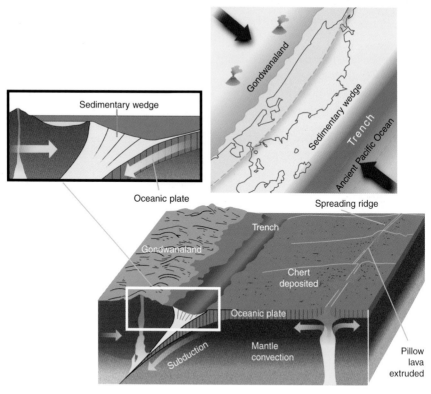

Auckland's greywacke rocks accumulated as sediment on the floor of the sea off the coast of Gondwanaland during the Age of Dinosaurs. The coast lay along the collision boundary between the crustal plates.

As the sediment layers built up in the trench, they were deformed by continual movement of the down-going Pacific Plate. Layers became stacked and progressively tilted towards Gondwanaland. Younger sediment, and sometimes much older underlying layers of chert and pillow lava, were scraped off the top of the Pacific Plate, as if by a giant bulldozer blade, and incorporated into the growing pile of sedimentary rocks. In this way a wedge of rocks formed and continued to thicken and extend oceanward for as long as subduction and the supply of sediment lasted.

As the sedimentary pile thickened, the older layers were compressed and hardened into greywacke. The deeper the rocks were buried, the more they were subjected to high pressures and temperatures, which started to metamorphose them. Mineral-rich waters passing through the rocks at depth deposited quartz and zeolite minerals in fractures to form the characteristic white veinlets of our greywacke rocks.

These greywackes are Auckland's most ancient rocks. We cannot trace the region's origins back any further in time.

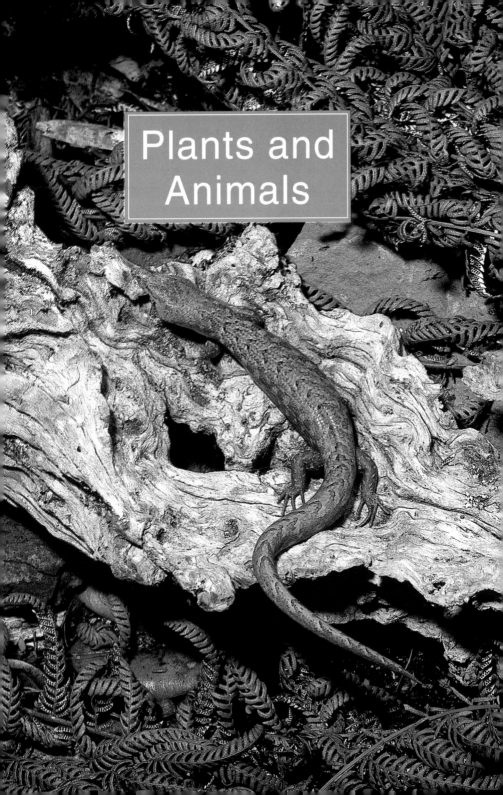

Plants and Animals

Plants and Animals

The Auckland region, although small in area, has an amazing diversity of habitats — from tiny islets to forested mountain tops, from black-sand beaches to wetlands, from wilderness areas to suburban back yards — supporting a rich and varied array of over 20,000 species of plants and animals. The most obvious are the 800 or so kinds of native vascular plants, ranging from tiny orchids to giant kauri. About 130 birds may be seen in the region, but the 17 species of frogs and reptiles are much less visible. By far the most abundant are the thousands of kinds of small creatures and plants such as insects, marine invertebrates, fungi, mosses, liverworts, lichens and algae.

Animals and plants introduced by humans add to the number of wild species, from escaped cage birds, such as the colourful eastern rosella, to ornamental plants, such as the wild ginger so prevalent in the Waitakere Ranges. The region's mild and wet climate encourages weeds, and Auckland has the distinction of being one of the weediest cities in the world. The Waitemata Harbour, New Zealand's busiest port, has more marine organisms that have been introduced by shipping than any other area in the country.

Auckland's ecosystems have been modified over the ages by natural processes such as fluctuating sea levels and volcanic activity, and more recently by humans. Since human settlement, logging, forest clearance for farms and houses, draining of swamps, and reclamation of salt marshes and mangroves have occurred unabated except in remote or reserved areas. However, small areas of virgin forest have survived, in places like Cascade Kauri Park (**44**), parts of Great Barrier (**140**) and most of Little Barrier. Other areas in the Waitakere Ranges, the Hunua Ranges, and on Little and Great Barrier Islands have regenerated well and are already on their way back to tall native forest. Although habitat modification by humans and introduced pests is steadily degrading many native animal populations, Auckland's numerous islands and islets offer 'life rafts' away from introduced predators for many insects, lizards and birds. Little Barrier Island has the most intact forest ecosystems containing several bird species which have survived nowhere else in the region. The restoration project on Tiritiri (**138**) offers the public a wonderful opportunity to see many of the nation's threatened bird species. On land, most of our remaining natural habitats and resources are now protected in a network of Regional Parks, Department of Conservation and local body reserves, the largest of which are in the Waitakere and Hunua Ranges and on Great Barrier Island.

The biota of the coastal marine environment, especially around Auckland, is under increasing pressure from human harvesting by people of diverse cultures, who collect and eat almost any marine life. However, around our coast, only a small fraction of one percent of our coastal seas and ecosystems have any protection. There are currently seven protected areas in the region where marine life cannot be harvested. There are three Marine Reserves, including the New Zealand's oldest at Goat Island Bay (**5**), and

Page 37: Chevron skink, restricted to Little and Great Barrier Islands.

others at Long Bay (**27**) and Pollen Island (**68**). The north coast of Tawharanui Regional Park (**9**) has been protected as a marine park for several decades, and three beaches, Karekare (**56**), Cheltenham and Eastern, are currently closed to any form of harvesting.

When we think of Auckland's vegetation, the images that come to mind are the crimson-flowering pohutukawa fringing the beaches and coastal cliffs; massive, spreading, mature kauri and the groves of slender young rickers in the Waitakeres and Hunuas; the mixed broadleaf-podocarp forest of the hill slopes; the manuka-dominated shrublands between forest and open ground; the olive-green mangroves on sheltered mudflats, clearly visible from all the motorways out of the city; the tumbling spinifex heads and golden pingao on exposed sand dunes, not to mention the large expanses of grass and plantings of exotic trees that constitute the many city parks.

Mature kauri with their spreading crowns often support epiphytes such as tank lilies.

Kauri with their massive heads above the canopy, from the Waitakere Dam (48).

Forests and Shrublands

Auckland's most extensive and accessible forests are in the Waitakere and Hunua Ranges. However, many smaller areas throughout the region contain equally impressive forest, such as Parry Kauri Park (**12**), Mt Auckland (**19**), Smiths Bush (**32**), Auckland Regional Botanic Gardens (**108**), Kirks Bush (**119**), Whakanewha (**136**) and Great Barrier (**140**).

Auckland's forests are characterised by evergreen trees that differ in form and colour to such an extent that they can be identified from a distance — for example, the massive heads of mature kauri; the shaggy, hanging branchlets of rimu; the erect fan-like branching of tree rata; dark heads of miro with wide branching; the narrow Lombardy poplar shape of rewarewa; the erect palm heads of nikau; and the large curving fronds of the mamaku tree fern. Trees range from fast-growing, short-lived primary colonisers such as kumarahou and karamu to slower growing, long-lived conifers like kauri and rimu. Only three deciduous species are present: kowhai, tree fuchsia and ribbonwood.

Coastal forest
Pohutukawa is a feature of coastal forest (**17**, **27**, **56**, **60**, **114**, **131**, **133**, **138**), but it is most noticeable clinging to cliffs along Auckland's coastline, for example along Tamaki Drive and Achilles Point (**89**). With roots often extensively exposed by erosion, they still manage to grow and seem invincible, except to damage by possums, which graze

Flowering pohutukawa are a striking feature of the Auckland coastline in early summer.

on their foliage. Hanks of reddish brown aerial roots are another distinctive feature of these marvellous trees. Pohutukawa covered in crimson flowers, visited by tui, with a clear blue sea below provide the classic picture of Auckland coasts at Christmas time.

Two particularly fine specimens can be seen on the Huia foreshore (**60**) and in Parnell Rose Gardens (**77**).

Coastal forest is characterised by a canopy of mixed broadleaf trees, including kohekohe, New Zealand's sole member of the mahogany family, which shows the tropical trait of flowering straight out of the trunk; taraire, which creates a distinctive carpet of large leathery leaves underneath the tree; titoki, whose brownish fruit capsule splits to reveal a shiny black seed embedded in crimson flesh; karaka, with shiny green leaves and scented, orange-coloured fruit; and puriri, with rich green leaves, pale bark, dark pink flowers and bright red fruit. All these trees have large seeds with a fleshy covering which attracts the native pigeon.

Kowhai bursts into golden yellow flowers in September before the leaves appear, producing a spectacular sight, especially along tidal banks or river margins (**10**, **42**). Tui relish this early nectar source. The yellowish brown seeds are eventually

Kowhai flowers appear before the leaves in September and are sought after by tui for nectar.

Large-leaved nikau on Great Barrier,

released from the beaded seed pods when the pod decays. Because of their waxy covering the seeds are well adapted to dispersal by water, including seawater, and they are frequently seen along the drift line of beaches. On Auckland's west coast (**52**, **53**, **63**)

Celmisia major *var.* major, *the grey-leaved daisy now confined to Auckland's west coast.*

there is a distinctive variety of kowhai (*Sophora microphylla* var. *fulvida*), which has a larger number of smaller leaflets.

New Zealand's only palm, the nikau, gives the coastal forest a tropical look. It is common in shaded valleys and fruits for most of the year. Native pigeons perch on the fruiting stalk to reach the bright red fruit.

Hardy shrubs of houpara, karo, cabbage tree and coastal karamu are usually present in low forest and on exposed margins. Kawakawa, with its heart-shaped, peppery tasting leaves, distinctively holey from being chewed by a small green native looper caterpillar, is often abundant. The daisy shrub, rangiora or bushman's friend, is usually present, with large leaves that are green above and white below.

Exposed forest margins or cliffs commonly feature clumps of flax. The reddish flowers, held well above the fibrous strap-like leaves in summer, are sought after by tui for their rich supply of nectar. Another species of flax, mountain flax, grows near the coast (**54**) and on rocky bluffs (**62**). It differs from common flax in its smaller size, yellowish flowers and hanging capsules. Also common are tussocks of *Astelia banksii*, a ground lily with long silvery leaves; rengarenga lily, which has showy white flowers held above the leaves in late spring; and mats of pink- to white-flowered ice plant, and fleshy-leaved native spinach. *Celmisia major*, which occurs on Auckland's west coast (**53**), is the region's only representative of this large genus of mainly alpine daisies with showy flower heads.

Ferns frequently found in coastal forests include the shield fern (*Polystichum richardii*), coastal brake (*Pteris comans*), true maidenhair (*Adiantum aethiopicum*), rosy maidenhair (*A. hispidulum*) and rasp fern (*Doodia media*). The latter two both have attractive reddish new fronds. *Asplenium haurakiensis* is common in the outer Hauraki Gulf, after which it is named.

Kauri forest

Kauri is New Zealand's most massive and longest-living plant. Trees have been measured up to 50 m tall and estimated to be some 2000 years old. There are few species that can rival the magnificence of mature kauri, with its enormous untapering trunks and massive spreading crowns. The smooth grey trunks remain clean by shedding wide pieces of bark, preventing vines or large epiphytes attaching. Older trees contain many epiphytes in the upper branches, especially tank lilies, ferns, orchids and even a few shrubs.

Both male and female cones are produced on the same tree. The male cones drop off annually after shedding their pollen, but the female cone opens in the first year to be pollinated and then closes for 1–2 years to mature. The ripe cones shatter on the tree, releasing the small, winged, seeds to spin sycamore-like to the ground.

Kauri grows north of Kawhia in the west and the Mamaku Range in the east. It was originally widespread throughout the Auckland area but in the 19th century most of the region's forests were systematically logged for all millable timber (see page 86).

Young kauri growing typically on a ridge top in the Waitakeres.

Although the real giants have gone, there are still some fine kauri remnants that are quite accessible, for example at Parry Kauri Park (**12**), Mt Auckland (**19**), Cascade Kauri Park (**44**) and at the end of the Arataki Nature Trail (**49**). The largest trees in the region are at Parry Kauri Park (**12**) and Cascade Kauri Park (**44**).

Despite this decimation, the forests are recovering with vigour, and today the best stands of young regenerating kauri are found in areas that have been most devastated in the past (**118, 122, 140** and parts of the Waitakere Ranges). Young, slender, conical-shaped kauri are known as rickers before they branch out and form a crown. At this stage podocarps, especially tanekaha, with its leaf-like branches resembling celery leaves, (**115, 122**) can be abundant as well, but few are able ultimately to compete with kauri. Rimu is also a common associate of kauri and is easily identified from a distance by its shaggy branches. Young rimu are one of our most graceful trees, with hanging branches of olive-green reaching to the ground.

Hard beech may be present with kauri although it is scarce in the west. The largest areas of beech in the region are in the Hunuas (**115, 118**) and on Little Barrier. Small, isolated stands are also present on the North Shore (**29**), Waitakeres, Mt. William (**122**), Waiheke and Ponui Islands. Its absence from Great Barrier is a mystery.

The fan-like branching of northern tree rata often stands out on the skyline (**51**) or can be seen more closely at Cascade Kauri Park (**44**). The red flowers appear around Christmas and can be viewed from the road down to Karekare. This species begins as

Pre-European kauri in the Waitakeres with the typical kauri grass ground cover. Note person in grass beside the trunk.

an epiphyte, frequently on a mature rimu or puriri. As it grows it also puts roots down to the ground and finally over-tops its host, killing it by shading rather than strangulation. These trees can become massive, 2–3 m in diameter near the base. As with pohutukawa, the foliage is sought after by possums.

Other trees associated with mature kauri forest include white maire, neinei (*Dracophyllum latifolium*) and mairehau (*Phebalium nudum*), which has the most fragrant leaves of any New Zealand plant.

The striking character of such forests is the massive kauri trunks arising from a tussock ground cover of kauri grass (*Astelia trinervia*), which is a lily, and cutty grass (*Gahnia xanthocarpa*), which is a sedge with sharp-edged leaves. This association is easily seen at the end of the Nature Trail at Arataki Visitor Centre (**49**). The climber kiekie is often present, its leafy heads reminiscent of cabbage trees, but the leaves are sharp-edged, and roots produced from the stem enables it to attach to tree trunks.

Characteristic ferns of kauri forest are: the climbing fern mangemange (*Lygodium articulatum*), unique in New Zealand with its twisting fronds which form hanging tangles of nylon strength; the miniature tree fern-like *Blechnum fraseri*, which grows in patches; fan fern (*Schizaea dichotoma*), which has a unique flat, fan-shaped frond; and *Lindsaea trichomanoides*, with fronds that are reminiscent in shape of tanekaha foliage. Tree ferns are usually present in all forest types.

Broadleaf-podocarp forest

This is the most widespread forest type in the region. Broadleaf trees such as tawa, taraire, rewarewa, kohekohe, puriri and mahoe are the main canopy species of the hill-slopes. Emerging above this cover are tall podocarps such as rimu and totara. Tawa generally grows in cooler sites and is uncommon in the Waitakeres but is the major canopy species of the Hunuas. Taraire grows in warmer sites (north-facing and lowland areas), but is restricted in the Waitakeres to the western valleys (**56**). The tree daisy, heketara (*Olearia rani*), can be a common species on ridges (**9**) and hill-slopes, especially above 200 m in altitude. Some years its leaves are virtually hidden by the prolific covering of white flower-heads in October. Clematis vines flower before the heketara and form a splashy white in August-September in low forest.

Male clematis stand out in the spring.

Gully forest

Gully bottoms or river floodplains are the most fertile sites and support the tallest trees. The Auckland City Walk at Cascade Kauri Park (**44**) is a good place to see many gully forest species. New Zealand's tallest tree, kahikatea, is typically present at such sites (**44, 49, 107**). Often associated with these giants are totara, pukatea and matai (**108**). A woody climber, supplejack, may form impenetrable thickets in these moist areas. Other plants of wet places are nikau, wheki, cabbage tree, flax, *Astelia grandis*, tree fuchsia or kotukutuku, cutty grass (*Gahnia xanthocarpa*), putaputaweta and kiokio. Many of these plants grow naturally along the stream margin at the Botanic Gardens (**108**) and Clevedon (**112**).

Forest pests

Wild introduced mammals are abundant in the region and have a large impact on the native flora and fauna. They include rodents (Norway rat, ship rat, mouse, rabbit, hare), mustelids (ferret, stoat, weasel), cat, hedgehog, possum, goat, pig, wallaby (four species on Kawau Island) and fallow deer. Possums are particularly destructive because they prefer certain plant species and even concentrate on particular individuals until they kill them. Some of these 'ice-cream' species include several of our best-known trees, such as pohutukawa, northern tree rata, kohekohe and totara. Kirk's daisy, with its showy flowers, is another sought-after species. These plants are being eliminated from our mainland forests by continual browsing. On parts of the mainland some of these pests are now being controlled, and on the important conservation islands eradication programmes are being carried out.

There are now more than 2,000 introduced plant species growing wild throughout New Zealand — about equal to the number of native species — and well over a third of these occur wild in the Auckland area. Most of these wild introductions are escapees from suburban gardens and thrive in Auckland's climate. On average over four new species become wild annually in urban Auckland alone; some 10% of these will become serious weeds requiring management.

A large number of weed species threaten forests. The sun-demanding species such as pampas grass are restricted to the forest margins. All vigorous vines are a threat because they can rapidly grow over the canopy and smother it. The best-known of these, old man's beard, was the first environmental weed to be gazetted as a noxious plant in New Zealand. On Auckland's warmer slopes jasmine is proving to be a difficult species to control as it spreads rapidly and roots wherever it touches the ground.

Shade-tolerant species establish more quickly in forest. Two species of wild ginger, Kahali and yellow, with their succulent root-like shoots (rhizomes), form an impenetrable layer up to 1 m thick over the ground, preventing germination of other plants. Wandering Jew propagates easily from stem fragments, forming a dense ground cover which inhibits regeneration of future canopy species. Possibly the worst weed of the region is climbing asparagus, because it spreads quickly over the ground, up tree bases and saplings, smothering and strangling all it encounters; it also has abundant small, fleshy-orange fruit attractive to birds.

Coastal cliffs are prone to weed invasion because they are naturally open places, especially the erosion-prone Waitemata Sandstone cliffs of Auckland. Dominant weeds in these areas include bone-seed (**87**), rhamnus (**132–135**), smilax and pampas grasses. Inland cliffs are the habitat of many native herbs (**51**), and weeds such as mist flower and Mexican daisy threaten these habitats.

Shrublands

Auckland shrublands are a transient stage between open ground and forest. They were once widespread in the region but most have succumbed to housing, farming or firewood extraction. Most are growing in previously burnt areas on poor clay soils where growth rates are retarded. These areas of gumland scrub (**29, 59, 67, 115**), partly induced by fire, once supported kauri forests but over many generations the kauri died off as the soil became impoverished, leaving behind buried kauri gum, which was the basis of an intensive and profitable gum-digging industry (see page 86).

Manuka is the dominant species in these associations. Typically growing with the manuka are shrubs of kumarahou (*Pomaderris kumeraho*), which remains in bud all winter and over a few spring days is suddenly covered in yellow flowers, tauhinu (*P. phylicifolia*), akepiro, *Dracophyllum sinclairii*, mingimingi, with its spiky narrow leaves, and glossy karamu. Without fire the aging manuka gives way to taller, longer-living species such as kanuka, tanekaha (or other podocarps) and kauri.

One of the Auckland region's endemic plants is the slender, pale-flowered kumarahou shrub, *Pomaderris hamiltonii*, which occurs on roadside banks east of Warkworth, south

Kumarahou, or golden tainui, a gumland shrub in full spring flower.

A winter-flowering ground orchid, Pterostylis alobula.

of the Hunuas and on Great Barrier. Two other endemic species are confined to shrublands of central Great Barrier Island. *Olearia allomii* is a shrub similar to the widespread akepiro (*O. furfuracea*). The low spreading kanuka relative *Kunzea sinclairii* has leaves clothed in silky hairs, giving its foliage a silvery sheen. It has masses of small, clustered flowers, making it an attractive garden plant. Both can be seen in open areas by Windy Canyon.

Ferns and fern allies are often common, such as umbrella ferns (*Gleichenia*), which form dense tangles, *Lindsaea linearis*, with its low sterile fronds and erect fertile ones, bracken fern, two tiny comb ferns (*Schizaea*) and an erect club moss, *Lycopodium deuterodensum*. Sedges are also an important part of gumland vegetation; most of the common species are virtually reduced to leafless flowering stems.

Ground orchids usually abound in manuka shrublands. They include the green-hooded orchids (*Pterostylis*), *Acianthus*, spider orchids (*Corybas*), and sun orchids (*Thelymitra*). Other typical gumland plants include sundews (*Drosera*), mats of bryophytes (mosses and liverworts) and lichens.

Shrublands are frequently rather open and prone to weed invasion by woody nitrogen-fixing species, such as gorse, wattles and oxylobium, and also by spiny hakea and willow-leaved hakea.

Forest birds

The native forest species ubiquitous in the region are native pigeon, tui, silver-eye, grey warbler, fantail, morepork and kingfisher. Common in forest, the large native pigeon is often first noticed by the heavy swish of its wing beats or by its cooing sound at rest. Seed of large fleshy-fruited New Zealand plants is dispersed solely by this herbivorous

Native pigeon

Kaka

Male tomtit with chicks.

pigeon because the fruit is too large for other birds to swallow.

The tui's song of full melodious notes to coughs and wheezes alerts most people to its presence. The whirring flight is another indication. It is an aggressive bird and a strong flier, often covering many kilometres to reach good nectar sources such as kowhai, flax, rewarewa or pohutukawa. It also eats insects and small to medium-sized fruit.

The silver-eye has a bristly tongue which enables it to drink nectar, but because of its short bill it often 'robs' the nectar by piercing the base of long tubular flowers, and therefore fails to pollinate such flowers. It forms small winter flocks. The trill of the male grey warbler is one of the commonest songs heard in the bush or suburban garden. Fantails are often seen flitting here and there to catch insects stirred up by walkers, giving the impression of a very friendly bird.

The morepork's presence at night is indicated by its 'more pork' call. It is usually only seen during the day when disturbed from its tree roosts.

Tomtits are present in the larger forest blocks (**9**, **14**, **19**, **48**, **51**, **118**). In September spring is heralded by the arrival of the migrant shining cuckoo from the Solomon Islands area to breed. More often heard than seen, its song is a series of upward whistles followed by fewer downward notes. A single egg is laid in a grey warbler nest and the warblers unknowingly raise the cuckoo chick to the detriment of their own offspring.

A population of kokako, an endemic threatened wattlebird closely related to the extinct huia, exists in the Hunua Ranges, and an established population on Little Barrier is thriving. A small number have recently been released on Tiritiri.

Kaka, the clown of the forest, is a remarkable parrot. It is worth visiting Great Barrier (**140**) just to watch and listen to these conspicuous birds. They are usually observed in small groups, moving noisily through the forest, even hanging upside down, practising their aerobatics, circling around screeching like a rusty hinge, or giving a beautiful liquid whistle. They eat fruit, nectar and insects, using their powerful beak to extract grubs from decaying wood. Kaka are strong fliers and they are being seen more frequently in mainland forests, such as around Leigh (**6**), and even occasionally in Auckland's city parks (**85**), presumably on a sojourn from Little Barrier.

Red-crowned parakeets are present on some of the islands and are most easily seen on Tiritiri. The threatened North Island brown kiwi is common on Kawau (**139**). Little spotted kiwi and kakapo have been established on Tiritiri and Little Barrier respectively. North Island robin, whitehead, stitchbird (New Zealand's smallest honeyeater) and saddleback (New Zealand's smallest wattlebird) all have natural populations on Little Barrier and have also been established on Tiritiri. Island populations of weka have long been established on Rakitu and Kawau Islands; at Mansion House Bay (**139**) they are virtually tame.

Many introduced bird species are found around the forest margins but a few live permanently in the forest. By far the most common is the blackbird. Others include song thrush, dunnock, chaffinch and occasionally redpoll. Interesting forest-margin species are the sulphur-crested cockatoo (**44**), kookaburra (**17**, **18**, **139**), and groups of brightly coloured rosellas, which noisily visit large trees in forest (**32**) and parks (**85**).

Invertebrates

Native landsnails, most of which are tiny, are often common in bush areas. Some 120 species are found in the Waitakeres alone, with up to an amazing 30 species in a square metre! The carnivorous kauri snail is the largest, up to 70 mm across, and shells of this may be found in the area around Mt Donald McLean (**62**).

Centipedes over 150 mm long are still present; they hide during the day under rocks and wood, and hunt at night aided by their poisonous claws. The caterpillar-like peripatus is thought to be a 'missing link' between the worms and the arthropods; they grow to about 50 mm long and live in rotting forest logs, in such places as Mt Auckland (**19**) and the Waitakeres.

The large male giraffe weevil (up to 75 mm long), or tuwhipapa; the 'neck' is much longer than in the female.

Insects are the most abundant animal group and

some of the more obvious ones are: tree weta, which lives in the bush and most Auckland hedges; a large cave weta (Waitakeres); a giant weta (Little Barrier); giraffe weevil; stick insects; and cicadas, abundant in bush and gardens and whose chirping song can be deafening in the summer.

Reptiles, Frogs, Fish and Mammals

A third of New Zealand's native reptiles (eight skinks, five geckos and the tuatara) are found in the Auckland region, mostly in shrubland and forest; the tuatara is known only from Little Barrier, where it is scarce. Geckos climb trees, have large eyes and their bodies are covered in small dull scales, whereas skinks generally remain on the ground,

have small eyes and possess shiny overlapping scales. Geckos and skinks mainly eat insects and spiders but most will also eat fleshy fruits, which assists seed dispersal; geckos also act as pollinators, visiting flowers for nectar.

The common green gecko is usually found in manuka-kanuka shrublands, where it is active during the day. Common, forest and Pacific geckos are a brownish colour and are most active at night. Copper skink, Auckland's commonest lizard, inhabits forested areas.

Sun-basking moko skink occurs on Auckland's mainland and offshore islands.

Some of the lizards are restricted to offshore islands where the threat from introduced predators is decreased. Great Barrier (13 species) and Little Barrier (12 species) have the highest lizard diversity of any of our offshore islands. One of our largest skinks, the endangered chevron skink, is endemic to these two islands. Marbled and striped skinks, and Duvaucel's gecko (one of the world's largest geckos) are present on Little and Great Barrier.

The small primitive native Hochstetter's frog occurs at several localities in the Auckland region (**9**, **14**, **140**), including the Waitakere and Hunua Ranges. This silent, endangered frog lives on the stream margins of undisturbed forest but is seldom seen.

Most bush streams contain eels and several species of kokopu (native trout), which begin life as whitebait.

Duvaucel's gecko now restricted to islands. Note red mites around the eye.

The small Hochstetter's frog is widespread in the Auckland region.

New Zealand's only native land mammals are two threatened species of bat. Short-tailed bats are common on Little Barrier. Long-tailed bats are more widespread but uncommon; they can be seen at dusk just downstream of Cascade Kauri Park (**44**) in the summer.

Wetlands

Although many swamps and lakes have been drained and converted to pasture, Auckland still retains some fine freshwater wetlands. The largest and most impressive are 266-ha Kaitoke Swamp on Great Barrier (**140**), 80-ha Bethells Swamp (**43**) and Whakanewha wetland on Waiheke Island (**136**). The catchment of these wetlands is generally protected by native forest. Smaller swamps are numerous in many of the regional parks (**24**, **130**), Whatipu (**63**), Hunua Ranges, Motutapu (**133**), Waiheke and Great Barrier.

Auckland's water-supply reservoirs in the Waitakere and Hunua Ranges are the largest lakes in the region. They are mainly deep sided with fluctuating water levels and fringed only by a narrow band of wetland vegetation. The main natural lakes are formed by sand dunes (**23**, **45**, **63**, **140**), or volcanic explosion craters (**33**). Lakes generally contain similar vegetation to the swamps, but it is limited to the shallow margins. The extensive open water of lakes allows more space for species with floating leaves than in a dense swamp.

The main swamp vegetation consists of emergents — plants rooted under water and protruding above it. They include: raupo, sedges, flax, rushes, swamp millet, swamp willow weed (*Polygonum*), swamp willow herb (*Epilobium*). Common in the shallow swamp margins are kiokio fern, an aquatic buttercup, giant umbrella sedge, pink bindweed, manuka, cabbage tree and regenerating kahikatea.

Tall spike rush (Eleocharis sphacelata) *a common emergent sedge in the Bethells Swamp.*

Pondweed (*Potamogeton*) is rooted under water and has floating leaves (like a water lily). Red pondweed (*P. cheesemanii*) is widespread, with leathery oval floating leaves. There are two submerged native milfoils (*Myriophyllum*) in the region, recognised by their finely divided whorled leaves. The native yellow bladderwort, *Utricularia protrusa*, is submerged and unrooted with showy yellow flowers held above the water. This species is just hanging on in Bethells Swamp (**43**) and also at Whatipu (**63**). The native free-floating surface species are limited to a fern (*Azolla rubra*) and the tiny duckweed and water-meal. The small azolla plants can completely cover a pond, forming a red floating mat by vegetative division.

Aquatic weeds are numerous and no wetland is entirely free of them. Most reproduce vegetatively, resulting in rapid expansion from fragments. Free-floating weeds include the sterile fern salvinia, which used to entirely cover Western Springs lake (**71**) until it was successfully eradicated in the late 1980s. The introduced azolla (*A. pinnata*) is replacing the similar native azolla (*A. rubra*). Submerged oxygen weeds (especially *Egeria*) have the potential to dominate the aquatic zone right down to 3–4(–8) m. Smothering weeds, such as Mercer grass and reed sweetgrass, are common. Alligator weed can cover shallow lakes as at Whatipu (**63**), and willows can dominate swamps or river margins as at Bethells Swamp (**43**) and Whakanewha (**136**). Weeds can also be attractive in spring when flowering as along the lower Whatipu Stream margin (**63**) with white flowering watercress, pink *Lythrum junceum*, blue water forget-me-not and white marsh bedstraw.

Wetland Birds

Freshwater wetlands are the main habitat for waterfowl (ducks, geese and swans). The most common and widespread ducks of the region are mallard (from Europe) and grey duck, which hybridises with the mallard. Less common are grey teal, New Zealand shoveler (look for them at Whatipu, **63**) and brown teal, which have their national stronghold on Great Barrier (**140**). Scaup, a small diving duck, is present in some of the Kaipara dune lakes (**23**) and also at Western Springs (**71**). Paradise shelduck is common, and is most obvious where pasture is adjacent to the wetlands (**24**, **133**). The larger waterfowl (geese and swans) are all introduced.

Pukeko are abundant and can reach high densities (**24**, **133**). The secretive marsh and spotless crakes are both widespread where there is sufficient dense cover. The Australian coot breeds at a few localities (**71**).

Black, pied and little shags are frequently seen in the water fishing, or perched drying their out-stretched wings. Other widespread wetland birds include the Australasian harrier, which glides over the reed beds looking for prey; the kingfisher, which perches and waits; the welcome swallow, which darts over the water and never seems to land; and the pied stilt, which wades in the shallows. The threatened New Zealand dabchick dives for insects and small shellfish in the dune lakes (**23**). The Australasian bittern is widespread but difficult to see; Whatipu (**63**) is a good place in autumn and winter to try and see it. In wetlands adjacent to shrubby manuka (**23**, **43**, **68**, **130**, **137**, **140**) the shy fernbird is often heard rather than seen.

Australian green and golden bell frogs are commonly heard and seen in Auckland's wetlands, and eels are usually present.

Pied shag.

Suburbs, City Parks and Open Spaces

Auckland's ideal growing conditions combined with New Zealand's largest human population has resulted in a wide range of cultivated exotic trees. Big trees are a real asset in any city, and the region's early settlers showed great foresight in their plantings 100–150 years ago. Auckland's often-quoted oldest-known cultivated tree is a 'red gum' (actually *Eucalyptus obliqua*) at Orua Bay on the Manukau Harbour, said to have been planted by Rev. James Hamlin in 1836, but there is some doubt about the date. The camphor tree and Queensland box (or brush box) planted in 1843 at 91 St Heliers Road may be our oldest surviving cultivated trees. The fine English oaks at Auckland University (**75**) were planted in 1844–45.

Older plantings are usually a mixture of exotic and native species, and are often associated with historic buildings (**78, 79**) or parks (**72, 74, 75, 77, 80**). Common exotic species are English oak, London plane, tulip tree, monkey apple, Dutch elm, Norfolk pine, Queensland box, various gums, holm oak, Port Jackson fig, Moreton Bay fig, Norfolk Island hibiscus, Canary Island palm, Chinese windmill palm, Lombardy poplar, pines, macrocarpa, laurel magnolia and silver birch. Common cultivated native species are pohutukawa, puriri, titoki, kowhai, karaka, kauri, totara, rimu and cabbage tree.

Tucked away among Auckland's gardens are some very unusual and attractive exotic trees, many represented by few individuals: for example *Ficus superba* (**69**), ombu (*Phytolacca dioica*) (**69**), Chilean wine palm (**139**), silk-floss tree (**80**), Illawarra flame tree (*Brachychiton acerifolium*) (**80**) and *Quercus acutissima* (**69**).

As well as softening the landscape, providing shade, adding colour and diversity of form, big trees offer a habitat and food for birds. Several native birds have colonised suburban gardens. Grey warbler, fantail and silver-eye are usual residents. Tui are common visitors, often feeding on plants rich in nectar such as kowhai and banksia. Epsom, with its many big trees, is one of the few central Auckland suburbs where native pigeons can be seen. Kingfisher, morepork and shining cuckoo may also be present if there is sufficient cover of large trees. Welcome swallow and the Australian magpie prefer more open areas. The introduced house sparrow,

*Auckland's best dragon tree, planted in c. 1898 (**78**), native to the Canary Islands.*

Thousands of South Island pied oystercatchers roost at Ambury Regional Park and back to Mangere Bridge during spring high tides in autumn and winter.

blackbird, song thrush, finches (chaffinch, goldfinch, greenfinch), starling and myna are all common. Small groups of colourful eastern rosellas frequent areas with mature trees.

In open pasture flocks of seed-eating finches, yellowhammers and starlings are common. Others include myna, magpie and skylark. Frequent native species in pasture areas are kingfisher, harrier, spur-winged plover, paradise shelduck, white-faced heron, and seagulls during storms. All these birds can be seen in the Regional Farm Parks (**24, 100, 114**). Cattle egret is an Australian migrant that may be seen in wet pasture in the winter.

The copper skink is common in suburban gardens, where it often finds refuge in rocky areas from cats and rats. Also found locally is the small introduced Australian rainbow skink.

Coastal Habitats

Sand dunes

Sand dunes are present behind many of the more exposed beaches along Auckland's coastline. Once active with wide swathes of bare sand, the majority have now been stabilised by the planting of exotic vegetation, such as marram grass, lupins and then

Whatipu is Auckland's stronghold for the golden pingao, growing with the silvery spinifex — our two native sandbinders.

pines, as at Woodhill Forest. The most extensive dune systems remaining are on Auckland's west coast (**1, 23, 45, 63**), with a few remnants on the east coast e.g. Pakiri (**4**) and eastern Great Barrier. The two native sand-binders that grow on our dunes are a grass, spinifex, and a sedge, pingao, both of which have long-running stems. A covering of silky hairs gives spinifex a silvery appearance; on the female plants the seeds are grouped in large spherical heads which detach and bowl along the beach when ripe. Pipits are a common sight among the spinifex on the West Coast foredunes (**43, 52**). The strong and golden pingao leaves are sought after by traditional Maori weavers. At Whatipu (**63**) only pingao and spinifex manage to establish on the exposed foredunes, with introduced marram grass relegated to the more stable dunes behind.

Sandflats that are inundated only by spring tides are sometimes found behind the mobile dunes. At Whatipu, for example, there are extensive wet flats which have a green turf of native herbs (**63**). One of these, a small leafless native sedge, *Eleocharis neozelandica*, is a nationally threatened species. It forms extensive reddish patches by the stream margins but becomes marooned when the stream changes course. The most widespread plant living in damp dune hollows is a small native sedge, *Carex pumila*, with a deep spreading stem which gives rise to separate tufts of pale green leaves. Small brown balls of a blue-green alga (*Nostoc*) may appear seasonally in these damp hollows.

On the more stable dunes small shrubs of aromatic tauhinu are common, and on the

Native shore bindweed, a spreading dune plant in the convolvulus family.

west coast the large sand toetoe (*Cortaderia splendens*) stands out. It is distinguished from the introduced purple pampas grass, now present on most of Auckland's dunes by its smooth-margined leaves and its flowering head which hangs to one side (not erect). Shore bindweed, with its glossy heart-shaped leaves and large pink and white trumpet flowers, is an attractive sight creeping over the dunes, such as at Pakiri (**4**). Prostrate sand coprosma is declining, but is still present along parts of both coasts (**4, 23, 56, 63, 129, 140**). Scrambling wire-vine is a ubiquitous dune species which manages to hold its own with most of the weeds as well. It is a host plant of the small copper butterflies, frequently seen fluttering around the dunes. A native yellow-flowered oxalis (*Oxalis rubens*) with reddish stems is a common dune and coastal cliff plant.

As the dunes become more densely clothed in vegetation, woody shrubs, such as manuka and kanuka, develop, with cabbage trees in the hollows. This stage can be seen on the young dunes at Whatipu (**63**). Dense tea tree stands can be seen by Lake Wainamu (**45**) and in Woodhill Forest, extending to South Head (**23**). They contain several shrubby species with interlacing branches (divaricating form), such as *Coprosma crassifolia*, korokio (*Corokia cotoneaster*), milk tree (*Streblus heterophyllus*) and *Lophomyrtus obcordata*. The final broadleaf coastal forest stage with mature trees growing directly in sand is best seen in the forest remnants at south Woodhill.

Open semi-stabilised dunes provide a suitable habitat for a wide range of weeds, including the well-known yellow-flowering tree lupin. Other aggressive dune weeds include: purple pampas grass, Kikuyu grass, buffalo grass, blackberry, boxthorn, marram grass, and in damp areas wandering Jew and mist flower.

Sheltered Harbour Shores

Sheltered harbours and tidal estuaries are a dominant feature of the region's coastline. Their sheltered upper reaches are commonly fringed with salt marsh, salt meadow and mangroves.

The salt marsh fringe consists of a variety of rushes and sedges, such as orange-tinted, jointed 'rush' (*Leptocarpus similis*), sea rush (*Juncus maritimus*) and *Bolboschoenus*. Their roots receive a dowsing of salt water only at the peak of spring tides. The usually secretive banded rail hunts for crabs, snails and insects among the salt marsh in some of the larger estuarine areas. It is unusually obvious on Great Barrier (**140**), which may reflect the lack of stoats on the island.

The secretive banded rail is common at Wenderholm (17).

The best examples of salt meadow in the region are at Pollen Island (**68**), Miranda (**116**) and north of Shelly Beach on the Kaipara Harbour. Glasswort (*Sarcocornia quinqueflora*) is the most common salt meadow plant in New Zealand, but above mean high-tide level it is frequently accompanied by other small plants such as the white-flowering selliera and sea primrose (*Samolus repens*), yellow-headed bachelor buttons (*Cotula coronopifolia*), and sea blite (*Suaeda novae-zelandiae*). Cord grasses (three species of *Spartina*) form widespread salt meadows, especially in the Kaipara Harbour. They were introduced from the northern hemisphere in the 1920s–1960s to aid land reclamation.

The most noticeable vegetation of our sheltered shores is the mangrove forest, which colonises harbour mud flats and the banks of estuary channels between mid- and high-tide levels. Unlike most mangrove forests elsewhere in the world, the New Zealand examples are composed of a single species (*Avicennia marina*) and never reach the height of their more tropical counterparts. Around Auckland, the average mangrove tree grows to a height of 1.5–3 m, with the tallest usually lining the banks of tidal channels. Low, stunted mangroves (less than 0.5 m high) are a feature of high tidal flats (**31, 68**).

Mangrove forests used to be despised and abused as smelly, unpleasant places, but they are now recognised as an important nursery area for some species of fish. Their aerial roots, trunks and lower branches, which are submerged at high tide, are often encrusted with tiny filter-feeding acorn barnacles (*Elminius modestus*), small black

*Low mangrove forest grows in the shelter of a shell spit on the fringes of the Waitemata Harbour at Pollen Island (**68**).*

Sea bird tracks and crab holes in the high tide salt meadow (glasswort) and salt marsh (rushes and sedges) at Pollen Island.

mussels (*Xenostrobus pulex*) and large clumps of Pacific oysters. Cat's-eye snails are often seen grazing on the surface algal film of the lower branches.

Around the mangroves in the upper reaches of tidal estuaries, the mud is often deep and soft, with a black anaerobic, sulphurous layer beneath the surface. Only a few organisms live here, notably the mud snail that crawls around on the surface ingesting the mud and extracting the goodness it can from it, and the mud crab (*Helice crassa*), whose abundance can be gauged by the density of their burrow holes.

Vast areas of our harbours are tidal sandy mud flats. People seldom venture out on them because of the perception that they are deep in soft, smelly mud. In most places, however, they are quite firm and relatively sandy and well worth a visit — try Meola Reef (**70**), Tahuna Torea (**90**), Ihumatao (**101**) or Awhitu Regional Park (**130**). These tidal flats are inhabited by abundant shallow-burrowing cockles and deeper-burrowing wedge shells. Numerous mud snails live on the surface near high-tide level and are replaced around mid-tide by dense patches of horn shells (*Zeacumantus lutulentus*). Two species of scavenging whelk (*Cominella adspersa, C. glandiformis*) and the herbivorous mudflat topshell (*Diloma subrostrata*) are also commonly seen.

The burrow openings of two species of mud crab (*Helice crassa, Macrophthalmus hirtipes*) are common, but may be mistaken at lower tidal levels for those of the orange-tinged snapping, mantis and sand shrimps. At least a dozen different kinds of marine worm burrow through the muddy sand in this habitat. The enormous abundance of spionid worms around low-tide level can be seen by the vast numbers of their tiny sand tubes that poke up just above the surface.

These harbour flats were once covered in green sea grass (*Zostera*), a marine flowering plant, but it was virtually wiped out in the Auckland region by a fungal outbreak 50–60 years ago. Today there are small patches scattered around the region's harbours (**70**).

A recent introduction to the low tidal flats around our eastern harbours and estuaries is the Asian date mussel. Each mussel grows to about 20 mm long and its byssal hairs extend out and gather a thick mat of mud or shell fragments around it. After about 18 months the mussels die and the mat breaks up and washes away.

Wading birds

Large flocks of wading birds are a familiar sight on the sheltered tidal flats of our harbours and along the Firth of Thames coast. Resident waders include variable oystercatcher, New Zealand dotterel, pied stilt and spur-winged plover. Thousands of South Island pied oystercatchers, wrybills and pied stilts, and many banded dotterels feed from late summer to winter on the abundant intertidal life before migrating southwards to nest, mainly in the South Island. As they depart they are replaced by the Arctic migrant waders, particularly the abundant bar-tailed godwits and lesser knots. Pacific golden plovers, turnstones and red-necked stints are quite common, and numerous uncommon migrants and vagrants from the Arctic, Asia, America and Australia have also been recorded from the Auckland region.

For the greatest number of birds and species, Miranda (**117**) cannot be surpassed. However, there are many other excellent wader areas (**1, 23, 90, 100, 140**). The different wader species do not directly compete with each other because the differing lengths and shapes of their bills

Variable oystercatcher and chick, resident waders of remote coastline.

enable them to seek out different organisms.

Small numbers of royal spoonbill and white heron are also sometimes seen on the harbour flats in winter. They too fly south to breed in the South Island. White-faced heron is common around the upper parts of harbours and in pasture and has a wide diet from fish to insects. It usually nests in tall conifers, unlike its less common cousin, the reef heron, which nests on the ground by the coast.

Sandy Beaches

The Auckland region is richly endowed with sandy beaches, which attract hordes of bathers during Auckland's hot and humid summers. The sheltered beaches of the inner Hauraki Gulf and harbours commonly support extensive beds of burrowing bivalves, particularly cockles, wedge shells and pipi. Living attached to or in the shelter of cockle shells on the beach are tiny limpets (*Notoacmea*), small anenomes (*Anthopleura aureoradiata*) and green chitons (*Chiton glaucus*).

Buried just below the surface in the fine sand close to low-tide level on these protected beaches we often find sand dollars and, if we are lucky, three burrowing snails — the ostrich foot, olive shell and arabic volute. The latter two are not as common around the Waitemata Harbour as they once were, because they have been poisoned by TBT anti-fouling paint.

On the more exposed east coast beaches of the Hauraki Gulf, and particularly the surf beaches of the west coast, the inhabitants are largely restricted to those that can burrow deeply into the sand and not be swept away by the large waves. Here the shallow-burrowing pipi is replaced by its cousins the tuatua and, more rarely, the larger toheroa. From spring low-tide level out to 5 m depth these sandy beaches are home to a group of burrowing bivalves collectively known as surf clams — coarse dosinia (*Dosinia anus*), trough shell (*Mactra discors*) and triangle shell (*Spisula aequilateralis*). Together with tuatua, these

Common inhabitants of Auckland's sheltered and exposed beaches.

are often the main shells washed up on our exposed beaches.

Also washed up on these beaches are marine snails — helmet shell, ostrich foot and knobbed whelk, that burrow through the sand just offshore. Often found washed up on the west coast beaches are fragile, spiral ram's horns, which are internal shells from small cuttlefish. Blue-bottles or Portuguese man-of-war and prized violet shells are both animals that swim and float about in the ocean and are periodically washed ashore.

The white-fronted tern is common along the coast, and the larger Caspian tern is widespread. The former roost in large flocks and the latter in much smaller groups. New Zealand's smallest and rarest tern, the fairy tern, is now virtually confined for breeding

These bird's foot-like marks on sheltered beaches indicate the presence of live wedge shells beneath. These are the feeding traces left by their siphons in the surface sand above them.

to two Auckland sandspits (**4, 23**). Red-billed and black-backed gulls are abundant along the entire Auckland coastline and particularly common on the beaches. Rangitoto Island (**132**) is a wonderful place to see nesting colonies of black-backs. Red-billed gulls mainly nest in smaller groups on more remote islets. Some black-billed gulls from lake areas to the south over-winter in the region, especially at Miranda (**117**), and more recently breed in the Kaipara Harbour.

Sheltered rocky shores

The range of organisms that live intertidally on our rocky shores is largely determined by the height they live on the shore with respect to the tides and the strength of the waves they are exposed to.

On the more sheltered coasts, the first organism most people notice is the sharp shells of the flourishing, introduced Pacific oyster. It arrived from Asia in the 1960s, possibly attached to barges, and quickly colonised our northern shorelines. Around parts of the Manukau and Waitemata Harbours (**70, 89, 96, 106**) it is still increasing in abundance to epidemic proportions. Sections of rocky and sandy coast that were previously pleasant places to walk or swim have now been overrun and require extreme care to avoid slipping over and being slashed by the oysters' razor-sharp shells.

High on the shore we find a number of algal-grazing snails, such as the tiny blue periwinkle, the rock-dwelling horn shell (*Zeacumantus subcarinatus*), several topshells (*Melagraphia aethiops*, *Diloma zelandica*) and the dark, shell-less, leathery sea slug (*Onchidella nigricans*).

Often living just above and around the oyster clusters at mid-tide are thousands of

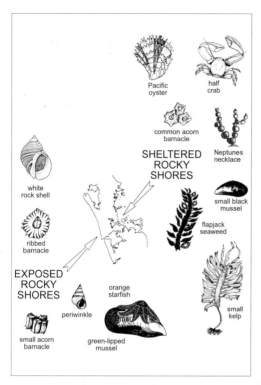

Common zoning organisms that live on the rocky
shores around Auckland.

the common acorn barnacle, clumps of the small black mussel and festoons of Neptune's necklace. Further algal grazers that are common among the oysters are the cat's-eye snail and the snakeskin chiton. Also present here, away from the areas that are worst affected by TBT poisoning, are numerous native oyster borer snails. There are several seaweeds that flourish seasonally on the sheltered intertidal rocks around Auckland. These include the dark green, convoluted sheets of *Codium convolutum* and the fragile, golden vesicles of *Colpomenia sinuosa*.

Two carnivorous starfish are common on our sheltered shores. The cushion star comes in a wide range of colours and occasionally has 4 or 6 arms rather than the usual 5. The many-armed greeny brown starfish (*Coscinasterias cala-maria*) is mostly seen as small individuals 5–12 cm in size. Softer rocky substrates, especially the Waitemata Sandstones, are often extensively bored on the lower part of the shore by several kinds of rock-boring bivalves.

A wide range of organisms take shelter beneath loose rocks and cobbles that lie on the rocky shore. Lifting a high-tide rock will often reveal fast-moving sea slaters, sand hoppers and the orange shore crab (*Cyclograpsus lavauxi*). Lower on the shore, most rocks shelter groups of blue-green half crabs and sometimes the larger, hairy crab (*Pilumnus novaezelandiae*).

At low-tide level the rocks commonly also shelter sucker fish and rock fish (*Acanthoclinus fuscus*), and in more open water the green sea egg, kina. Where it is sandy beneath the rock, brittlestars and several kinds of colourful marine worms are often found lurking. Frequently attached to the undersides of these low-tide rocks are numerous brightly patterned chitons (*Ischnochiton maorianus*), slipper limpets and orange, purple or brown seasquirts.

On most sheltered rocky shores, the low-tide level has a fringe of brown seaweeds

A cushion starfish and brightly coloured sponge occupy the underside of a boulder at spring low-tide level on Meola Reef (70).

that extends out below low tide. The most common are the branching, narrow-leaved *Carpophyllum flexuosum*, *C. maschalocarpum* (flapjack), *Sargassum sinclairii* and *S. scabridum* and the small kelp *Ecklonia radiata*. Around their holdfasts the low-tidal rock is usually painted pink by the calcareous film and turf of the red alga *Corallina*.

Richly coloured sponge gardens, more usually seen only by scuba divers at depths of 10 m or more, are exposed during spring low tides along some of the sheltered rocky shores of our harbours, where they are swept clean of sediment by strong tidal currents. The sponges live in these shallows because of the suspended sediment in the harbour waters which greatly reduces light penetration, thus reproducing conditions more usually encountered at greater depths. The most common sponges here are the spiny, brown spheres of *Aaptos aaptos* and the orange golf ball sponge. Small yellow finger sponges are frequently seen on exposed low-tide reefs. Unusually under rocks, but sometimes on their sheltered sides or growing in the shade beneath wharves, are numerous brightly coloured sponges — often as sheets, but sometimes subglobular, fluffy, erect or branched. Some places where these sponges can be seen are Meola Reef (**70**), alongside Tamaki Drive (**87**), and along the Birkenhead and Devonport coastline (**29, 38**).

New Zealand is unusual in possessing 12 species of shag. Five breed in the Auckland region and all are found along the coast, often perching on rocks. Only spotted shags are confined to coastal waters and they reach their northern breeding limit on Auckland's west coast (**46**) and the inner Hauraki Gulf. They nest on cliffs and mainly fish in deep water. Black, little black, little and pied shags feed in generally shallow fresh or salt water and nest in trees overhanging water. They often nest communally (**30**, **71**, **94**).

Exposed rocky shores

On more exposed rocky shores, like at Goat Island Bay (**5**) and on the west coast of the Waitakere Ranges (**40, 55**), the intertidal zone is more extensive because of the height waves and splash extend up the rock faces.

In the splash zone above high tide, two species of periwinkles graze — the small blue *Littorina antipoda* and the larger brown-grey *L. cincta*. Moving down the shore, rocks are usually covered in barnacles that come out of their shelly houses to filter feed when the tide is in. Three species are normally present on our exposed shores — tight

clusters of small acorn barnacles, *Chamaesipho columna*, and its larger cousin *C. brunnea*, and the tall, ribbed barnacle *Epopella plicta*. Sometimes present at this level, especially when they can find shelter under boulders, are the globular black nerita snails and the deep red anenome *Isactinia tenebrosus*.

The large orange starfish clings tenaciously to rocks on exposed shores, where it feeds on clumps of mussels.

Close to low tide there is often a wide belt of green-lipped mussels, almost always accompanied by its predators, the large orange starfish, *Stichaster australis*, and the large, spirally ribbed, white rock shell. Clinging tightly to the rocks at mid- to low-tide levels are several species of grazing limpets — the variably patterned *Cellana radians* and the white-beaded *C. ornata*. Sometimes also present is New Zealand's largest chiton,

Giant straps of bull kelp flail in the surf where they are attached to rocks on the west coast of the Waitakeres (55).

Eudoxochiton nobilis, which can grow up to 10 cm long.

Often seen scurrying into rocky crevices are the large purple shore crab and at lower levels the red spiny surf crab. Living in slightly more sheltered, shelly pools are numerous hermit crabs, and the richly coloured jewel anenomes and the large pink, yellow to lime-green anenome (*Isocradactis magna*), which studs its outer wall with shell fragments.

As with the sheltered shores, the low-tide zone is encrusted with pink coralline algae and is fringed by a wide belt of brown seaweeds. The two most common are branched, tough and leathery *Xiphophora chondrophylla* and *Carpophyllum angustifolium*. In the cooler waters of the west coast, the giant straps of the bull kelp are attached by large holdfasts to the rocks.

The small blue penguin is common along the exposed rocky coasts of the mainland and islands, but in built-up areas dogs threaten this bird. For a closer view of these penguins, visit Tiritiri (**138**), where you can see into the penguin nesting boxes.

Sea birds and marine mammals

An amazing 10 species of petrels and shearwaters breed in the region and many others feed here. They are common in Auckland's exposed waters and can often be seen as close in as Rangitoto Lighthouse. The most frequent in the Hauraki Gulf are Buller's, fluttering and flesh-footed shearwaters, and the much smaller white-faced storm and common diving petrels. All these, except Buller's shearwater, nest on various islands in the region. Also nesting in the region are sooty and little shearwaters, black (**140**), Pycroft's, Cook's, and grey-faced (**46, 138**) petrels. Albatrosses, mollymawks, giant petrels, Cape pigeons and prions are winter visitors to the region.

Australasian gannets nest on small islands in the Hauraki Gulf and on the mainland at Muriwai (**40**). They are a wonderful sight diving for small fish from a great height. In the summer fishing flocks of white-fronted terns are frequently harassed by the migrant Arctic skua, forcing them to drop their catch to these pirates.

Grey-faced petrel, or oi, is widespread nesting on islets in the region. Chicks leave the burrows in December to January.

Fur seal pups near Muriwai are now a frequent sight on rocks or sand. They are usually only resting so please leave them alone.

Seven marine mammals are frequently seen in the region. The New Zealand fur seal is increasing in numbers and is mostly seen along the west coast (**40, 56**), although they are not breeding there yet. Both common and bottlenose dolphins are frequent, often venturing right up the harbours. Large schools of dolphins may be encountered further out to sea. The main whales seen are orca, Bryde's, short-fin pilot and sperm.

Blue penguins nest on all Auckland's exposed rocky coasts.

History

History

Although recent by world standards, the human occupation of the Auckland region extends back a millennium. Successive waves of migration, conquest and occupation have left the region with a rich human history, and a landscape covered by a complex and unique assemblage of historical and cultural sites. Many of these places relate to the 200-year European association with the land. The majority of the region's historic places, its oldest placenames and traditions are, however, concerned with its much longer Maori occupation.

The historic places described in this book are samples that reflect the chronology and diversity of Auckland's human history. They tell us about the successive communities who have lived on the land and of the nature of their occupation. Collectively these sites chronicle the origins of the present community and define the place that is Auckland.

Nga Purakau me nga Tikanga a Iwi: Myths and Traditions

The traditions of the iwi (tribes) of the Auckland region reflect the long Maori occupation and provide cultural explanations for the origins of the region's distinctive structures, landforms, seascapes and ecology. They link the past with the present and link today's tribal groups with the land. Maori tradition offers a very different explanation of the region's origins from that offered by present-day European scientific understanding.

Te Ika Roa a Maui : The Great Fish of Maui

In the mists of ancient time the heroic demi-god Maui Tikitiki a Taranga hauled a great fish (the North Island) from the depths of Te Moana nui a Kiwa (the Pacific Ocean). The body of Maui's fish settled on the surface of the ocean, with part of it forming what is now the Auckland region.

Maui's brothers proceeded to beat the huge fish in order to subdue it and to claim the most prized portions for themselves. Their strenuous efforts left Auckland as a narrow and undulating landmass lying between two great oceans. The scales of the fish were scattered, forming the larger offshore islands like Aotea (Great Barrier, **140**).

Into the wounds of Te Ika a Maui poured the surrounding seas. Thus the land and sea became interwoven, giving the Auckland region its pervasive maritime character. Maui and his family are forever preserved as the islands now known as the Hen and Chickens, which are visible from the Mangawhai Cliffs Walkway (**3**).

Over the centuries that followed, the deities of the Maori pantheon continued to shape and modify this new land. The forces of Tangaroa and Hinemoana sculpted the coastal environment, creating the region's long sandy beaches and large sheltered

Page 69: A finely carved canoe stern post (taurapa) photographed by Reverend John Kinder at Mechanics Bay c.1863. The Swan Hotel is in the background on what is now the corner of Stanley St and Parnell Rise.

harbours, with their distinctive broad intertidal flats. Tawhiri Matea brought Auckland its warm, moist climate and ever-changing weather patterns.

The wrath of Mataaho flowed from deep under the earth, creating Auckland's distinctive volcanic landscape (see tradition p. 138). Rangitoto, his most recent creation, stands as a guardian over the land. It acts as an enduring symbol of the region's rich heritage and the link between the ancestral deities of the Maori and the landscape we know today. In time the children of Tane Mahuta clothed the land, bringing the ecological diversity for which the region is renowned.

The era prior to the human occupation of the land is referred to as Te Ao Kohatu, 'the age of stone'. It was a time when inanimate objects possessed animate qualities. Rocks and mountains traversed the land until, like Paratahi, the errant child (the island off Karekare, **56**), they became frozen in place when humans came to inhabit the land.

Te Ipu a Mataaho, 'the foodbowl of Mataaho' (Mt Eden crater).

Nga Turehu: Those who Arose from the Earth

The traditions of the iwi of the region tell of its first human occupants, the Turehu, who are sometimes also referred to by specific names like Ngaurukehu or Maewao. Those seen as taking a less material form are also referred to as Tahurangi and Patupaiarehe.

The Turehu are referred to collectively in tradition as being fair skinned, clever and resourceful, and capable of superhuman feats. Tiriwa, a Turehu chieftain from the Waitakere Ranges, is credited, for example, with moving Rangitoto Island from Mercer Bay, Karekare, to its present position at the entrance to the Waitemata Harbour.

The love affair between Hinerangi, a Turehu woman of Hunua, and Tamareia of Waitakere led to the first major battle in the region. Hinerangi, like a number of her

Te Unuhanga o Rangitoto: the chasm from which Rangitoto was drawn by Tiriwa (Mercer Bay).

contemporaries, was turned to stone. She reclines as a guardian rock on Maraetai Beach. Yet other Turehu influenced cultural practices. An example was Hinerehia, a Turehu woman from Motuihe Island (**135**), who taught later peoples the culinary arts and the art of weaving.

Tamaki Herenga Waka: Tamaki the Mooring Place of Canoes

The iwi of the region all claim descent from the Turehu. Their specific tribal identity is, however, generally based on descent from the crews of the ancestral voyaging waka (canoes) that visited the region. One of the earliest of these ancestors was Toi te Huatahi, who is commemorated in such names as Te Hauturu o Toi (Little Barrier Island), Te Moana Nui o Toi (the northern Hauraki Gulf) and Te Whanganui o Toi (St Heliers Bay). His niece Pareira settled near Wai-pareira (Henderson Creek), while a companion, Uika, settled on Maunga a Uika (North Head, **39**).

Another illustrious ancestor, Kupe mai Tawhiti, visited Aotea (Great Barrier, **140**) where he reprovisioned his canoe. After crossing the Tamaki Isthmus he said karakia (incantations) and left the mark of his paddle at Whatipu (**63**). He then created Nga Tai Whakatu a Kupe, 'the upraised seas of Kupe' (the rough seas of the west coast), to throw off enemies who were pursuing him. Matahaorua, a small bay near Kaipara South Head (**23**), commemorates his canoe.

Many famous waka were to follow. The Moekakara, commanded by Tahuhunui o Rangi, reached land at Wakatuwhenua, near Motu Hawere (Goat Island, **5**). The Aotea, commanded by Turi, called and named Aotea (Great Barrier Island, **140**). After rounding North Cape it visited the Kaipara Harbour (**21**), where its lashings were retied at Aotea

*The Tainui Memorial at Te Haukapua (Torpedo Bay, Devonport, **38**) commemorates the landing of the Tainui canoe over 600 years ago.*

(Shelly Beach). The Arawa, under the command of Tamatekapua, visited the eastern and northern parts of the region. Here some of its crew left descendants and many important placenames such as Wai-te-mata, O-kahu and Kai-para.

The waka that had the greatest ongoing impact on the region was the Tainui, commanded by Hoturoa. It made landings at many places, e.g. Waihihi (**115**), Whaka-kaiwhara (**111**) and Te Haukapua (**38**), and was then portaged across the isthmus to the Manukau. The Tainui and its crew left placenames and other associations at many places. Most notably they left descendants, who were collectively known as 'Ngaoho'. Over time they developed individual tribal identities, although their genealogical unity was a fundamental reason for the ongoing peace in the region prior to the 17th century.

From this time the Ngaoho people were affected by three important migrations. From Kawhia came Marutuahu, the ancestor of the Hauraki tribes. Also from Kawhia came Maki and Mataahu, whose Kawerau people were to settle throughout the area north of the Tamaki Isthmus. From the north came the tribal group who became known as Ngati Whatua. These peoples secured land in the region through both intermarriage and conquest. From them and the earlier inhabitants emerged the many tribal groups who occupy Auckland today.

The Archaeological Record

The long Maori occupation is not only recorded in tradition, but it is also graphically reflected by the region's remarkable archaeological record. This record shows that pre-European Maori society and culture was clearly Polynesian in character, being based around a seasonal cycle of agriculture, fishing and shellfish gathering. It also shows that the Auckland region has been settled by humans for as long as any other part of the country, and that it was always relatively densely settled in the pre-European period. This was particularly the case for fertile Tamaki Makaurau, 'Tamaki desired by many', the Auckland Isthmus.

The Auckland region offered an amazing array of natural resources that must have stunned its first human inhabitants. Its long coastline, offshore islands and three large harbours provided easy access to a wealth of marine resources. The mainland was clothed in luxuriant sub-tropical forest, which offered food, medicine, building and weaving materials, and teemed with wildlife.

The ripening bracts of the kiekie, a favourite seasonal delicacy from the abundant resources of the forest.

It also had extensive tracts of volcanic loams that were well suited to Polynesian gardening practices. Everywhere in the region the resources of the land and sea lay in close proximity to each other, making it the perfect living environment, as is summed up by the following whakatauki or traditional saying:

He wha tawhara ki uta, he kiko tamure ki tai.
The edible bracts of the kiekie on the land, the flesh of the snapper in the sea.

Nga Kakano: The Seeds

The oldest known settlement sites in the region are found on the coastline, especially around river or harbour mouths, e.g Papakanui (**23**), or on the offshore islands of the Hauraki Gulf. These 'archaic sites', which date back approximately 800 years, reflect a marine-based society and a seasonal resource-gathering economy. They also provide evidence of an environment much richer than that found several centuries later, after forests had suffered the impact of fire and many species had become extinct through hunting, forest clearance and the introduction of the Polynesian rat and the dog.

A notable example of an archaic site is provided by the Sunde site near Rauporoa (Administration Bay) on Motutapu Island (**133**). Here an archaeological excavation revealed a thin occupation layer beneath the volcanic ash. It contained the remains of 10 species of sea bird, six species of bush bird and several extinct bird species including moa, crow and eagle. There were also the remains of tuatara, seal, dog, and large quantities of fish bone. Most importantly, human footprints were found to have been preserved in the ash, showing that the site was occupied when Rangitoto (**132**) erupted.

Archaeological investigation in the region, although far from complete, reveals a remarkable degree of continuity in cultural and economic practices. At the same time it also reveals change, as an identifiably Maori culture developed and adapted in response to a modified environment and a growing population.

Throughout the pre-European era, fishing and shellfish gathering remained predominant economic activities. As the population grew and made an impact on the ecology of the region, horticulture appears to have become increasingly important. It is

*Maori village on Motutapu (**133**) engulfed by ash during the Rangitoto eruption.*

also clear that the pre-European Maori community was highly mobile, with whole communities moving from their horticultural bases in an ongoing cycle of hunting, fishing and resource gathering.

The Archaeological Assemblage

Urban development, quarrying, rural land use and public works have modified or destroyed many of the region's archaeological sites. Nevertheless, Auckland still retains a remarkable Maori archaeological assemblage. The most common site types are midden or refuse heaps associated with food processing and cooking, and terraces, which were generally residential areas and sometimes gardens.

Another commonly seen site type is rectangular pits, which were used as subterranean storage facilities for kumara (sweet potato), and sometimes as dwellings. Kumara, and other tropical crops, such as taro and hue (gourds), required underground storage in order to protect them from being damaged by winter cold and damp.

To the untrained eye the old cultivations themselves are often not apparent, consisting of indistinct earth rows on warm, north-facing slopes. They take their most spectacular form in the unique stonefield gardens estimated to have once extended over 8000 ha of the volcanic field. The stonefields consist of a complex landscape of drystone walls, stone alignments and boundary markers, retaining walls of houses and terraces, and stone heaps. The latter were constructed to clear garden plots, or when mixed with soil were used as raised mounds on which to grow hue (gourds).

Less than 200 ha of the stonefields remain and they continue to be modified. The two largest remnants, Matukurua and Otuataua, are not included in this book as they are privately owned. An example of stone garden mounds can be seen within the crater of Mangere Mountain (**98**), and a small stonefield garden system is located at the eastern

A group of kumara pits photographed on Maungarei (Mt Wellington) by H. Boscawen in 1899.

end of Motukorea (**134**). A unique alluvial river flat stonefield garden containing remnant clumps of introduced Polynesian taro can be seen at Tapapakanga Regional Park (**114**).

Many of these occupation areas and gardens also feature remnant examples of introduced species of ti (cabbage tree), and groves of the distinctive shiny-leafed karaka. Its fleshy orange drupes were harvested in autumn and processed as a winter food supplement. Particularly fine examples of karaka groves are found at Lake Pupuke (**33**), Anawhata (**52**) and Waharau (**115**).

Quarries and areas used for the manufacture of stone implements and weapons are found at several places in the region, most notably at Muriwai (**40**), Motutapu (**133**) and Aotea (Great Barrier, **140**). There are also many tapu or sacred and restricted places located throughout the region. These include burial areas, places of worship, or sites associated with important events and ancestors.

Te Toka Tuwhenua, a rock pillar that held the 'mauri' (spiritual essence) of Te Tatua a Riukiuta (Three Kings). It was re-erected in Cornwall Park by Sir John Logan Campbell in c.1895.

The most intact Maori archaeological landscapes are those found on the Hauraki Gulf Islands. Motukorea (**134**) retains a largely unmodified site assemblage, while Motutapu (**133**) has a spectacular cultural landscape that spans the entire period of human occupation. However, the best-known and most accessible archaeological assemblages are those found on Auckland's volcanic cones.

The Volcanic Cones

Archaeological evidence suggests that the cones were terraced as gardens and occupation sites from the 14th century. In time they became important focal points at the hub of expansive garden systems, and from the 17th century they began to be increasingly fortified. However, even the largest cones such as Maungawhau (**81**), Maungakiekie (**85**), Maungarei (**92**) and Mangere (**98**) are essentially sprawling townscapes located at the centre of major garden areas. Their fortified pa are generally a small part of the wider complex and are confined to their upper crater rims. These fortifications were largely constructed in the 1700s at a time when the Waiohua occupants of the region faced increasing pressure from the Hauraki tribes of the south-east and Ngati Whatua from the north-west.

The volcanic cones, like the other dominant mountains of the region from Atuanui (**19**) in the north to Pukekohe (**124**) in the south, were, and are, of major symbolic and spiritual importance to the tribal groups of the region.

Rarangi maunga tu te ao, tu te po; Rarangi tangata ka ngaro, ka ngaro.
A mountain range stands day in day out; while generations of people are forever lost.

The hills and mountains of the region were dominant features in a landscape which was intimately known by its inhabitants, and in which every feature was named. These names, which lay over the land in an intricate mosaic, reflected a millennium of human occupation. They described the topography of the land, its natural resources and their usage (e.g. **8**, **18**, **52**, **70**, **90**, **124**). They also commemorated specific ancestors and traditions (e.g. **9**, **23**, **28**, **38**, **47**, **61**, **96**).

To those familiar with them, these names and their historical associations act as 'tohu' or symbols that are central to the identity of the region's tribal groups and reminders of the past. In conjunction with tradition they bring the natural and archaeological landscape to life.

A view of a massive kumara pit and the lower tihi on Maungawhau (Mt Eden).

Te Ao Hou: The Modern World

Cultural Contact and its Impact

Into the isolated and strictly regulated world of the Maori sailed Captain James Cook on the barque *Endeavour* in November 1769. After a brief visit to the Firth of Thames, Cook sailed north along the south-western shores of the Hauraki Gulf. He went ashore briefly on the Orere-Kaiaua coast, where he found 'neither inhabitants or anything else worthy of note.' He then sailed past the Waitemata during a gale and made no other comment on the region.

Cook left behind placenames, such as Little and Great Barrier Islands, Cape Rodney and Bream Tail, which are still in current use. His visit also had several important long-term indirect influences. Cook introduced the pig and the potato, which were widespread among the iwi of the region by the 1780s. Most importantly, his journals stimulated interest in the natural resources of the region, in particular timber, throughout Britain and North America.

Following the foundation of a British penal colony in New South Wales in 1788, the Auckland region began to be visited by Sydney merchants and British naval vessels seeking kauri masts and spars. The visit by the missionary Rev. Samuel Marsden further publicised the timber resources of the region and drew attention to the existence of the region's three large harbours. Whaling and sealing vessels reprovisioned in the inner Hauraki Gulf during this period, and the first European traders arrived in south of the region in the mid-1820s.

These intermittent European visitors had a direct impact on the iwi of the region through the introduction of iron tools and utensils, and most importantly through the introduction of epidemic diseases such as influenza. Their main impact was, however, to come in the form of muskets, which were first introduced in large numbers to the tribes of Northland. Between 1818 and 1826 the iwi of the Auckland region were devastated by northern taua (war parties) armed with muskets. Many sought refuge in the Waikato and they only began to return to their old homes in the mid-1830s. As a result, Europeans who visited Auckland in this period found a region devoid of inhabitants.

The Missionaries

In 1833 the region's first European village developed around Gordon Browne's spar and sawing station at Browne's Bay on the Mahurangi River. From that time an increasing number of timber-trading vessels visited the region, and the Bay of Islands-based Anglican and Wesleyan missionaries began to visit the now-scattered Maori communities of the district. Missionaries like Rev. Henry Williams travelled up and down the coast in small cutters, taking shelter at such places as Omaha Cove (**6**) and Te Haruhi Bay, Whangaparaoa (**24**). This was a risky business, as illustrated by the drowning of Rev. John Bumby when the canoe in which he was travelling capsized in a squall near Tiritiri Matangi Island (**138**). The missionaries brokered a fragile peace between Ngapuhi and

Omaha Cove (6) as sketched by Rev. Henry Williams in 1831.

local iwi, and acquired tracts of land on which to found mission stations.

The first of these was Orua Bay Mission Station (**131**), founded by William Woon at Awhitu in 1834. It was followed by Robert Maunsell and James Hamlin's Moeatoa Mission (near Waiuku, **128**) in 1836, and the Maraetai Mission founded by lay preacher William Fairburn in 1837. Part of the farm of this latter institution is now Omana Regional Park (**110**). In this period the Wesleyan missionaries visited Maori villages such as Pehiakura (**131**) from northern bases such as Tangiteroria. They later founded missions at Auckland in 1842, and Ihumatao and Three Kings in 1848.

The missionaries introduced Christianity to the iwi of the region, who adopted it with zeal. They also brought important economic change through the introduction of farm animals, the plough, cereal and vegetable crops, and fruit trees such as peaches and figs. Remnant examples of such trees can be seen on Motutapu Island (**133**) and at Omeru Pa (**20**). Following the missionary land purchases, individual timber traders such as William Webster purchased land on the Gulf islands of Waiheke and Great Barrier (**140**). These traders provided the Maori with increased access to European utensils and tools, while also introducing tobacco and alcohol.

1840: The Foundation of Auckland

The year 1840 was to be pivotal in the region's history. At that time it was still largely in Maori ownership apart from a few scattered land blocks claimed by private purchasers. Early in 1840 many local chiefs signed the Treaty of Waitangi at Karaka Bay (**89**),

Tara Te Irirangi the Ngai Tai chief who accompanied Brown & Campbell to Motukorea and oversaw the construction of their first nikau homes in 1840.

Mangere and Awhitu. Leading Ngati Whatua chiefs, then resident at Okahu Bay (**87**), invited William Hobson, Lieutenant Governor of New Zealand, to come to the Waitemata to establish a capital for the new colony. William Brown and John Logan Campbell had by this time purchased Motukorea (**134**) from Ngai Tai and had established a rudimentary home and pig run on the island.

After inspecting the Whangarei, Mangawhai and Mahurangi Harbours, Hobson was quickly convinced of Auckland's suitability as a capital. He noted in a dispatch to the Secretary of State for the Colonies that Auckland was sited 'on the shores of a harbour, safe and commodious, and easy of access, and within five miles of Manukau, certainly the best harbour on the whole of the western coast of New Zealand — within fifteen miles of the harbour of the Kaipara, into which four considerable rivers discharge themselves — at no great distance from the Waikato which waters the fertile and extensive plains of the Waipa, on the western side of the island — and the fertile valley of the Thames on the east . . .'

The establishment of Auckland as the capital of New Zealand was formalised when the Union Jack was raised on Point Britomart (**75**) on 16 September 1840, although the land purchase was not concluded with Ngati Whatua until two days later. Hobson named the new settlement after his naval commander George Eden, Lord Auckland.

The 1840s: Formative Years

The Town

Auckland was to be the colony's political focal point as the seat of government, 1840–65. In the 1840s the Imperial Army's headquarters of Fort Britomart (**74**, **75**) and the Admiralty Naval Station at Flagstaff (Devonport, **38**), were the colony's premier military installations. During the 1840s Auckland also became the provincial headquarters for the Anglican (**78**, **91**) and Wesleyan missions.

From its foundation, the town was focused around Commercial Bay (Fort St-Shortland St area), while Official Bay, below Government House (**75**), was the centre of administration. Auckland's main industrial area was Mechanics Bay, at the foot of

A sketch of Mechanics Bay by Government Surveyor Charles Heaphy.

Stanley St. Here were located sawpits, a rope walk, a flour mill, and several shipyards. Freeman's Bay to the west of the town, also had saw pits, a brick kiln, and a slaughter house.

The pattern of Auckland's early European settlement was more haphazard than in any of New Zealand's other large settlements. Cornwallis (57), the region's only large planned settlement of the 1840s, failed within a year. The first large wave of European settlers, who arrived 1842–43, were a polyglot group dominated by English, Irish and Australian immigrants. Many soon moved on to other parts of the colony. Others, however, settled in the growing town, or on tracts of nearby land acquired after Governor Fitzroy removed the Crown's pre-emption on land purchases in 1844.

The Hinterland

Farms soon covered the Tamaki Isthmus, and villages developed around road junctions at New Market, Mt Eden, Epsom and Onehunga. William Swainson, Attorney General of New Zealand 1841–56, was able to comment that by the mid-1840s most of the Tamaki Isthmus was 'now in cultivation, not a stump of a tree is left in the ground.' These farms produced meat for local sale and large quantities of wheat, which was ground at Bycroft's Mill near Mt Eden (81). Other focal points of settlement were the Anglican Church institutions located at Parnell (78) and Purewa (St Johns, 91).

In the wider Auckland hinterland the only European settlements of note to develop in the 1840s were those which grew around large industrial enterprises. These included the Kawau Island (139) and Great Barrier (140) copper mines, although most were

The Riverhead Mill, one of colonial Auckland's most important industrial sites, is here photographed in 1914 with a scow alongside.

timber mills. The latter were generally located near a reliable source of water power and where they could be served by bulk water transport. Prime examples of such enterprises were Thomas Henderson's 'Dundee Mill', Henderson (**66**), and Erasmus Brereton's Riverhead Mill (**41**).

A Time of Insecurity

The Maori communities of the region played a vital role in Auckland's early development. They provided the bulk of the town's produce during its founding years and were to be involved in large-scale trade with Auckland over the next decade. They also provided labour for settlers and the construction of public works. Maori-European relations were generally cordial in this period, although the settler community's unease was exemplified by the development of military fencible settlements, 1847–52, at Onehunga (**97**), Otahuhu, Panmure and Howick (**104**, **106**).

When fighting broke out between British troops and Maori in Northland and Wellington, 1845–47, the town's insecurity increased. Auckland grew into an observably 'garrison town' with the construction of Albert Barracks (**74**, **75**) and the arrival of additional British regiments. Although the Auckland economy was depressed in the late 1840s, the town continued to expand. By 1847 it had a Colonial Hospital and a network of Government Reserves, including the Government Domain (**80**).

The 1850s: Land Purchase and the Expansion of Settlement

The 1850s were a time of expansion and prosperity for both the Maori and European communities of the region. Auckland continued to be the colony's main military base, and its administrative importance was secured when the General Assembly (**75**) was opened near Government House in 1854.

A key feature of the 1850s was the Crown purchase of a huge acreage of Maori land in the region after the formation of the Native Land Purchase Office in 1852. However, local Maori still retained large native reserves and were heavily involved in both local and Pacific trade. The availability of land for settlement, and the attraction of the Government's 40-acre free-grant scheme, saw the spread of European settlers to all parts of the region in the 1850s. Villages sprang up on the periphery, for example at Waiuku (1851, **128**), Wairoa South (1852, **112**), Warkworth (1853, **10**), The Wade (1855, **25**) and Drury (1855). The location of these villages beside navigable waterways illustrated the role that water transport was to play in the region's development over the next 70 years.

The S.S. Weka *at Waiuku Wharf; in the background is the Kentish Arms Hotel.*

The 1860s: The Land Wars

The Build-up to War

The 1860s, while a time of expansion and growth, was also a time of great tension for the region's inhabitants. The Maori King Movement (Kingitanga) had been founded in the Waikato in 1858, with Potatau Te Wherowhero (**80**) at its head. This movement, which continues in strength today, was essentially a commitment by the Tainui tribes to resist further land acquisition within their territory.

The Crown responded to this perceived threat by constructing a series of military blockhouses and stockades on Auckland's southern perimeter, 1860–61. Some of these installations, like the Onehunga (**97**) and Blockhouse Bay (**95**) blockhouses, were constructed to thwart attack. Most, however, like Alexandra Redoubt (**125**), were erected to facilitate the construction of the Great South Road and the intended invasion of the Waikato by government forces.

The Conflict and its Aftermath

After government forces crossed the mouth of the Mangatawhiri River in July 1863, fighting broke out between Maori and European. Most of the major battles waged over the next few months were fought in the Waikato itself. Several battles were, however, fought in South Auckland at places such as: Red Hill (**120**), Clevedon (**112**), Pukekohe East (**123**), Paparimu, and elsewhere within Franklin District. One Tainui war party, recognising the strategic importance of the Paratutai Signal Station at Whatipu (**63**), crossed the Manukau Entrance and chopped down the signal mast in 1863. In an unconnected incident the Captain of the British warship HMS *Orpheus* failed to heed the signal set by the same station, resulting in New Zealand's worst maritime disaster.

The Settlers Stockade (Wairoa South) Clevedon, 1863.

During this brief but tragic episode of fighting the tribes of South Auckland were devastated. They suffered heavy casualties in the ongoing campaign and many remained in exile in the Waikato for over a decade. All of the South Auckland iwi who were deemed to have been in 'rebellion' also had the bulk of their remaining land confiscated by the Crown in 1865.

Tainui always disputed that they were 'rebels'. They asserted that they were simply defending their land and referred to the war as Te Riri Pakeha, 'the white man's anger'. Major General Sir James Alexander (1803–1885) noted in 1863, 'For my part I never considered the Maoris as rebels, or they had not acknowledged, that is, few of them, the Queen's Authority. They fought so as not to be swallowed up by the white settlers.' The consequences of this tragic era in Auckland's history are still being addressed .

Many settler farmsteads were damaged, and South Auckland was largely deserted for nearly a year. Some settlers sold up and sought their fortune elsewhere. Those who decided to remain were paid compensation for property damage, although it would take them a decade to recover economically. The town of Auckland had, on the other hand, undergone a relative boom in 1863–64 as it catered for the needs of up to 10,000 troops. Some of Auckland's leading entrepreneurs also amassed small fortunes through investment in the vast confiscation blocks in the Waikato.

Special Settlements

In order to boost European settlement in the region, the Government had encouraged ethnically based Special Settlements in the early 1860s. Examples were the Bohemian settlement of Puhoi (**16**) and the non-conformist English settlement of Albertland (**2**), both established in 1862. Following the Land Wars the Government took the opportunity to establish further Special Settlements on land confiscated from Maori in South Auckland. Scots, English and South Africans were settled variously at Otau (near Clevedon), Tuhimata (south of Drury), Bombay, Pukekohe, Patumahoe, Tuakau and Pollok (**131**).

The Landscape Transformed

By the end of the 1860s the town and much of rural Auckland had been transformed. Shingle-roofed, kauri homesteads, typically with a verandah, dotted the landscape. It was during this period that many of the region's distinctive rural 'Selwyn Churches' were commissioned by Bishop George Selwyn in the gothic revival style (**112, 126**).

Numerous exotic bird species like the song thrush, blackbird, sparrow and myna had been introduced. Extensive plantings of exotic trees like the common English oak, elm, London plane, *Pinus radiata* and the Norfolk pine covered the land. Wealthier landowners like Judge Gillies, George Owens and Sir George Grey (**139**) planted internationally important aboreta on their properties, and the Acclimatisation Society Gardens were begun in Auckland Domain (**80**). Animal pests like the rabbit and goat became common, and each parish in the region had a thistle inspector from 1863.

The 1870s: Economic Consolidation

Following the Land Wars the Auckland region underwent a brief period of depression after the Imperial Regiments withdrew and the capital was re-located to Wellington in 1865. The Auckland economy received an unexpected boost after gold was discovered at Thames in 1867, although the next decade was to be a period of consolidation rather than spectacular growth.

The Importance of Extractive Industries

In the 1870s Auckland's economy was firmly based on extractive industries, such as timber milling, gum digging and brick making. The firewood industry was also important as vast quantities of fuel were needed for domestic and industrial purposes. Manufacturing industries like flour milling, brewing and publishing also grew in importance. It was the age when water power was superseded by the steam engine, and Auckland's first reticulated water-supply system was commissioned (**71**).

Timber milling was to remain the region's most important industry until the farming boom that resulted from the widespread introduction of refrigeration in the late 1880s. It was to continue to be a major industry until the 1920s. During this period Auckland's forests were systematically stripped of their kauri and other millable timber. Vast quantities of logs were hauled by bullock team, steam hauler and tramway (**45, 56, 63** , **140**), or washed downstream by driving dams (**42**).

The scow Kauri *ghosting into Mechanics Bay with a full load of kauri logs in 1904.*

A related industry which had been of importance to Auckland from the 1840s was ship building (e.g. **4, 6, 7,13, 38, 140**). The 1870s saw the construction of the first of the ubiquitous Auckland scows, the *Lake Erie,* built at Big Omaha by Septimus Meiklejohn in 1873. These flat-bottomed bulk cargo carriers (**76, 128**) were based in design on vessels operating on the Great Lakes of North America. They were ideal for crossing harbour bars, and for navigating the region's shallow tidal creeks and estuaries. Scows were to play a major part in Auckland's economic development for many decades.

In the same period small coastal steamers began to make scheduled runs to the region's many small ports. The steamer services boosted trade, as well as tourism at places like Wairoa South (Clevedon, **112, 121**), and the region's premier tourist destination, the Waiwera Hot Springs (**18**).

Consolidation of the Agricultural Base

The 1870s also saw the consolidation of the region's agriculture base. Much of the better quality land had been cleared of its forest cover, and extensive areas of pasture were established on the lowlands. The farms of the period were generally small, semi-subsistence family units producing a remarkable diversity of products in order to survive.

Auckland's small farms received a major boost with the development of the Auckland-Drury and Harkins Point (Riverhead)-Helensville railways, constructed as part of the Vogel Government's programme of public works in the early 1870s. The regional railway made the local market more accessible to farmers, bringing stability to farm incomes for the first time.

The 'F' class tank locomotive 'Maccallum Mhor' which worked throughout the Auckland region in the late 19th century.

The 1880s: Boom, Bust and Insecurity

Economic Growth in the early 1880s

The early 1880s saw the continued expansion of the region's infrastructure. The rail link between Kaukapakapa in the north and Te Awamutu in the south was completed. Large industrial enterprises like brick making and freezing works relocated beside the railway at places like New Lynn and Westfield. Auckland's new cemetery was located beside the railway at Waikumete (**67**), and villages sprang up around the region's many new railway stations.

When refrigeration became widespread in the late 1880s farming patterns changed. Local creameries were built all around the region as dairying became more important, and growing numbers of fat lambs were produced for the export trade. Farm prices, however, remained low, and the rural economy was to be depressed for a decade.

Timber production was at its peak in the early 1880s, with Helensville (**22**) being the region's main timber port. The trade was however to go into decline from 1885 as timber prices fell sharply and many mills went into receivership. In 1888 the timber industry became subject to a monopoly as the Melbourne-based Kauri Timber Company (**45, 140**) acquired most of the region's mills and all of its large remaining forest stands.

From 1888 the main KTC mill was located on the Auckland foreshore west of the main wharves in what was then New Zealand's main industrial area. Here were located timber mills, shipyards, flour mills, a boot and shoe factory, a freezing works and cannery, and numerous warehouses and offices (**76**). The Colonial Sugar Company Refinery was also established on the opposite shore at Chelsea (**30**). A graving dock had operated for many years near the site of the Tepid Baths. In 1888 it was superseded when the massive Calliope Dock was built near Devonport (**38**).

Although it was a time of economic uncertainty, Auckland continued to grow. The town now had 8000 inhabitants, and approximately 20,000 people lived on the isthmus. Suburbia spread when a horse tram service was established between Auckland and Ponsonby, and later extended to Newmarket. During the decade many large commercial buildings were erected, along with important public buildings like the Customhouse (**76**), and the City Library and Art Gallery (**74**).

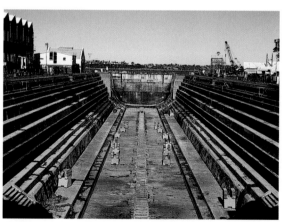

When it was constructed in 1888 the Calliope Dry Dock was regarded as one of the finest facilities of its type in the world.

The Russian Scare

As in previous decades the insecurity of the colony again became apparent during the 'Russian Scare' of 1885–86. From the 1870s an increasing number of Russian commercial and naval vessels were observed in the Pacific. As Russian naval activity increased further in the early 1880s, military officials decided to build a series of fortifications to defend the port of Auckland in case of attack. Fort Bastion was built at Bastion Point, Fort Takapuna was built at Takapuna Head, and both North Head (**39**) and Mount Victoria (**37**) were fortified. A torpedo boat base was established at Devonport (**38**), and a controlled minefield was installed at the harbour entrance.

The 1890s: The Seddon Years

By the 1890s Auckland was no longer a rough colonial town. It had a sophisticated town centre and it was the nation's main industrial centre and port. A visitor of 1895 commented on the cosmopolitan nature of Auckland's population, noting, 'as you saunter about you may hear half-a-dozen languages, from Maori to Gaelic.' Auckland had long had a small and influential Jewish community. It was now also home for growing numbers of immigrants from places like France, Germany, Italy, China and India. Many Maori still brought vegetables or kauri gum to sell in the city, often staying at the Mechanics Bay Maori Hostel. It was, however, a time of depression for the small Maori communities of the region, whose population and land base continued to decline.

Life in Auckland was greatly influenced by the election of New Zealand's first party-based government when the Liberal Party came to power in 1891. Under the leadership of Richard John Seddon, 1892–1906, the Liberals introduced a series of social and economic reforms that created international interest. In the rural area they encouraged the development of small farm units, and their leasehold land schemes opened up much of the region's marginal land. A regional dairy industry was now firmly established, and the West Auckland orcharding and viticultural industries began to develop (**65**).

Women received the vote for the first time in 1893, and the residents of Onehunga elected the Empire's first woman mayor (**97**). New labour legislation brought better wages and a 40-hour working week. Most importantly, it gave workers Saturday afternoons and Sundays off, leading to a remarkable growth in leisure activities. Organised sports competitions emerged for the first time at venues such as Auckland Domain (**80**). Weekend steamer excursions to places like Devonport (**38**), Motutapu (**133**) and Motuihe (**135**), became increasingly popular, as did horse racing, brass-band concerts, walking and cycling. As the Victorian era came to a close, Aucklanders at last had time to explore their region.

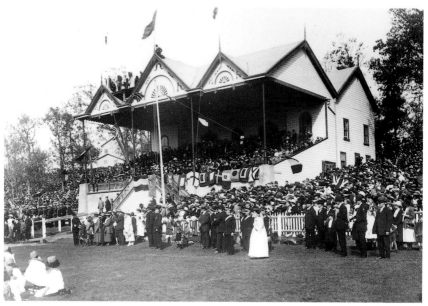

Auckland Domain Grandstand (1893) at the time of the Prince of Wales' visit, 1920.

The Edwardian Era: Optimism and Change

The death of Queen Victoria in 1901 was mourned with great displays of public emotion by the community. The coronation of King Edward VII in 1901 signalled the beginning of a new age and was marked by almost every community. Devonport, for example, renamed its foreshore road after the new monarch and built a commemorative seawall and steps (**38**).

The Edwardian era was to be a time of optimism and great change in the region. A remarkable growth in butter and meat exports to Britain stimulated the rural economy and led to growth in the region's many small towns, which were now served by the telegraph and the penny post. Auckland's growing importance as a manufacturing centre and export port also stimulated growth in the urban area. New suburbs like Herne Bay, Grey Lynn, Sandringham and One Tree Hill developed as the electric tramway network (**71**) expanded over the isthmus. Suburban growth also took place on the North Shore with the construction of the Takapuna Steam Tramway in 1910.

The city's confidence was reflected by the construction of the internationally acclaimed Grafton Bridge (**73**) and an unprecedented number of new public buildings, including: the Ferry Building (**76**), Chief Post Office, Magistrates Court and the Town Hall. Recreation continued to grow in popularity. Aucklanders flocked to the newly created local body parks network, which now included Cornwall Park (**85**), and to other publicly funded facilities like the Parnell Salt Water Baths (**77**).

The barque Bjarne *loading kauri gum at Queen St Wharf in 1904.*

The Great War

The euphoria of the Edwardian age was brought to an abrupt end with the outbreak of the First World War in 1914. Thousands of young Aucklanders served overseas 1914–18. When the 'Great War' ended on 11 November 1918, thousands of them had been killed and many others wounded. This had a traumatic impact on every community in the region, as illustrated by numerous country war memorials and the construction of the Auckland War Memorial Museum (**80**). Returning soldiers introduced the 1918 Influenza Epidemic. It led to the long-term closure of Auckland's schools and churches, although remarkably the pubs stayed open. Nearly 2000 people were

Grafton Bridge, hailed as one of the world's finest ferro-cement structures when it was constructed in 1910.

buried in mass graves in Waikumete Cemetery (**67**). The epidemic hit the region's Maori communities particularly hard, with their death rate being seven times that of the rest of the population.

The 1920s: The Machine Age

After the trauma of the First World War, the region's inhabitants began to forge a strong identity as Aucklanders and New Zealanders for the first time. The 1920s were to bring them economic stability and further social change, much of this resulting from the introduction of mechanisation and the motor vehicle.

The kauri timber industry which had been so important in Auckland's economy for a century came to a close with the completion of the Kauri Timber Company's operation on Great Barrier Island (**140**). Pastoral farming and associated secondary industries now dominated the regional economy.

Farming had become more scientific and productive. Pasture quality was improved through the use of better grass-seed varieties and artificial fertiliser, and selective breeding improved livestock, thus increasing yields of meat and milk. The greatest change, however, came from mechanisation. The introduction of the stationary engine, milking and shearing machines, and tractors freed up labour and made the operation of larger farm units possible. It was a time of innovation in agriculture which saw new fads like ostrich farming being tried, and the expansion of West Auckland as an orcharding and viticultural centre.

Remains of the massive timber driving dam built by George Murray in the Kaiarara Stream Valley, Great Barrier in 1924.

The lives of both rural and urban Aucklanders were permanently changed through the introduction of the telephone and the motor vehicle, which soon replaced horse transport. The widespread construction of metal roads opened up access to rural areas and sounded the death knell of coastal shipping. The commissioning of the Upper Nihotupu (**51**) and Upper Huia (**60**) Dams brought urban Aucklanders a reliable water supply for the first time. Wealthier Aucklanders were connected to electric power, although the mainland rural area was not to be completely connected until the 1950s.

King St, Pukekohe, on a busy day c.1930.

The 1930s: Economic Depression and the Welfare State

A dramatic downturn in export prices for farm produce in the late 1920s heralded the onset of a five-year economic depression. Thousands of Aucklanders became unemployed and were placed on relief work. Hard manual labour saw the improvement of many local parks, such as Blockhouse Bay Reserve (**95**), and school grounds, such as those of Mt Albert Grammar School. Larger projects included the development of Chamberlain Park Golf Course and part of the Scenic Drive (**50**), as well as the planting of much of the Woodhill and Riverhead pine forests.

Frustration with relief work and ongoing food shortages led to a major riot in Auckland in April 1932. Queen Street's shops were looted, and a force of 2000 police and troops was needed to bring order. Aucklanders were obviously seeking change. This came with the landslide election of the first Labour Government in 1935. Led by Michael Joseph Savage, MP for Grey Lynn, this administration introduced sweeping social and economic reforms based on the concept of the 'welfare state'. Its most visible long-term outcome was growth in the region's educational and health facilities, and the emergence of state-housing suburbs. However, the economic recovery of the late 1930s was to end abruptly when the Second World War broke out in 1939.

The 1940s: War, Recovery and Social Change

The Second World War, 1939–45

Once again, thousands of Aucklanders volunteered to serve in a war which was to last six years. The many citizens who died in the conflict were again commemorated by numerous memorials and the extension of the Auckland War Memorial Museum (**80**).

Apart from the sinking of the steamer *Niagara* when it struck a German mine near the Mokohinau Islands, the war did not reach Auckland directly. In order to defend the port from a major seaborne attack, the authorities decided to construct a network of large coastal gun batteries (**24, 28, 39, 132, 137**) and many smaller defence installations. After the Japanese entered the war in 1941, large numbers of US servicemen were based in Auckland. They established camps and hospitals throughout the region, e.g. at Auckland Domain (**80**) and Cornwall Park (**85**).

In the midst of conflict Auckland had celebrated its centenary in 1940 in a remarkable way by creating the Centennial Memorial Park in the Waitakere Ranges (**49**).

War graves at Waikumete Cemetery.

The Post-War Boom

After the war the regional economy was buoyant, as there was a world-wide demand for primary produce. The most striking feature of Auckland in the late 1940s was the development of large state-housing suburbs like Mt Roskill, Mt Wellington and Glen Innes.

Auckland began the 1950s by hosting the Empire Games (1950) and celebrating the coronation of Queen Elizabeth II (1953). These two events provided an appropriate beginning for two decades of remarkable prosperity and growth. For Aucklanders it was an age of amazing material progress as many came to own their own homes and a motor car for the first time. Most households now had a radio and household appliances like refrigerators and electric stoves. The whine of the motorised lawnmower became a symbol of the suburban weekend.

It was an was era of unprecedented growth in the region as the population of the urban area climbed to over 630,000 by 1970. This growth resulted from the post-war 'baby boom', along with both internal and external immigration. Many rural people sought work and the 'bright lights' of the city, and large numbers of Maori migrated to Auckland for the first time.

In the 1950s many European immigrants arrived in the region from countries like Hungary, Holland and Yugoslavia, bringing Auckland more cosmopolitan tastes and its first proper restaurants. In the 1960s the government encouraged large-scale immigration from the Pacific Islands in order to staff the region's growing industrial base, which included the New Zealand Steel Plant, opened at Glenbrook in 1967. Most immigrants who arrived in this era continued however to be government-assisted British immigrants.

In this period the shape of urban Auckland changed as the motorway network was progressively constructed from 1953. It created the many dormitory suburbs of south and west Auckland and made Aucklanders increasingly reliant on the motor car. The construction of the Auckland Harbour Bridge and the Northern Motorway in 1959 led to the urbanisation of the North Shore. In 1955 the first Hunua water-supply dam was commissioned at Cossey's Creek (**121**).

Auckland Harbour Bridge (1959), a symbol of the post-war boom.

Rural Auckland continued to rely on dairying, with sheep and beef production predominating in the hill country. Prices for dairy produce were stable on the British market and wool prices boomed during the Korean War. A revolutionary development in farming came with the introduction of aerial topdressing in the early 1950s. This transformed the productive capacity of the region's marginal hill-country properties.

A key feature of the 1960s was the decision of Auckland's many local bodies to form the Auckland Regional Authority in 1965. It was to co-ordinate regional planning and to develop the region's service infrastructure, including the construction of the Mangere Sewage Purification Plant (1960) and Auckland International Airport, Mangere (1966). An important heritage outcome of the establishment of the ARA was the progressive development of Auckland's magnificent regional parks network, beginning with the purchase of Wenderholm Regional Park (**17**) in 1965.

Recent Decades

The 1970s and 1980s were decades of economic stagnation for the region following the international oil crisis of 1974 and the sharemarket crash of 1987. A notable heritage gain was the creation of New Zealand's first marine reserve at Goat Island Bay (**5**). The 1990s have been a period of economic growth and social change in a new deregulated 'market forces' economy. The region's population has continued to climb steadily throughout the period, adding 119,000 people 1991–96, or the equivalent of Dunedin's total population, passing one million for the first time in 1996.

Auckland's rural area has been subjected to major change. Large areas near the urban edge have been subdivided into 4-ha 'lifestyle blocks', and many new forms of land use ranging from tropical fruit production to ostrich farming have emerged. During this period the urban area continued to sprawl across the countryside in association with the extension of the motorway network.

The inner city has been subjected to major intensification through infill housing and the development of large numbers of city apartments. Auckland has become increasingly cosmopolitan. It has long been the largest Polynesian city in the world, and has become home for a growing number of ethnic groups. As in other parts of the country, there has been a renaissance of Maori identity.

In 1990 the region commemorated the 150th anniversary of both the signing of the Treaty of Waitangi and the foundation of Auckland. Aucklanders have become less self-conscious about their origins and more interested in the region's past. They have become aware that Auckland's identity is the legacy of many strands of history woven over a period of 1000 years.

Te toto o te tangata he kai: te oranga o te tangata, he whenua.
Food supplies humans with physical sustenance; their spiritual wellbeing comes from the land.

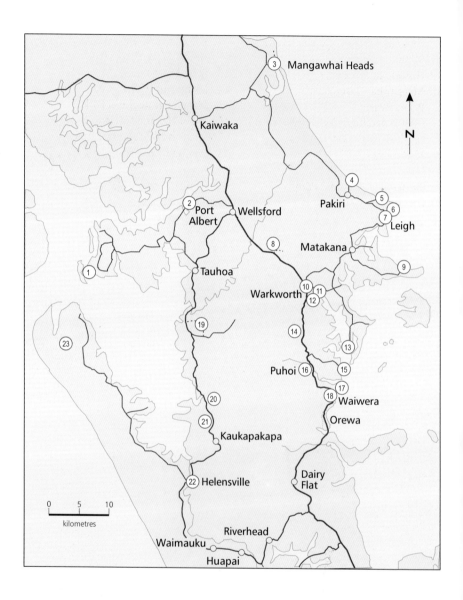

Mangawhai Heads

③

Kaiwaka

④

⑤
⑥
② Port Albert ○ Wellsford   Pakiri   ⑦ Leigh
①   Matakana
⑧
① Tauhoa   ⑨
                ⑩ ⑪
Warkworth ⑫
⑲   ⑭
㉓   ⑬
        Puhoi ⑯ ⑮
⑳   ⑰
㉑   ⑱ Waiwera
Kaukapakapa   Orewa

Dairy Flat
㉒ Helensville

0   5   10
kilometres

Riverhead
Waimauku ○
Huapai

North

1. Taporapora, Okahukura Peninsula
2. Minniesdale Chapel via
   Historic Port Albert
3. Mangawhai Cliffs Walkway
4. Pakiri Beach
5. Goat Island Bay Marine Reserve
6. Leigh Harbour (Omaha Cove)
7. Mathesons Bay Fossils
8. Dome Forest Walkway
9. Tawharanui Regional Park
10. Historic Warkworth
11. Wilson's Cement Works
    Ruins
12. Warkworth Museum & Parry Kauri
    Park
13. Scott Point
14. Moirs Hill Walkway
15. Mahurangi Regional Park
16. Puhoi Historic Village
17. Wenderholm Regional Park
18. Waiwera Hot Springs
19. Mt Auckland Walkway
20. Omeru Scenic Reserve
21. Kaipara Harbour Lookout
22. Historic Helensville
23. Kaipara South Head

*The Mangawhai Cliffs Walkway (3) traverses the white sands of Mangawhai Heads Beach
before climbing up through pasture to a clifftop ridge with inspiring views.*

*Page 97: Pohutukawa trees provide a stunning display in early summer along the coastline
north of Auckland.*

Accessible from Wellsford via Port Albert, then follow the signs to Tapora; turn right for access to the coast from Journeys End Rd, or left and take Te Ngaio Pt Rd for access to the south shore.

Sand-dune island off south-west corner of Tapora flats, with oioi in a dune hollow.

Okahukura Peninsula takes its name from Kahukura, a chief from the Takitimu canoe who visited the Kaipara area six centuries ago. The density of archaeological sites indicates intensive occupation over many generations. At the west end of the peninsula is the extensive sandy area known as Taporapora. According to tradition it was an important occupation area that was largely eroded away several centuries before it was occupied by Ngati Whatua.

The peninsula was purchased by the Crown from Ngati Whatua in 1862, except for the Maori Reserve at Kakaraea, and sold to Thomas Fitzgerald in 1876. He built a post-and-rail fence across the narrowest part of the peninsula on the old Opou portage and farmed the property as one large cattle run. Kauri timber rights were sold to McLeod's of Helensville (22), and the whole farm was dug over for kauri gum. In the 1950s the peninsula was developed into smaller farm units by the Lands and Survey Department.

All the flat and gently rolling land around Tapora is grassed sand dunes that have accumulated in the last 7000 years (see p. 21).

Today, patches of regenerating kanuka are scattered through the farmland, occasionally with taraire, puriri, kahikatea or kauri rickers.

Off the south-west corner of the Tapora flats is a large sand island, with low dunes, oioi-filled dune slacks and a few small stands of kanuka, which are being buried by moving sand. The golden pingao and silvery spinifex are common on the dunes. Shrubs of spicy-scented tauhinu are present, although sadly the native coastal toetoe is being replaced by South American pampas grass. In the upper tide zone are extensive salt meadows of glasswort, selliera, shore pimpernel, saltwater paspalum and native lobelia.

The area is a haven for shore birds and waders. In March large flocks of godwits and knots build up before departing for the Arctic. Dotterels, wrybills, oystercatchers, pied stilts, pipits, black swans, gulls, swallows and white-faced herons are all common.

Port Albert, 11 km from Wellsford along Port Albert Rd. Toilets, picnic area.
Minniesdale Chapel, 6 km from Port Albert via Wharehine Rd, signposted from Pah Hill Rd.

Several historic sites can be observed en route to Port Albert: Port Albert Hall, Port Albert Church, and a memorial stone on the site of the first Port Albert Cemetery (1862–70). The Albertland Museum, located under the grandstand at Port Albert Domain in Wellsford Valley Rd, houses a collection of photographs and local memorabilia. It may be visited by arrangement locally.

Present-day Port Albert consists of an isolated group of houses on a headland overlooking Port Albert Wharf and the Oruawharo River. When founded in 1863 'Albert Town' had been planned as the port and focal point for the large settlement of 'Albertland'. Named in honour of Prince Albert, the late husband of Queen Victoria, it was one of the last 'Special Settlements' sponsored by the Colonial Government. The Albertland Special Settlement Association was organised in Birmingham by a journalist, William Brame, with the intention of settling 1000 Non-Conformists from the English Midlands on 30,000 acres chosen by Wesleyan missionary Rev. William Gittos.

Eight shiploads of 'Albertland' settlers arrived (1862–65) to take up land under the 'Free Grant' system. Only half took up land at 'Albertland' because of delays in land survey and allocation, isolation and the transport difficulties associated with the tidal Kaipara Harbour. 'Albertland' never became the settlement that Brame and his fellow settlers had intended, although many of their descendants remained in the district, which flourished with the arrival of dairying and all-weather roads in the 1930s.

Among those who settled in 'Albertland' were Rev. Edwin Brookes and his wife Jemima, who brought with them the framing, window glass, joinery and bell for the construction of a small chapel, which was erected in 1867. It and the Brookes' homestead became known as 'Minniesdale', after Jemima (Minnie) Brookes. The Brookes family and many other 'Albertlanders' are buried in the cemetery that surrounds this beautiful little church. The restored Minniesdale House, near the church, is privately owned but may be visited by arrangement.

Minniesdale Chapel

Access from the end of Mangawhai Heads Rd. Changing sheds, surf patrol in summer, campground nearby. Walkway (3 hrs return) crosses private land (closed August and September for lambing).

At its northern end, Mangawhai Cliffs Walkway passes through a natural rock arch on the foreshore.

The walkway is signposted from the Surf Club carpark that overlooks Sentinel Rock and the oft-changing entrance to Mangawhai Harbour, which was a busy 19th-century timber port. Mangawhai estuary is enclosed by a magnificent sandspit that is a wildlife refuge and nesting and roosting place for a wide variety of birds including Caspian, white-fronted and fairy terns and the New Zealand dotterel.

The first section of the walkway passes below the highly modified Mangawhai Pa and then follows the beach for 1 km. The track turns inland following marker poles up a ridge to the clifftop track. It passes remnant patches and solitary trees of coastal forest dominated by pohutukawa, totara, gnarled puriri, nikau and in places taraire. There are magnificent views to Bream Tail (Paepae o Tu), Sail Rock and the Hen and Chickens Islands (see p. 70) beyond, with inland views over farm country to the Robert Hastie Scenic Reserve on the forested Brynderwyn Hills.

The track zigzags down to the foreshore, 1 km south of Bream Tail. Here there is a pied shag colony in a large pohutukawa tree and a natural arch in light-coloured dacite rock. Walkers can return following the same route or via the rocky foreshore. This latter route includes some scrambling around rocky reefs; avoid at high tide.

The arch is close to the contact between an intrusive dome of dacite and thick, concretion-bearing Waitemata Sandstone beds to the north. About 800 m south of the arch is a delightful white sandy beach on the southern margin of the intrusive dacite body. Here the rocks are known as the 'Giant's Staircase' because of their spectacular, columnar cooling joints, but a closer look also reveals beautiful, sometimes folded flow-banding.

From here to Mangawhai Heads beach the coastal rocks are ancient greywacke. Blocks of limestone (basal Waitematas, p. 26) have fallen down the cliffs to the beach.

Access from the end of Pakiri River Rd, off the Leigh-Wellsford Rd, 10 km north of Leigh. Surfing, changing sheds, swimming, surfcasting, campground and store.

Pakiri Beach extends 24 km from Pitokuku Reef in the south to Mangawhai Sandspit in the north. The beach and sand dunes have formed in just the last 6500 years (see p. 21). The white sand is mostly the mineral feldspar derived from rhyolite eruptions around Taupo and carried into the gulf by the Waikato River, when its course flowed through the Hauraki Plains.

Pakiri Beach was traditionally called Nga One Haea o Pakiri, 'the gleaming white sands of Pakiri'. The name Pakiri originates from the pa located on the headland at the mouth of Pakiri River. This area has been the home of the Ngati Manuhiri subtribe of Ngati Wai since their ancestor Tahuhunui landed at Goat Island Bay (**5**).

The numerous shell middens found along the beach indicate that it was a rich source of seafood over many generations. From the 1860s, a timber mill was located near the

The native sand-binding sedge pingao at the mouth of Pakiri River. Little Barrier Island looms up offshore.

site of the present motor camp and a number of sailing vessels were constructed near the river mouth. Thousands of kauri logs were floated down the river and towed in rafts to Auckland mills. Pakiri was not accessible by all-weather road until the early 1900s.

Variable oystercatchers and New Zealand dotterel nest sparingly in the dunes. Trumpet and helmet shells, scallops, tuatua, horse mussels, volutes, ostrich feet and wheel shells are commonly washed up on the beach from just offshore.

Pingao and spinifex dominate the foredunes, often with bright-green patches of shore bindweed. On more fixed dunes, harestail grass and leafy rosettes of hawkbit are present. The presence of mangroves and salt marsh show that the Pakiri River is tidal for at least 1 km. Reef and white-faced herons, pied stilts, little shags, banded rail, paradise shelducks and kingfishers are present in this estuarine habitat.

At the end of Goat Island Rd, 3 km north of Leigh. Changing sheds, snorkelling and scuba diving, swimming, short walkway.

The Cape Rodney to Okakari Point Marine Reserve is New Zealand's oldest marine reserve. It was established in 1975 after years of effort by Bill Ballantine and his colleagues from Auckland University's marine laboratory, which is located up the driveway at the end of the road.

Since the reserve's establishment, fish and rock lobster numbers have dramatically increased. Schools of fish, particularly blue maomao, red moki, snapper, parore, trevally, blue cod, spotties and leatherjackets, can often be seen from the rocks or by wading in the water. The best way to appreciate the rich marine life is by donning a snorkel and mask or scuba gear and venturing out. A glass-bottomed boat operates on busy days.

The shore platforms to the right of the beach are sandy conglomerate (basal Waitemata Group, see p. 26) containing pieces of fossil oysters, sea-egg spines, lamp shells and calcareous algae. The high cliffs north-west of the beach are thick Waitemata Sandstone beds with packets of thin-bedded siltstone that accumulated in the Waitemata Basin.

Goat Island has a native forest cover dominated by tall pohutukawa on the south side, some of which pied shags nest in. In winter grey-faced petrels nest in burrows.

Goat Island Bay (Wakatuwhenua) is of traditional importance to the northern tribes

A large snapper investigates divers in Goat Island Bay, New Zealand's first marine reserve.

as the landing place of the Moekakara canoe commanded by Tahuhunui o Rangi. Motu Hawere (Goat Island) was so named as it was likened to an ear pendant. The area at the end of the road was occupied by Ngati Wai until the early years of this century, and the valley behind was farmed by the Matheson family (7).

Walk up the University laboratory driveway and follow the signs that lead up the hill behind to a short clifftop walkway. It passes through clumps of coastal forest and provides excellent views out to sea to Little Barrier and beyond.

Access to the walkway around the upper cove is down the boat ramp from Leigh Wharf carpark, at the north end of the township. A more difficult walk is south around rock platforms at low tide or via steep steps at the end of Harbour View Rd.

Leigh Harbour (Omaha Cove) is a picturesque, deep-water cove. Sheltered from all but the strongest south-west winds, it provides a safe anchorage for a permanent fishing fleet and recreational craft. Traditionally the harbour was known as Omaha, which can be freely translated as 'the place of plenty'. It has been home for many generations to Ngati Wai, who maintain the ancestral Te Kiri Marae and a cemetery on the northern side of the cove. In the 1830s, Omaha was the favourite camping place for Rev. Henry Williams and his fellow missionaries as they travelled up and down the east coast. Williams and his party camped on the sandy flat that is now occupied by the Fisherman's Inn at the head of the cove (see p. 79). A number of sailing vessels were constructed on the same spot at McQuarrie and McInnes's shipyard (1865–76).

The village of Leigh was surveyed by Heaphy and Baber in 1858 and named in honour of the Wesleyan missionary Rev. Samuel Leigh, who began work in New Zealand in 1817. It was settled by Nova Scotians from 1859 and English immigrants from 1863. The graves of many of them may be seen in the old Leigh Cemetery at the end of Harbour View Rd. This spot offers excellent views over the cove, and beyond to Panetiki, Little Barrier (Hauturu) and Great Barrier (Aotea) Islands.

The shoreline walk around the upper cove passes through Leigh Scenic Reserve with its large overhanging pohutukawa. The regenerating coastal forest is quite diverse. Ponga, coastal karamu and houpara are common with taraire, puriri and nikau and a few kauri. Kaka may sometimes be seen, as well as endless bush-framed harbour views.

Omaha Cove from Leigh Scenic Reserve.

Turn right just before Leigh, down Grand View Rd. Picnic area, changing sheds, safe swimming.

Mathesons Bay, known traditionally as Kohuroa from the sea mist which sometimes hangs in the bay, has a sheltered sandy beach suitable for swimming at all tides. The area received its present name from the Matheson family, who arrived from Nova Scotia in 1859. A memorial seat at the south end of the bay records that Captains Duncan and Angus Matheson opened a shipyard, developed farms and built homes in the bay, which they called 'Seaside'. Angus Matheson's original house is still in use as a private residence at the north end of the bay.

The cliffs and shore platforms north and south of the beach are one of the best places in the region to see fossils. It is also an excellent place to view the buried 20-million-year-old shoreline of the Waitemata Basin.

The irregular ancient coastline of greywacke stacks and small bays can be seen eroding from the modern cliffs, where it is buried beneath bouldery breccia and layers of grey pebbly sandstone. These sedimentary rocks accumulated as coarse talus fans, pocket beaches and sand on the floor of shallow bays. The thick fossilised shells of huge oysters and numerous pebbles encrusted in laminae of calcareous algae are common in the coarse breccia lenses. The pebbly sandstone, in the cliffs 100 m south of the beach, is rich in fossil lamp shells, sea-egg spines and unusual, cup-shaped corals. The 10–20 cm deep, vertical feeding burrows of ancient rays are present here.

These coarse basal Waitemata group sediments are overlain by siltstone and fine sandstone that accumulated in the deepening sea as the Waitemata Basin subsided to a depth of 1–3 km (see p. 26).

Other places to see fossils: Motutapu Island (**133**), Motuihe Island (**135**) and Ihumatao Fossil Forest (**101**).

Fossilised plates of giant barnacle (up to 12 cm long) can be seen in the rocks at the north end of Mathesons Bay.

Access from Dome Tearooms carpark, at top of the hill on SH1, 7 km north of Warkworth. Walk to lookout (40 mins return); to Dome summit (1.5 hrs return); or to Waiwhiu Kauri Grove (3 hrs return).

The track climbs to the lookout with views across the Hauraki Gulf and Mahurangi Peninsula. From here the track is a lower standard, descending and then ascending steeply to the rocky Dome summit (336 m) with views northwards across exotic pine plantations and the outer Hauraki Gulf and Hen Island.

The Dome was traditionally known as Tohitohi o Reipae, or 'the prominent landmark of Reipae'. This famous Tainui ancestress is said to have travelled to the north on a bird with her sister Reitu, who was seeking the hand of a leading northern chief, Ueoneone. En route they alighted at Tohitohi o Rei before proceeding to Whanga a Reipae (Whangarei Harbour).

The Dome and surrounding ridges are made of exceedingly thick, erosion-resistant beds of Waitemata Sandstone. These sandstone layers north of Warkworth are much thicker (3–10 m) than those around Auckland (0.3–1 m), because they were nearer the source of the turbulent

Easter orchid (Earina autumnalis)*, a common perching plant along the Dome Walkway, usually detected by its strong, sweet scent.*

slurries (turbidity currents) that deposited them on the ancient seafloor (see pp. 26–27).

From Dome summit the track descends gently to Waiwhiu Kauri Grove, where some 20 large kauri are present flanking the ridge. Oddly, kauri are absent along the rest of the track.

The first part of the track is through kanuka forest with good regeneration underneath. Along the ridge, heketara, a tree daisy and tall rimu are common in association with Hall's totara, totara, miro, kohekohe, hinau, rewarewa, lacebark, tawa and pigeonwood. Beside the track, well before the lookout, is a single tall northern tree rata and a kawaka. The kawaka particularly stands out with its rich-reddish peeling bark and straight trunk. Common shrubs include New Zealand gloxinia (taurepo), koromiko (*Hebe macrocarpa*) and forest cabbage tree. On the ground are native irises (*Libertia* species) and dwarf cabbage trees. Epiphytic orchids are common and sweet-scented when flowering in spring (*Earina mucronata*) and autumn (*E. autumnalis*).

Access signposted off Warkworth-Leigh Rd. Last 8 km of the route is gravel road. Picnics, toilets, camping, peninsula walk (2.5 hrs), ecology trail (1.5 hrs), swimming, surfing and snorkelling at Anchor Bay.

Tawharanui is the region's largest (588 ha) and most spectacular coastal farm park. It was purchased by the ARA from the Georgetti family in 1973. Tawharanui Peninsula consists of folded and uplifted greywacke overlain by Waitemata Sandstone. The western flats consist of gravel and sand that has accumulated in the last 6500 years.

The park is largely pasture, although it includes kanuka patches with regenerating forest of pohutukawa, puriri, taraire, totara, tanekaha, tawa, kahikatea and nikau. Kauri and rimu are less common. A fantastic fallen puriri which has continued to grow, near the stream on the uphill side of the Ecology Trail, stretches down the hill for 30 m and has 14 erect branches. This valley is dominated by large puriri, dense taraire and nikau palms. Kauri and tanekaha regeneration with kanuka, totara, rimu and rewarewa are the main trees by the upper end of the trail. Walkers to Takatu Point are rewarded with great views of the gulf and, on the clifftops, prostrate manuka, which is botanically unique in the region. A raupo wetland is located in the Mangatawhiri Stream valley, and pingao and spinifex, the native sand-binders, grow in the dunes behind the main ocean beach.

Beautiful Anchor Bay, named after the anchor of the Phoenix, *wrecked in 1879.*

Jones Bay Lagoon, Tawharanui, was created by a century of shingle extraction.

Birds of particular interest are the reef heron, spotless crake and bittern, which inhabit the wetlands, and New Zealand pipit and New Zealand dotterel, which nest on the north-west edge of the park. The presence of pasture and wetland has provided an ideal habitat for New Zealand's endemic paradise shelduck, which abounds in the park in pairs or flocks. Females are white-headed and have a shrill call, males are greenish, black-headed with a deep call. They feed on pasture grasses, clover and aquatic vegetation. New Zealand's first Marine Protected Area (1981) safeguards the marine ecology of the reefs and sandy northern coastline.

Tawharanui has a long history of human occupation. Until the 1870s the park was occupied by subtribes of Ngai Tahuhu and Kawerau descent. Its environs provided the Maori with a rich variety of marine and forest resources, as illustrated by the name Tawhara-nui, 'the abundant bracts of the kiekie vine'. A fine ridge-top pa is located above the park entrance, and a headland pa can be seen at Anchor Bay.

Tawharanui was purchased from its Maori owners, 1873–77, and developed as a farm in the 19th century by the Martin, Jones and Young families. Kauri timber was milled in the 19th century, and manuka firewood was cut for many years. Shingle was extracted for a century, creating the large Jones Bay Lagoon. Locality names like 'Phoenix Reef' reflect the fact that nine vessels were wrecked on the Tawharanui coastline, 1871–1978.

69 km north of Auckland on SH1. Public toilets and picnic areas in Kowhai Park and on the River Walk.

Warkworth is located at the head of the Mahurangi River beside the falls, known traditionally as Puhinui, 'the great plume'. The township area was settled in 1843 by John Anderson Brown. A decade later, Brown subdivided his farm and offered sections for sale in the village he named 'Warkworth', after his birthplace in Northumberland. Its original streets were named after the noble families of Northumberland and the villages surrounding Warkworth in England. Timber merchants and the Royal Navy visited the area seeking spars and timber from c.1830, and a water-powered mill operated near the falls from c.1843. Excellent deposits of limestone occur in the vicinity of Warkworth, which was one of New Zealand's most important lime-producing areas for over 70 years. Other economic activities in the area were boat building, orcharding and farming.

The historic places of Warkworth are best seen on foot. A good place to begin is Kowhai Park, on the northern edge of town. Here a short signposted walk leads through a fine coastal forest remnant past the remains of lime kilns that operated during the 1880s. In Elizabeth Street is Auckland's oldest functioning courthouse (1880) and Bridge House (1912), located on the site of J.A. Brown's original home. Cross the old bridge (1914) over the falls (of Waitemata Sandstone) and take the 'Nathaniel Wilson Steps' to the River Walk, which begins at the weir located on the site of Brown's Flour Mill Dam (1844). From here the River Walk runs beside the Mahurangi River to the site of the former Warkworth Wharf. Proceed up Kapanui St (named after a coastal steamer that serviced Warkworth in the 1920s) to Mill St. Buildings of interest here include Stubb's Family Butchery (1922), opposite it one of the town's oldest shops (now the ASB), and the Warkworth Inn (1862). In front of the inn is a Norfolk pine planted by the hotel owner, John Southgate, to commemorate the birth of his first child in c.1868. Just beyond the end of Mill St in Baxter St is the Masonic Lodge (1883). At the eastern

The Warkworth Bank of New Zealand, built in 1929.

end of this street is Lucy Moore Park, which has short walks and fine views over the Mahurangi River.

From Baxter St return to Neville St. At 'Roberts Corner' is the former Hinemoa Boardinghouse, and next to it is 'Broomfield House', named after an early owner, A.G. Broomfield. Further south along Neville St is the BNZ (1929), the Post Office (1911), and the Town Hall (1911). This building is of interest as it was constructed from glazed ceramic building blocks made at Clark's Potteries, Hobsonville. At the southern end of Neville St is the Methodist Church (1859), above which is a cluster of historic buildings in the area known as 'Church Hill'. They include: the Band Hall (1883), the Band Rotunda and War Memorial, Christ Church (Anglican, 1876) and the old cemetery. St Columba Church (Presbyterian, 1876) is in nearby Whitaker St.

On the north side of the Mahurangi River opposite Warkworth township is the Puhinui Scenic Reserve. Here tall regenerating forest on a steep slope is dominated by totara, kowhai, kanuka and mamaku tree ferns, with tanekaha and occasional pole kauri. The estuarine nature of the river is reflected by mangroves along its southern shore. Caspian terns, black and pied shags fish the river right up to the township. A trip down river is popular in springtime to view the abundant kowhai in full flower.

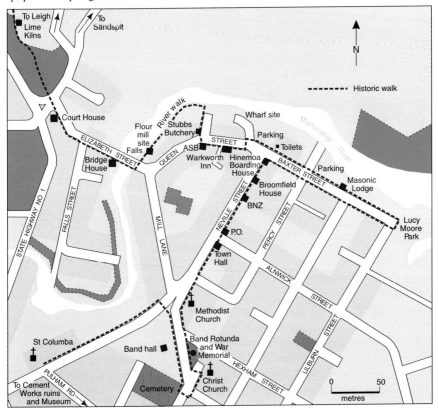

Located at the end of Wilson Rd, Warkworth; accessible via Pulham Rd or from McKinney Rd off SH1. Toilets, picnic area, boat ramp.

Remains of Wilson & Co. Cement Works and flooded open-cast mine (1866–1928) — Auckland's most impressive and picturesque historic industrial site.

The Wilson & Co. Cement Works ruins is one of the region's largest and most impressive historic industrial sites. Founded by Nathaniel Wilson in 1866, it was the first cement works of its type in the Southern Hemisphere and the first to produce 'Portland Cement'. The works operated until 1928, when much of the plant was removed to Portland, Whangarei. The abandoned works were used during the Second World War by the Home Guard and US Forces to practise demolition techniques. This created the picturesque present ruins, a popular venue for events and with filmmakers and photographers. Although the ruins are generally stable, visitors are advised to treat them with caution.

The 3-ha site contains the remains of a large number of concrete buildings, kilns, chimneys, ball mills, laboratories, workshops, etc. These structures reflect the development of cement-manufacturing technology over a period of seven decades. The large-scale production of high-quality cement by Nathaniel and later John Wilson at this plant played a very important part in the introduction of the use of concrete in building construction in New Zealand. Early Auckland structures constructed from Wilson's 'Star Brand' cement included: the Parnell Rail Tunnel, Rangitoto Beacon, Grafton Bridge (**73**) and the Upper Nihotupu Dam (**51**). Wilson & Co. promoted the use of their cement in the construction of some of New Zealand's earliest concrete houses. A fine privately restored example may be seen near the works and in Nathaniel Wilson's own mansion, 'Riverina', near the junction of Wilson and Pulham Rds. The raw material, quarried on site, was muddy limestone in a giant block of Northland Allochthon (see pp. 33–34), which had slid into the Waitemata Basin during a major seafloor failure 20 million years ago.

Signposted from Pulham Rd, or from McKinney Rd on the southern edge of Warkworth. Museum (open daily 9 am–4 pm; toilets, picnic tables, short walk.

One of the region's best local museums is located at Parry Kauri Park, which was purchased by local residents in order to preserve the fine remnant of kauri forest. In front of the museum is a picnic area dominated by two huge kauri trees.

The Warkworth and District Museum is impressively organised by historical theme and contains a wide range of artefacts and memorabilia. A feature of the museum is the Tudor Collins Room. It contains the photographic equipment and many of the photographs of Tudor Collins, as well as displays of polished kauri gum and native timbers. Collins was one of the best-known chroniclers of the kauri timber-milling and gum industries, and played a prominent part in the preservation of the Parry Kauri Park. Outside the Museum are related displays and several small colonial buildings including the old Warkworth Jail.

Over 2 ha of regenerating bush is associated with the two large kauri. Native conifers in the podocarp family are particularly common, especially kahikatea, which is present in dense stands near the kauri. Just behind the McKinney tree is an advanced stand of regenerating kauri over 20 m tall. Two short loop tracks through the bush are well formed, with a boardwalk along much of the route, protecting the tree roots.

Native pigeons and tui are common in the area, and noisy rosellas are usually present.

Picnic area at the entrance to Warkworth Museum. On the left stands one of the region's largest kauri, the 800-year-old McKinney Kauri, with a diameter of 2.4 m.

At the end of Ridge Rd, south from Algies Bay and Snells Beach. Boat ramp. Foot access along the foreshore to historic Scott House and at low tide to Casnell Island Scenic Reserve (Maunganui Pa).

Scott Point takes its name from the Scott family, who settled on 3.2 ha at Scott Bay in 1853. Here Thomas Scott and his sons Thomas Junior and Benjamin established a home and a shipyard, which operated 1855–70. They also built a hotel, known as the 'Richmond Arms', catering for local shipyard and timber workers, as well as many sea-going travellers. The inn burnt down c.1873 and was replaced in 1877 by the boarding house now known as 'Scott House'. A wharf was built at Scott Point and the boarding house accommodated travellers on the Mahurangi River until 1910. 'Scott House' was then used as a family residence and holiday home until it was purchased by the ARA in 1971. The house has been progressively restored.

An interesting walk can be made around the foreshore to Te Kapa Inlet, once the location of three of the region's busiest ship-building yards, 1865–80. At the eastern end of the beach vertical layers of Waitemata Sandstone can be seen in the cliff, and beds of Parnell Grit form the shore platform. At low tide shell banks may be crossed to the well-preserved Maunganui Pa, located on Casnell Island.

Casnell Island Reserve supports a diverse native flora for its small size (6.8 ha). Regenerating kanuka is the main vegetation with pohutukawa, kowhai and tawapou. Tawapou is an attractive coastal tree native to northern New Zealand and Norfolk Island. Its large fruit go through a rainbow of colours before turning black. The Maori used their hard shiny seeds for necklaces.

Gulls, gannets, white-fronted and Caspian terns frequent this part of the coast.

Two cottages are available for short-term rental and Scott House is available for accommodation or as a meeting venue through the ARC Regional Parks Service. Nearby Burton Wells Scenic Reserve is also worth a visit. It contains a well-preserved ring-ditch pa under regenerating coastal forest.

Scott House (1877), the region's oldest remaining coastal boarding house.

Signposted on SH1, 9 km north of Puhoi turnoff, just below the Pohuehue Viaduct, or via exotic plantations from Moirs Hill via Redwoods or Mahurangi Rds. The southern part of the walkway is closed during logging operations. From SH1 walks include a gravel track to a stream lookout (40 mins return); a 2-hr loop; or the walkway to Moir Rd (3–4 hrs return) — the latter two can be muddy when wet.

Moirs Hill was named after two Scottish brothers, Henry and Alexander Moir, who farmed the Moirs Hill area from 1859 until 1927. Their home on the western side of the hill was a well-known resting place for travellers on the old Great North Road.

From SH1 the walkway ascends through the spectacular Pohuehue Scenic Reserve, which is named after several forest vines. The reserve stretches from the Pohuehue Stream in the valley bottom to the ridge top and is visible to all who use the highway. From the roadside the emergent northern tree rata with their fan-like branches stand out on the skyline, tall rewarewa have the form of Lombardy poplars, mamaku tree ferns are abundant in the canopy with taraire, tawa and kohekohe. The native conifers of kauri, kahikatea, rimu and totara are less common. Heads of rata vines and perching puka (with shiny leaves) can also be seen in the canopy.

The lookout track follows a stream up to a waterfall flowing over Waitemata Sandstone. The dampness of the bush along this track is reflected in the abundance of filmy ferns, mosses and liverworts on the ground and on tree trunks, the herb paratanıwha with its rough-surfaced leaves (coppery when young), nikau and the scrambling climber kiekie. Three tree ferns are common: mamaku, ponga and wheki. Look for towai trees that usually start their life as an epiphyte on tree-fern trunks. The autumn-flowering rata vine (*Metrosideros fulgens*) with its showy orange-red flowers is common. Taraire and kohekohe are the most frequent trees along this lower track.

Tall rewarewa, tree rata and tree ferns stand out in the regenerating native forest of the Pohuehue Scenic Reserve.

Access signposted off SH1 (3 km north of Puhoi) down Pukapuka Rd. Changing sheds, safe swimming, picnics, BBQs, farm and beach walks, camping.

Mahurangi regatta day at Sullivan's Beach on Auckland's anniversary weekend. Pudding Island is in the distance.

The park is located on either side of the entrance to Mahurangi Harbour (Mahurangi East is accessible only by boat). The harbour formed when a forested Ice Age river valley was drowned by rising sea levels, c.7000 years ago (see pp. 20–22). Sea erosion since then has cut into the ends of spurs and ridges forming low cliffs of Waitemata Sandstone rocks. These are fringed with pohutukawa. Coastal walks abound when the tide is out; even Pudding Island can be reached at low tide.

The park was part of the ancestral domain of Ngati Rongo, from the 17th to the 20th century. Reminders of their occupation are an open settlement site on Tungutu Point and four fortified pa sites on Opahi, Cudlip and Te Muri Points, and above Otarawao Bay. A sea captain, John Sullivan, married Merehai Kaipuke, one of the principal owners of the land, and settled at Otarawao (Sullivan's Bay) in the 1870s. Their descendants farmed the area for nearly a century and built the two current rangers' houses c.1900.

Te Muri was an important Ngati Rongo settlement until the death of the chief Te Hemara Tauhia in 1891. More than 100 Maori and Europeans are buried in the little Te Muri graveyard, which is shaded by two tapu pohutukawa. A nearby chimney marks the site of a small church established by Rev. Wiremu Pomare, c.1872. In 1920 Te Muri was purchased by the Schischka family. They farmed it until it was purchased for the regional park in 1973.

Patches of coastal and podocarp/hardwood forest are present on Cudlip and Te Muri Points and north of Te Muri Estuary. These are dominated by kanuka, taraire, puriri, karaka, and kowhai, with some taller kahikatea, totara and tanekaha, and occasional kauri. Forest birds include native pigeon, grey warbler, fantail, tui, shining cuckoo, kingfisher and rosella. In the open pasture, harriers, swallows, magpies and mynas occur. The inner reaches of Te Muri estuary feature mangroves, with sea rush flats closer to the mouth. Pied stilt, variable oystercatcher, white-faced heron and pukeko are common.

Places of historical interest are mapped on a sign just beyond the Village Hall, 2 km up Puhoi Road from SH1.

Puhoi Village is nestled in a narrow valley facing the upper tidal reaches of Puhoi River. The name Puhoi stems from the 'slow flowing' nature of the river. The settlement was founded by Bohemian immigrants as part of a Colonial Government Special Settlement Scheme (see p. 85) arranged by Captain Martin and Emily Krippner, who had settled at Orewa in 1861. The migrants, who came from villages surrounding the town of Staab in former Czechoslovakia, arrived in three groups, 1863–73. After receiving initial assistance with food and shelter from the local Ngati Rongo people, the settlers hacked farms from the dense forest. Timber extraction was an initial focus, with seven million feet of kauri being floated down the river. Within several decades pastoral farming had become the most important activity.

Wayside Calvary erected in 1953 as a memorial to the Puhoi pioneers.

Puhoi lacked all-weather road access until the mid-1920s and relied on coastal cutters and steamers that came upriver to the original wharf opposite the Hotel. Puhoi's isolation gave rise to the colloquial saying 'up the boohai', meaning 'at the back of beyond'. This isolation meant that the Bohemian settlement retained its own close-knit sense of community and ethnic identity.

Buildings of interest in historic Puhoi village include: Church of Sts Peter and Paul (1880), Presbytery (1906), Convent (1923), Convent School (1923), Public Hall (1900) and Puhoi General Store & Post Office.(1940). The former Convent School now serves as the Puhoi Historical Society Bohemian Museum.

The best-known building is the Puhoi Hotel, which was originally licensed in 1879 as the 'German Hotel'. This tavern houses a remarkable collection of colonial artefacts and memorabilia. On Friday evenings it is home to the Puhoi Band, which plays traditional Bohemian music on instruments such as the dudelsack. Opposite the hotel are its original stables. A short distance beyond the village is the Puhoi Cemetery, where the graves of the original settlers with names such as Bayer, Schollum, Straka, Schischka, Wech and Wenzlick can be seen.

Access off SH1, 1 km north of Waiwera. Picnics, BBQs, changing sheds, safe swimming, kiosk, walks, high-tide boat ramp, historic Couldrey House, camping.

Wenderholm from a lookout on one of the tracks through forest on Wenderholm Hill.

Wenderholm's abundant natural resources made it a favourite living place in prehistoric and early European times for the subtribes of the Kawerau confederation. Te Akeake village was on the flat at the mouth of the Puhoi Estuary and Kakaha Pa on Maungatauhoro (Wenderholm Hill) to the south.

Robert Graham, a well-known Auckland politician and entrepreneur, was the first European owner. In c.1868 he built a homestead on the flat to use while at his Waiwera Hot Springs resort in winter. It was thus named Wenderholm (Winter Home).

Graham planted many of the large exotic trees seen near the homestead today, including Moreton Bay fig, holm and cork oak, Caucasian fir, bunya bunya pine, magnolia, olive and coral trees. He preserved several pohutukawa growing on the sandspit, and established what is New Zealand's largest 19th-century planted grove of pohutukawa behind the foreshore in c.1880. The restored homestead is named after its last owner, Mr H.W. Couldrey, and is open for visitors. Wenderholm was opened as Auckland's first regional park in 1965.

The extensive grassed sand flat and low dunes between the beach and the estuary built up across the mouth of the Puhoi River c. 4000–6500 years ago, after the sea level rose to its present height at the end of the Last Ice Age.

Several steep tracks lead up through the coastal forest on Wenderholm Hill, where spectacular views of the gulf are obtained from clifftop lookouts. Here native pigeon are particularly common, often seen feeding on large fruit of taraire, puriri, nikau, tawa, karaka and shoots of kowhai and lacebark. Also present are rewarewa, kahikatea, rimu, totara, tawapou, white maire, kohekohe, and a wide-leaf form of tawa. Other frequently encountered forest birds include tui, fantail and grey warbler.

Along the Puhoi Estuary margins are extensive mangroves, sea rush flats and shore ribbonwood, which provide a home for secretive fernbird and banded rail. Kookaburra, descended from birds released by Sir George Grey on Kawau Island in the 1870s, are sometimes seen in the trees around Wenderholm.

On SH1, 10 mins north of Orewa. Safe swimming, picnic area, changing shed, hot pools.

Waiwera is an abbreviation of the traditional name Waiwerawera, meaning very hot water, after the hot springs that used to bubble to the surface at the southern end of the beach. The sandstone block base of the first Waiwera bath house can be seen at the back of the beach near the original springs. It was constructed by Robert Graham in 1844 as part of New Zealand's first spa and tourist facility. With the advent of a regular steamer service from Auckland in the 1870s, Waiwera became one of Victorian Auckland's most popular tourist destinations. The springs ceased to flow when the first artesian bores were sunk in the 1870s. At this time Graham bottled large amounts of 'Waiwera Mineral Water' for sale throughout New Zealand.

Unlike the hot springs around Rotorua and Taupo, which get their heat from deep magma, the Waiwera springs are fed by deep thermal ground water that has risen rapidly to the surface up a fault-line of shattered rocks. Today there are no natural springs, but the hot water is tapped by several bores to feed the public pools.

The cliffs and shore platforms at the southern end of Waiwera Beach are accessible at mid- to low tide. A 6-m-thick, graded bed of Parnell Grit forms a prominent band with numerous cobbles and pebbles of dark basalt at its base. It also contains rarer pebbles of crystalline limestone, diorite and altered basalt, all eroded from the Northland Allochthon. These indicate that the submarine lahar which brought in this Parnell Grit came from the Kaipara Volcano, rather than Waitakere (see p. 32).

In some places the bedded Waitemata sandstones and mudstones are complexly folded and cut by numerous faults, including a large, low-angle fault, 5 m beneath the Parnell Grit bed. Most of the disruption to these beds is thought to have occurred as a result of a huge seafloor subsidence that occurred on the northern slopes of the Waitemata Basin 20 million years ago (see p. 29).

Thick Parnell Grit bed overlying bedded Waitemata Sandstone in the Waiwera cliffs.

Access from State Highway 16, 22 km north of Kaukapakapa, or 3 km up Kaipara Hills Rd from SH16. The latter is the more gentle ascent, summit 3.5 hrs return or 3.5 hrs right across (8 km). (SH16 access closed August–September for lambing.)

Mt Auckland Walkway passes through broadleaf forest with large puriri, nikau and tree ferns.

From Kaipara Hills Rd the track traverses pasture for 30 mins before entering taraire forest with nikau palm understorey and occasional trees of kahikatea, rimu, puriri and rewarewa. Native pigeons are present with a good range of bush birds. The track climbs steadily following a rather narrow ridge. Three short side tracks drop down to small stands of large kauri. The Mt Auckland forest was logged in the mid-19th century although it has never been damaged by fire. It was protected as a State Timber Reserve in 1887.

A pale-brown ground orchid (*Danhatchia australis*), the size of a pencil, was discovered on Mt Auckland in 1963. It appears in December, feeds on decaying litter (it has no green tissue) and is almost always found under taraire.

Mt Auckland (305 m) is the highest point in Rodney District. Its Maori name is Atuanui, meaning 'great deity', and the mountain continues to be of special symbolic and spiritual significance to Ngati Whatua. On its summit an extensive fortified pa provided refuge for the sub-tribal groups of the district during times of major crisis in pre-European times. The walkway passes through its large defensive ditches, and scattered shell midden is visible beside the track.

Around the trig the young vegetation is mostly flax and cabbage trees with kanuka, New Zealand broom, karamu, kohuhu, hinau, rewarewa, mapou, koromiko and young kahikatea. Climb the lookout platform to look down on the northern boundary of the forest, the Hoteo River, which is the largest river in the region. Other visible landmarks include Little Barrier and Hen Islands, Whangarei Heads, Maunganui Bluff and the Kaipara Harbour.

The descent to the west takes an hour, with the last part through pasture where paradise shelducks and spur-winged plovers may be present.

On SH16, 8 km north of Kaukapakapa. Features signposted at entrance. Parking, toilets, BBQ, picnic tables. Short walks, swimming if the stream is not in flood.

This beautiful scenic reserve was gifted to Rodney County by the late Sir Basil Orr in 1971. It features the Waitangi Falls, and a small terraced pa located on a hillock in a bend of the main stream. The smaller Omeru Stream forms the western boundary of the pa and joins the Waitangi Stream at the north end of the reserve. Omeru Pa was the focal point of the important Ngati Whatua settlement known as Waitangi, which was occupied until the 1860s. The settlement was visited by early missionaries, and one of the district's first trading stores was sited nearby. Old fig trees associated with the early settlement remain. On the left, just beyond the first bridge, an impressive and unusually sited group of kumara storage pits may be seen on a narrow point between the two streams.

From the swing bridge located at the far end of the picnic area, a 15-minute walk leads past several cascades to the Waitangi Falls. This sometimes muddy walk passes through a fine stand of regenerating native forest featuring totara, kauri (up to 1 m diameter), kowhai, kanuka, rimu and titoki in which native pigeon and tui are often seen. Shrubs of *Coprosma areolata* up to 4 m tall with small roundish leaves are locally abundant. Around the pool at the foot of the falls are moisture-loving plants such as tree fuchsia, pate and the climber kiekie.

The 8-m-high falls are held up by hard beds of Albany Conglomerate, formed of gravel that was swept down submarine canyons and deposited on the northern slopes of the Waitemata Basin, c. 20 million years ago (see p. 28).

The grass-covered earthworks of Omeru Pa dominate the reserve.

On SH16, 4 km north of Kaukapakapa.

View of the southern arm of Kaipara Harbour.

From this rest area motorists have a chance to view most of the southern half of New Zealand's largest harbour. Two million years ago this was a large embayment wide open to the Tasman Sea. Since then a series of high sand dunes have built up across the mouth of the bay forming the North and South Kaipara barriers, which now enclose the harbour. This period coincided with the Ice Ages with its alternating low and high sea levels. Thus the Kaipara Harbour has been alternately present as a large inland waterway during warm periods, or replaced by forested river valleys during cold periods. It is just 7000 years since today's harbour was last formed as the sea level rose after the end of the Last Ice Age.

The harbour was named in the 14th century by the Arawa chieftain Kahumatamomoe, while visiting his nephew Taramainuku at Pouto, near the harbour entrance. Kahu was so impressed with the cooked root of the para fern served by his hosts that he decreed that the harbour and district should be called Kai-para.

Over the centuries the Kaipara was visited by many ancestral canoes and settled by a number of tribes. Since the 16th century it has been the home to Ngati Whatua, who still maintain many marae around its shores. From earliest times the harbour, and particularly its entrance, was treated with great caution and respect. An ancient saying is 'Kaipara whakatahuri waka, whakarere wahine' — 'Kaipara which overturns canoes, and leaves women as widows'.

In 1820 Rev. Samuel Marsden confirmed that the harbour entrance was navigable, although the first European vessel did not enter until 1836. Even though the entrance was the site of many shipwrecks, the Kaipara became one of New Zealand's busiest harbours in the late 19th century. Sailing vessels exported vast quantities of kauri timber from Helensville (**22**) and the Northern Wairoa to Australia and North America. The Kaipara was also an important centre of ship building and fish canning.

Grassy flats that extend out into the harbour are former salt marsh and mud flats that have been reclaimed in the last 50 years with the assistance of the introduced cord grass, *Spartina*.

Self-guided heritage walk. Helensville Pioneer Museum signposted in main street (open daily 1–3.30 pm).

Helensville was founded in 1863 when John and Helen McLeod established a farmstead and timber mill beside the Ngati Whatua village of Te Awaroa. Their home, 'Helen's Villa', provided the origin of the town's name, which came into common usage from the late 1860s.

In the late 19th century Helensville was an important transport centre and one of New Zealand's busiest ports. It was linked by rail to Riverhead (1875) and Auckland (1881), and was serviced by numerous coastal steamers. The town's vibrant economy was based on flax milling, gum digging and in particular timber milling. Timber was towed by steam tug from the Kaipara Harbour's many tributaries to the town's mills. Sailing vessels were towed in from the Kaipara Harbour entrance to load millions of feet of sawn kauri for export.

When the kauri milling industry went into recession around 1890, Helensville declined in importance. From that time the town has largely been a service centre for the surrounding farming district, with the major employer being the Kaipara Co-op Dairy Co., 1911–88. Helensville is often visited in association with the nearby Parakai Hot Springs. It has recently come to be valued for its heritage buildings that reflect its Victorian heyday.

The town's historical focal point is the Helensville Pioneer Museum. It is housed in a relocated homestead (1898) and the former Helensville District Courthouse (1864), built using kauri from McLeod's Mill. This beautifully preserved little building was the venue for the Maori Land Court and the local District Court until 1980. It was relocated from its original site near the Kaipara River in 1982.

A pamphlet for a 40-minute main street heritage walk may be obtained from the Museum. It features such buildings as the former Helensville Town Board Office (1911), the Commercial Road Shops (1883–1910), and the former Helensville Post Office (1911). Visitors may also visit the historic Helensville Cemetery in Garfield St, or to view the many heritage buildings located in the town's side streets.

Helensville Pioneer Museum.

Access to Lake Ototoa 22 km north of Parakai on South Head Rd. Access to Waionui Inlet via Inland, Tasman and Trig Rds, off South Head Rd. Access to Papakanui Spit (4WD) via Muriwai Beach at low tide (50 km) or Woodhill Forest via Rimmer, Inland and Link Rds. When the airforce is bombing, access is forbidden. A red flag is flown at the 40 km mark on the beach and at Tasman Rd.

The South Kaipara barrier was formed by a series of overlapping sand dunes that have built up along the coast over the last 2 million years. Five belts of sand dunes have been added behind Muriwai Beach in the last 6500 years. Several of these ponded a line of dune lakes (e.g. Lake Ototoa). In local Maori tradition these lakes are collectively known as Nga Tapuwae o Kawharu, 'the footprints of Kawharu', a famous ancestor.

These lakes are important wildlife habitats with New Zealand dabchick, New Zealand scaup, grey duck, shoveler, pukeko, fernbird, bittern, black, pied and little shags present at Ototoa. Raupo and *Elaeocharis sphacelata* form the main lake vegetation, and five species of green algae (stoneworts) line the lake bottom. Freshwater crayfish (koura) and introduced fish are also present. The lake adjoins the largest and most diverse native forest on the peninsula, but feral fallow deer and pigs are having a major impact on its regeneration.

At South Head, Papakanui Sandspit is a roosting site for migratory waders. Here threatened species, such as Caspian, white-fronted and fairy terns, nest in a wildlife refuge. South of the spit is the best remaining active dune system in the region, which is periodically used by the airforce as a bombing range. The head of Waionui Inlet is bordered by sedges, rushes, oioi and manuka, and is home to fernbirds and several threatened plants, such as *Mazus novaezeelandiae*, and two ferns (*Cyclosorus interruptus, Thelypterus confluens*). Beside Waionui Inlet are several archaic middens which indicate that it was one of the earliest settled Maori sites in the region.

The narrow, curved Papakanui Sandspit, named because of its similarity to a 'large crab's' pincer, forms a barrier between the Kaipara Harbour entrance and Waionui Inlet.

North Shore

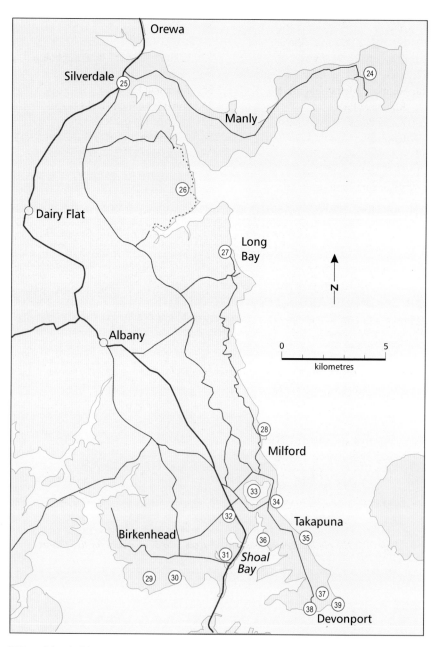

North Shore

24. Shakespear Regional Park
25. Silverdale Historic Village
26. Okura Bush Walkway
27. Long Bay Regional Park
28. Kennedy Memorial Park & Rahopara Pa
29. Kauri Point Park & Chatswood Reserve
30. Chelsea Sugar Refinery
31. Onepoto & Tank Farm Explosion Craters
32. Smiths Bush
Legend: Te Riri a Mataaho
33. Lake Pupuke & The Pumphouse
34. Takapuna Reef Fossil Forest
35. Takapuna Cliffs
36. Shoal Bay Shell Banks
37. Mt Victoria & Mt Cambria
38. Devonport Waterfront Heritage Walk
39. North Head Historic Reserve

Shoal Bay

Page 125: The old brick pumphouse in Killarney Park is now used for live theatre.

Access from Whangaparaoa Rd, at the end of Whangaparaoa Peninsula. Farm park, three safe swimming beaches at Okoromai, Army and Te Haruhi (Shakespear) Bays; changing sheds, picnic areas, BBQs, walks, summer camping.

When Rev. Henry Williams visited Whangaparaoa ('Bay of Whales') in 1833 the peninsula was occupied by a subtribal group known as Ngati Kahu. Their main settlements and cultivations were located between sheltered Te Haruhi (literally 'weak breath') and Army Bays. Both areas were protected by fortified pa whose earthworks can still be seen. The wetlands and tidal flats of Okoromai Bay were an important source of eels, shellfish and weaving materials.

Whangaparaoa was purchased by the Crown in 1853, although a small group of Ngati Kahu lived at Okoromai Bay until the 1890s. Two Scots, Findlay McMillan and Duncan Campbell, developed grazing runs at Te Haruhi Bay from 1854. Most landholdings between Hobb's Bay and the end of the peninsula were acquired (1882–1901) by the Shakespear family after whom the park is named. For a time (1897–1910) they lived on Little Barrier but returned in 1910 to build the large Shakespear homestead that still stands on the point between Te Haruhi (Shakespear) and Okoromai Bays. The family farmed the land until 1967, when it was sold to the ARA for a regional park.

Land north of the park was acquired by the army during the Second World War and still remains Ministry of Defence land. During the war, a gun emplacement was sited above Army Bay and an observation post was built high on the hill overlooking Army and Okoromai Bays.

Most of the puriri in Waterfall Gully are at unusual angles, because they have partly or completely fallen over but continued to grow. They were probably blown over when there was little surrounding forest to protect them.

Most of the park is grassland with tea tree scrub, occasional forest patches and raupo wetlands. Waterfall Gully Track, up the valley due east of Army Bay, passes through regenerating forest dominated by large puriri and taraire. Other canopy trees include kowhai, karaka and kohekohe. Tank lilies, *Collospermum hastatum*, are frequent epiphytes high on the puriri branches. Many kowhai and cabbage trees grow along the bush margins. By the stream, tangles of bare stems of supplejack are common 'hanging' from the canopy. Shrubs of mapou, putaputaweta and milk tree are frequent. Birds in these forest patches are mostly native pigeon, tui, fantail, grey warbler, silver-eye, blackbird, rosella and sometimes bellbird. Bellbirds have only recently spread here from Tiritiri (**138**); this is the only mainland site north of the Waikato where they currently breed.

Originally horizontal, Waitemata Sandstone beds at Shakespear Head have been pushed up to vertical.

The road to Okoromai Bay crosses a salt meadow of glasswort, clumps of sea rush, bachelor's button and an occasional patch of selliera. Pied stilts and kingfishers regularly feed on the salt meadow. A tidal creek runs north from the meadow to the freshwater duck pond. The creek margin is lined with the summer-green sedge, bolboschoenus, flax and, in places, marsh ribbonwood. Adjacent to the creek, in fresh water, 3-m-tall raupo is present. The duck pond is frequented by many ducks, as well as little shags, swallows and black swans. A walking track traverses these wetlands.

On the farmland common birds include greenfinch, yellowhammer, starling, myna, sparrow, magpie, harrier and peafowl at Te Haruhi Bay. The pukeko population is extremely high. They are territorial and form family groups of three to six.

The cliffs from Army Bay to Shakespear Head are made of Waitemata Sandstone and contain some of the most interesting folded and structurally complex strata to be seen in the region. The crumpled and tightly folded strata indicate compression and sliding from the north-west, consistent with their having been deformed during a giant seafloor slide on the Waitemata Basin's northern slopes (see p. 29).

An unusually thick (10–20 m) Parnell Grit bed forms the cliffs and shore platforms 0.5–1.5 km east of Army Bay. It contains large blocks of Waitemata Sandstone, ripped up from the seafloor as the turbulent flow passed, and two huge blocks (10–30 m across) of columnar-jointed basalt, which must have been carried along in the powerful submarine lahar from its source on the slopes of the Kaipara Volcano, 30–40 km away.

Located immediately west of Silverdale township; access from SH1 via Silverdale Rd. Museum, open Sundays and most public holidays.

Silverdale Historic Village is located in a small reserve beside the former Silverdale School (1878) and opposite Holy Trinity Anglican Church (1885). It includes a number of colonial buildings that have been relocated from the surrounding district and restored by local volunteers. They include the former Silverdale Schoolhouse (1907) and the Methodist Parsonage (1887).

Of particular interest is the Wesleyan Chapel, which is thought to be one of New Zealand's oldest remaining churches. It was built in Parnell in c.1845 and then in c.1856 transported by sea to the Wade, as Silverdale was known until 1911. The chapel was reconsecrated and opened for worship on 8 April 1860.

Beside the chapel is a small museum displaying items and information pertaining to the history of the Hibiscus Coast area, as well as a display of early agricultural machinery. A gumdigger's whare, a saw pit and a bushman's shanty are reminders of the two industries which dominated life in the district in the colonial era. A colonial herb garden is maintained by the Pioneer Herb Society. The village includes a large oak and several other trees planted in the original Silverdale School grounds last century.

Opposite the village in Wainui Road is the beautiful little Holy Trinity Anglican Church (1885) and historic cemetery.

Silverdale Methodist Parsonage (1887).

Starts at Haighs Access Rd off East Coast Rd, or from Stillwater at the end of Duck Creek Rd. Picnic area and toilets at Dacre Cottage, swimming at high tide; toilets and camping at Stillwater. Walk from Haighs Access Rd: 2 hrs to Dacre Cottage, further 1 hr to Stillwater.

From Haighs Access Rd, the track crosses a footbridge over the mangrove-lined upper reaches of the Okura Estuary. Once across the bridge, look for large native passionfruit vines on the tall kahikatea. The track climbs up to Okura Bush Scenic Reserve — an excellent example of coastal forest featuring taraire, kohekohe, puriri, nikau, and some fine kauri. It is home to a wide range of forest birds including native pigeon. After 30 minutes the track descends to the edge of the estuary again, where shell middens provide evidence of former Maori occupation.

Further on, at Dacre Point, the well-preserved earthworks of Okura Pa may be seen. Here the track descends to the tidal flats of Karepiro Bay, where coastal and migratory sea birds congregate. Behind the beach is historic Dacre Cottage, named after its first occupants, Henry Dacre and his father Captain Ranulph Dacre, a sea captain and timber merchant who purchased surrounding Weiti Station in 1848. The cottage, which has been restored by the New Zealand Historic Places Trust, was built (c.1855) using locally made bricks.

From here the walkway crosses a stream and rises through regenerating coastal forest and an old terraced Maori occupation site to the top of a headland, with extensive views over Karepiro Bay and Whangaparaoa Peninsula. The track follows the clifftop and descends to the Weiti Estuary. A feature of this section of the walk, which passes over some private land and may be very wet in winter, is the sequence of five shell spits. They provide a high-tide roost for wading birds, and the actively forming southern spit is the summer nesting site for New Zealand dotterel. The spits are of international significance in the study of sea-level change over the last 6500 years.

Kowhai and tall kahikatea line the bank where the walkway footbridge crosses the Okura Estuary.

Park entrance at the end of Beach Rd, Long Bay. Toilets, changing sheds, kiosk, restaurant, playground, miniature railway, BBQs, picnic areas, safe swimming, clifftop walk to north.

Long Bay is Auckland's most popular regional park. Swimming is possible on Long Bay beach at all tides. Patchy beds of cockle and tuatua live in the beach sand but are protected as the park's entire shoreline is a marine reserve, opened in 1996.

At mid-tide or lower, it is possible to walk northwards around the coast to three smaller beaches, often visited by nudists. Intertidal pools reveal an interesting mix of crabs, sea anenomes and sea snails. Two species of barnacle plus the Pacific oyster live cemented to the rocks, whereas clumps of small black mussels cling on with their byssus threads. Neptune's necklace and sea lettuce are two of the more common seaweeds.

An interesting round trip is provided by a return along the clifftop track with excellent views out over the gulf. The track descends at the north end of the beach through native bush dominated by large pohutukawa and younger regenerating karaka, kowhai, karo, rangiora, kawakawa, coastal karamu, hangehange and flax. A short distance inland from here is a small patch of large mature puriri and taraire.

Spinifex, the native sand-binding grass, is common at the northern end of the main beach. The rest of the beachfront is bordered by the South African ice plant which forms succulent mats. Kikuyu and buffalo grasses form thick swards behind.

The cliffs at both ends of Long Bay are composed of Waitemata Sandstone (see p. 26). Scattered through the sequence are thin black layers of broken-up twigs and wood, which were swept into the sea from the surrounding land during storms. The burrows of animals that lived in these sea-floor sediments long ago are visible in some of the rocks.

Te Oneroa (Long Bay) was occupied by a small Maori community until the 1850s. The homestead at the northern end of Long Bay has recently been restored. It was the home of the Vaughan family, who farmed the property from 1862.

View south over the unusually deserted Long Bay beach.

On Beach Rd, between Castor and Campbells Bays. Picnic areas, toilets, short coastal walk, steps down to coast.

J.F. Kennedy Park was developed as a memorial to the US President assassinated in 1963. This peaceful spot contains the remains of two defensive fortifications constructed many centuries apart. During the Second World War a coastal gun battery was constructed on the site to defend Rangitoto Channel in conjunction with the North Head and Fort Takapuna batteries. Two of the Castor Bay Battery's key structures remain: the 6-inch gun emplacement and magazine with its distinctive 'frying pan' roof, and the Battery Observation Post.

A unique feature of this military installation was its disguise as a civilian housing area. The main gun emplacement was encased within the shell of a weatherboard house with its 6-inch gun protruding out the front door. The disguise was so effective that the military received complaints about the construction of army seaside holiday homes. The installation remained in use as an army supply depot until 1964.

A 10-minute walk south along the clifftop, with excellent views over Rangitoto Channel, leads to the well-preserved headland pa Te Rahopara o Peretu. It is associated in tradition with Peretu, an early Maori ancestor after whom a number of places in the district are named. The archaeology of this pa indicates that the site was adapted over many generations. It has two defensive ditches, and its house terraces and kumara-storage pits are clearly visible under a beautiful pohutukawa grove. The pa is said to have been sacked in the 17th century by Kapetaua, an important ancestor of the Tamaki tribes, as revenge for being marooned on Te Toka o Kapetaua (Bean Rock) as a child. The pa was to have been used as fill for a marina but was preserved in 1965 after strenuous lobbying by archaeologists and local residents.

Just north of the park is a trail through regenerating bush at Centennial Park, Campbells Bay. Leaflet available from North Shore City.

The two-storeyed Observation Post, which has the outward appearance of a typical state house of the 1940s, was constructed over a thick concrete bunker and still stands in Kennedy Memorial Park.

Access to Kauri Point Centennial Park from three marked entry points off Onetaunga Rd, Birkenhead. Information shelter, bush tracks, beach. Nearby Chatswood Reserve has many entrances; we recommend two — the end of Mappin or Langstone Places, both side streets off Porritt Ave. Information leaflet available from North Shore City.

Regenerating kanuka forest with tanekaha, toru and glossy karamu, Kauri Point Centennial Park.

Kauri Point Centennial Park was created in 1986 to mark the centenary of Birkenhead Borough. From the ridge top the land slopes down to the Waitemata Harbour. The coast is lined by cliffs of Waitemata Sandstone except for Kendall Bay, which is a shallow swimming beach. To the east is the Chelsea Sugar Refinery property (**30**) linked to Kauri Point by a clifftop track.

On Kauri Point is the well-preserved headland pa named Te Matarae a Manaoterangi, 'the headland of Manaoterangi of Ngati Poataniwha'. The pa and Ngutuwera village located behind Rongohau (Kendall Bay) were important summer fishing settlements occupied when the pioke shark schooled off the point.

The reserve is recovering from past clearances and an invasion of pines. Maritime pine, and to a lesser extent radiata pine, form the dominant canopy over half the park, but native species are regenerating well beneath them.

Close to the road, areas of low 'gumland' vegetation grow on the poor clay soils. The main components are manuka, *Dracophyllum sinclairii*, kumarahou, mingimingi, umbrella fern, blueberry, shining karamu, dwarf cabbage tree and native sedges (*Schoenus tendo, Lepidosperma laterale*). Adjacent to these areas are tall kanuka stands, usually over-topped by pines. Vigorous tanekaha regeneration is common in such areas, frequently with toru, mapou, *Coprosma spathulata* and glossy karamu. Pohutukawa grows along the cliffs, usually with houpara and kowhai.

Unlike Kauri Point, nearby Chatswood Reserve has several imposing kauri trees and regenerating kauri stands on the flanks of the stream valley with kanuka, tanekaha and hard beech. The cool valley bottom is dominated by moisture-loving plants such as ferns (including the uncommon *Loxsoma cunninghamii*), kanono, kiekie, supplejack and nikau.

At the end of Colonial Rd, off Mokoia Rd near Highbury shopping centre; foot access from Chelsea Bay. Picnics, walks.

The water-supply lakes for Chelsea Sugar Refinery are frequented by Australian coots, ducks, black swans, little shags, pied shags and little black shags, as well as picnickers.

In 1883 the Colonial Sugar Co. of Australia selected Chelsea Bay as the site for New Zealand's first sugar refinery, because of its deep-water shipping access and plentiful supply of fresh water. It had been the site of Phillip Callan's brick kiln in the 1840s and was farmed for many years by the De Jersey Grutt family. The refinery was constructed using 1.5 million bricks fired on the site, and was formally opened in September 1884. Three water-supply lakes were impounded by brick dams constructed 1884–1917.

The refinery's isolation meant that it was necessarily self-sufficient. It had its own carpentry shop, blacksmith's shop, cooper's shop and stables. The refinery employed a large workforce and was the focal point for the Auckland region's largest 19th-century company town, which incorporated a school, reading room and store, as well as 35 company cottages. The company found the cottages difficult to maintain so they were demolished or sold for removal in 1908. Some can still be seen in nearby Birkenhead.

In 1909 the company constructed a manager's house behind the refinery and four duplex two-storeyed brick cottages in lower Colonial Rd. They housed specialist tradesmen who were on call at night and during weekends. Interestingly, they incorporated some of the first flush toilets in Auckland. These distinctive Edwardian houses have been beautifully restored by the New Zealand Sugar Co. and can be seen alongside the access road, which is bordered with many planted trees.

The refinery itself is only accessible by arrangement. The water-supply lakes and their surrounds are open to the public through the generosity of the refinery. They feature pleasant walks through stands of regenerating kanuka forest with tracks connecting to Kauri Point Park and Chatswood Reserve (**29**). The lakes contain mosquito fish, large koi carp and rudd. Pied shags nest in several trees overhanging the lower lake.

Drive into Onepoto Domain off Sylvan Ave, 100 m north of intersection with Onewa Rd. Adventure playground, pond for model-boat sailing. Tank Farm viewing platform at end of St Peters St, off College Rd, Northcote.

Tank Farm and Onepoto are well-preserved explosion craters formed by volcanic eruptions in a shallow valley about 30,000 years ago, when sea level was considerably lower than it is today. The eruptions threw out clouds of ash and debris that accumulated as circular tuff rings around them. Sylvan Ave, Exmouth Rd, College Rd and Akoranga Dr run along the tuff-ring crests.

Mature forest that grew in the valley at the time was decimated and buried by these volcanic eruptions. Hollow moulds of some of these trees were uncovered beneath the ash of Onepoto tuff ring during quarrying operations in the 1950s. This quarrying provided fill for the nearby Northern Motorway approaches to the harbour bridge and removed the south-western and north-eastern sectors of Onepoto and Tank Farm tuff rings respectively.

The tuff rings dammed stream valleys that had formerly flowed out through Shoal Bay, forming a lake. This slowly filled with silt to form the flat area now occupied by Wairau Valley industrial estate. Overflow from the lake was diverted around the northern edge of the Pupuke lava flows and through Wairau Estuary at the northern end of Milford Beach.

Onepoto and Tank Farm craters also originally contained freshwater lakes. As sea level rose to its present level at the end of the Last Ice Age, the craters were invaded by the sea and became tidal lagoons with mangrove forests. In recent decades Onepoto lagoon has been reclaimed and turned into playing fields. Tank Farm contains its original low mangrove forest with a narrow fringe of salt marsh. Millions of horn shells and mud snails live in the muddy film among the mangroves' aerial roots.

The name 'Tank Farm' arose from the installation of bulk fuel storage tanks near the foreshore during the Second World War. See Legend of 'Te Riri a Mataaho' (p.138) for Maori traditions associated with the creation of these craters.

Tank Farm (foreground) and Onepoto (beyond) are two well-preserved volcanic explosion craters in Northcote. The surrounding tuff rings are now covered in houses.

Access from Onewa Domain Carpark, Northcote Rd. Informally tracked.

The first European owner of this magnificent remnant of original North Shore kahikatea forest was Alexander Mackay, who purchased it in 1849. Amazingly, he and his son-in-law Thomas Drummond preserved it at a time when similar forest was being milled and cleared throughout the district. The reserve is named after James and Catherine Smith, who owned and conserved it 1909–34.

Cathedral Grove in Smiths Bush has several large puriri 20–25 m tall.

It was acquired as a public reserve in 1942. Sadly, the integrity of Smiths Bush was seriously compromised when it was bisected by the Northern Motorway in 1960. Its public ownership had ironically made it a cheap and easy option for the region's transport planners. Even today large puriri are dying near the motorway due to road widening over 25 years ago.

The most impressive area, Cathedral Grove, is near the motorway in the larger southwest remnant. This rather open area has several very large puriri and little else except for ground-cover plants. The fern *Asplenium lamprophyllum* forms attractive patches on the ground with its shiny fronds. Fragrant, thread and jointed fern all tend to clothe the tree roots and panic grass forms low mats on the ground.

Tall taraire trees surround the grove and the only large kahikatea is present on the motorway side. This straight-trunked tree is buttressed at the base and its snake-like roots spread out up to 20 m away. Admire this tree — it is a beauty! Tank lilies are common in puriri branches, and occasionally vine-like furrowed roots growing down a tree trunk advertise the presence of a perching puka above.

Other areas of the bush are more dense and younger in age. Pole kahikatea, with its bluish green branchlets, is particularly abundant, forming pure stands along the bush margins. Common among these younger stands is totara, matai, kohekohe, karaka, pigeonwood, mahoe, mamangi, hangehange and cabbage tree.

The usual Auckland bush birds are present, with tui and rosella particularly noticeable by sound.

Te Riri a Mataaho — The Wrath of Mataaho

Creation of the volcanic features of the North Shore is described in a tradition known as 'Te Riri a Mataaho'. In ancient times an ancestor called Matakamokamo lived on Te Rua Maunga, a mountain standing on the site of Lake Pupuke. He instructed his wife, Matakerepo, and her maid, Tukiata, to weave him some new garments but was dissatisfied with the finished product and argued bitterly with his wife. While they were arguing their house fire went out and it could not be rekindled. Matakamokamo then cursed Mahuika, the goddess of fire, with the result that she called on her fellow deity, Mataaho, to send a volcanic eruption to punish the quarrelsome couple.

Mataaho caused Te Rua Maunga to sink beneath the earth, leaving Pupuke Moana (Lake Pupuke) in its place. At the same time he caused Rangitoto to rise from the sea offshore, and it was this island that Matakamokamo, Matakerepo and Tukiata fled in panic. On reaching Rangitoto they realised that in their haste they had left their twin children at the southern end of Waiwhariki (Takapuna Beach). Tukiata was ordered to return to rescue the stranded children with instructions not to look up for fear of further wrath of Mataaho. After leaving Rangitoto, Tukiata forgot her instructions and she and the children were turned to stone. Tukiata became a rock pinnacle beside Rangitoto Beacon. The twin children, Hinerei and Matamiha, became the rock pinnacles at the southern end of Takapuna Beach.

Nga Mahanga: the twin rock pillars Matamiha and Hinerei (now fallen) at the south end of Takapuna Beach.

Matakamokamo and Matakerepo returned to the mainland where the wrath of Mataaho was again directed upon them. They were turned to stone and sank beneath the ground by the western foreshore of Shoal Bay. Their demise was associated with violent volcanic explosions which formed Onepoto and Tank Farm Explosion Craters. The southern crater is Te Kopua o Matakerepo ('the tidal basin of Matakerepo') while the northern crater is Te Kopua o Matakamokamo ('the tidal basin of Matakamokamo'). The three peaks on Rangitoto are said to represent the three adults who fled to the island. The mist and cloud that sometimes covers the summit of Rangitoto are the tears of Matakamokamo and Matakerepo as they weep for their old home and for their children waiting on the opposite shore.

The Pumphouse is in Killarney Park with access off Killarney St or Manurere Ave; other access to Lake Pupuke is from the end of Eric Price Ave, Sylvan Park Ave (toilets) and Northcote Rd.

Pupuke Volcano is one of the oldest in the Auckland field, possibly as old as 150,000 years. Early activity built a low shield volcano of thin, overlapping basalt lava flows fed from a lava lake. Withdrawal of the lava back down the volcano's throat probably resulted in the creation of a large collapsed crater. Subsequent explosive eruptions threw out ash, which

Lake Pupuke

formed a low tuff ring around the crater. Hurstmere Rd runs along the eastern crest of this tuff ring.

On the western flanks, minor fire-fountaining of frothy lava built up a small scoria mound (mostly removed by Smales' Quarry). Here the fine scoria layers are rich in light green crystals of olivine, a mineral that had crystallised out of the magma and was erupted with the semi-molten scoria.

The crater subsequently filled with fresh water to form Lake Pupuke (104 ha, 55 m deep; see 'Te Riri a Mataaho' opposite). The name is a shortened form of Pupukemoana, meaning the overflowing lake. Its level is controlled by natural outlets that occur around Thorne Bay (**34**).

The old brick pumphouse in Killarney Park was constructed in 1894 to provide a water supply to Devonport Borough. It housed steam engines that pumped water to a reservoir on Mt Victoria. Small pumping stations were also developed at Lake Pupuke by Northcote Borough (1908) and Birkenhead Borough (1913), with the result that the supply became inadequate and of poor quality from the 1920s. The North Shore boroughs were required to connect to the Auckland bulk supply from 1941 and the old Devonport Borough Pumphouse ceased operation in 1944.

Sylvan Park on the north side of Lake Pupuke has several fine stands of karaka and kohekohe with puriri, taraire and kowhai. An unusual introduced water weed, *Vallisneria*, with 1-m-long strap-like leaves, carpets the lake bed. Introduced Australian black swans feed on the weed where they can reach it.

Adjacent to the boat ramp and car park at the end of The Promenade, northern end of Takapuna Shopping Centre and beach. Safe swimming, pleasant coastal walk around to Milford Beach.

The intertidal reef beyond the seaward end of the carpark has one of the best examples in the world of a forest killed and fossilised by a passing lava flow.

The forest of numerous small trees and a few larger kauri was growing here around 150,000 years ago at a time when sea level was considerably lower than at present. Several lava flows from the initial eruptions of Lake Pupuke volcano flowed into the forest and set it on fire. As the lava flowed through, it cooled and solidified as a thick crust around the lower part of each tree trunk. The remaining molten lava flowed on, leaving behind the metre-high, cylindrical moulds of hundreds of tree trunks. They have hollow insides where the original wood slowly burned away. In some places miniature basalt arches between tree moulds are the remains of a solidified crust that formed on top of the lava flow and wasn't carried away as the lava flowed on.

Around the coast to the north there is a metal grill over the top of the hollow mould of a large, 1.5-m-diameter kauri tree that was surrounded and burned by a 4-m-thick flow. Further on, where the path runs along a concrete pipeline, there are numerous horizontal hollow moulds of tree trunks and branches that were engulfed and carried along in the lava flow. Their shape was captured in the rapidly cooling basalt lava, before the wood was slowly incinerated away.

Further north at Thorne Bay, freshwater overflow from Lake Pupuke pours out of cracks in the intertidal rocks. The water has flowed underground through the numerous fissures and joints in the basalt flow.

Behind the northern end of Takapuna Beach is Te Uru Tapu ('the sacred grove'), one of the finest mainland pohutukawa groves remaining in the Auckland region.

A passing lava flow produced the hundreds of hollow, cylindrical, basalt tree moulds now seen on Takapuna Reef.

Access down steps from the end of St Leonards Rd, beside Takapuna Grammar School, or by walking around the shore at low tide from southern end of Takapuna Beach.

The cliffs between Takapuna and Narrow Neck Beaches are made of Waitemata Sandstone (see p. 26). Scattered throughout the sequence are thin layers full of black specks of broken up twigs, wood and leaves. One layer about 100 m north of the St Leonards Rd steps is up to 20 cm thick and contains large carbonised pieces of flattened branches. These layers record storms on land, when flooded rivers carried trees and leaf litter into the sea. Here it became waterlogged and sank to the seafloor and was buried by further mud and sand layers.

A rock platform, halfway between St Leonards and Takapuna Beaches, contains exquisite examples of various trace fossils. These are the burrows made by mostly sediment-feeding, marine animals as they squirmed and tunnelled their way through the mud and sand just beneath the sea floor, some 20 million years ago. Some of these burrows are 3–5 cm in diameter with convoluted, meandering courses within a single layer of mudstone. They were probably made by a heart urchin that back-filled its feeding burrow with curved meniscus-shaped layers of sediment as it went.

Other radiating or branching burrows have been cemented with rusty orange limonite, which makes them stand out from the grey-coloured sandstone and mudstone. Until a few decades ago, these branching trace fossils were mistakenly thought to be fossilised seaweeds.

Takapuna cliffs were known as Paringawhara, the 'crumbling cliffs'. At their northern end are the two rocks known as Nga Mahanga, 'the twins' (see 'Te Riri a Mataaho', p.138)

The sea cliffs of the East Coast Bays, Hibiscus Coast and most of the Waitemata Harbour show similar exposures of Waitemata Sandstone.

Just south of the foot of St Leonards Rd steps, a narrow rock platform juts out into the beach. It contains a 1-m-thick unit of tightly folded and broken layers of thin sandstone and mudstone sandwiched within an unbroken sequence. The deformed layer is thought to have been a plastic horizon upon which a large block of the overlying rocks slipped shortly after being laid down on the seafloor.

Access from the bottom of Charles St; a shell path gives dry access to the shell bank except at high tide. You can walk both directions along the shell bank.

Glasswort and needle tussock grow on an older, stabilised shell bank at Shoal Bay.

The traditional name of Shoal Bay is Waipaoraora, loosely meaning 'heaped-up shell banks on tidal flats'.

The path to the shell bank passes through high tidal flats with low mangroves, and small patches of sea rush and the sedges bolboschoenus and *Baumea juncea*. Also living here in great abundance are mud snails and mud crabs.

Cockles live in large numbers just below the surface of the sandy mud in the adjacent tidal flats. When they die, the cockle shells split apart and are gradually washed shorewards by waves, where they accumulate in banks near high-tide level. Mud accumulates behind the banks, and mangrove forest often establishes itself in these sheltered enclaves. Storms sometimes push the shell banks closer to shore, often advancing them into the mangroves, which usually die as a result. As more shells arrive, new banks may form further seaward and the shoreward bank then stops moving. As the banks age, the surface shells crumble and compact down, making it more suitable for plants to establish.

Low mangrove forest is extensive inside the shell banks and in places outside as well around the head of Shoal Bay. In autumn the small four-parted, orange mangrove flowers are present, scented like pineapples. Needle tussock, named for its needle-tipped leaves, is abundant along the tops of the banks. Low mats of glasswort containing scattered patches of sea blite and orache are common. All three species are frequently reddish. The small sprawling, white-flowered herb, sea primrose, is usually present along the front of the glasswort. A few shore ribbonwood, with interlacing branches, are present among the needle tussock.

The shell banks provide roost sites for waders and shore birds at high tide. At low tide the birds feed out on the extensive mud flats.

See Pollen Island (**68**), Tahuna Torea (**90**) and Miranda (**116**) for similar areas.

Road up Mt Victoria starts at the corner of Victoria Rd and Kerr St. Mt Cambria Domain is between Vauxhall Rd and Church St, Devonport. Gentle walks, Devonport Museum (open weekend afternoons).

Mt Victoria was named after Queen Victoria and Mt Cambria after an old name for Wales, as it was purchased by a syndicate of Welshmen in 1874. Mt Victoria was traditionally known as Takarunga ('the hill standing above') and Mt Cambria as Takararo ('the hill standing below'). Both were important Maori pa over many generations, with earthworks still visible on some slopes of Mt Victoria.

Mt Victoria across Torpedo Bay from North Head.

The French navigator D'Urville climbed Mt Victoria in 1827, and the strategic importance of the mountain was recognised when the signal station for the port of Auckland was sited there in 1841. The mountain has been a public reserve since 1880, although a muzzle loader gun fort was constructed on the summit in 1885 and it was used for military purposes until after the Second World War.

Sixty-metre-high Mt Victoria dominates the Devonport landscape and provides visitors with spectacular views over the Waitemata Harbour. The road winds up through a mixture of planted native and exotic trees. Natives include pohutukawa, karo, puriri, lacebark, karaka and kapuka, and exotics include weeping agonis, Chinese poplars and a silky oak.

The scoria cones of Mt Victoria and Mt Cambria were formed by fire-fountaining of frothy, gas-rich lava around 20,000 years ago. Lava flowed down Mt Victoria's southern side and cooled to the dark basalt rock which now forms the rocky coastline east of Devonport. A small part of Mt Victoria's scoria cone was rafted away by this flow and came to rest near the present-day foreshore as Duders Hill, a prominent knoll that was quarried away prior to 1960.

Mt Cambria, a substantial, 30-m-high, scoria cone just north of Mt Victoria, has also disappeared. A century of quarrying, initially by private operators and later by Devonport Borough Council, ceased in 1977. The flattened site has been rehabilitated as a public park.

King Edward and Queens Parade, Devonport. Jackson's 'Muzeum', Victoria Rd (open daily). Naval Museum, Spring St (open daily).

Part of the original Signal Station Flagstaff from Mt Victoria stands in Windsor Reserve.

Devonport is Auckland's most historic seaside suburb. The heritage sites located along its waterfront span the entire period of the district's human history. Devonport developed a rich maritime heritage after the establishment of a Signal Station on Mt Victoria (1841) and a Naval Station (1842). A feature of Devonport are its fine villas, examples of which can be seen on the walk which follows King Edward and Queens Parade, named after the coronation of King Edward VII and Queen Alexandra in 1902. The sites on the heritage walk are here described east to west.

Torpedo Bay was named after the Torpedo Boat Base built during the 'Russian Scare' in 1885 (**39**). A plaque at the east end of the bay recalls that the French explorer Dumont D'Urville landed there in 1827. The Tainui Memorial commemorates the visit of the Tainui canoe in the 14th century. It anchored in Te Haukapua (Torpedo Bay) while its crew visited Maungauika (North Head). The Tainui later stranded on the sandspit Te Ranga o Taikehu (now Windsor Reserve), named after Taikehu, the chieftain who swam ashore through the waters known as Te Kauanga o Taikehu ('the swim of Taikehu').

Duders Beach was named after Thomas Duder, the Mt Victoria Signalman (1842–75). His home is located at 11 Church Rd, and the general store operated by his twin sons Robert and Richard is still standing opposite the Masonic Hotel. The hotel was built in 1866 by shipbuilder George Beddoes and owned for many years by John Duder.

Duders Beach seawall was constructed c.1935 using a bequest from local resident Alex Watson, as is commemorated by the Memorial Clock opposite Church St. Further west is the Calliope Sea Scouts Hall (c.1895), formerly the North Shore Rowing Clubhouse. A nearby plaque commemorates the fact that the Devonport foreshore was New Zealand's busiest shipbuilding area 1850–1920s. Sailing vessels, steamers and recreational craft were built by shipbuilders including Holmes, Beddoes, Niccol, Logan, Bailey and Le Huquet.

Devonport Yacht Club has occupied its present site since 1927. Its entrance features a massive hand-forged sailing-ship anchor. Lava flows from Mt Victoria (**37**) are a feature of the adjacent foreshore. Opposite May's St is the site where Joseph Burns was executed for the murder of the Naval Station Commander Lt. Robert Snow, his wife Hannah and child.

The Coronation seawall, archway and steps commemorate the 1902 Coronation and the peace secured at the conclusion of the South African War. The stone alignment visible near the steps at low tide is the remains of 'Tiller's Wharf' (1856). It was named after John Tiller, who traded from it in his cutter *Fortune Castle*. Opposite this site is the former Wrens Home 'Elizabeth House', previously the Ventnor Private Hotel.

Flagstaff Terrace recalls the fact that the suburb was originally named Flagstaff after the Mt Victoria flagstaff. When the village was surveyed in 1859 it was named Devonport after the British Naval port, although the name was not formally adopted until 1868. The land between Flagstaff Terrace and the foreshore was an Admiralty Reserve (1841–97). 'The Triangle' is dominated by historic trees, including two massive Moreton Bay figs planted in 1896, and includes a fine First World War memorial.

Windsor Reserve was the site of Auckland's Naval Station (1841–97) and the initial station of New Zealand's Hydrographic Survey. A plaque recalls the fact that Devonport has maintained a scheduled ferry service with Auckland since 1854. The Memorial Clock honours the contribution of the Alison family to the development of Devonport. A hotel has been located on the site of the Esplanade Hotel (1903) since 1864. Visitors may wish to divert to inspect the historic Victoria Rd shops or Jackson's Muzeum of Automobilia, Sounds, Victoriana and Collectables.

The heritage walk continues west along Queens Parade past the Victoria Wharf ferry terminal. Queens Parade Seawall (c.1920) is the best example of its type in the region. The Anne St-Garden Terrace foreshore was the site of Holmes shipyard (1875–90) and Nicol & Son's shipyard (1864–70). Garden Terrace recalls the 'Bear Garden' built by George Quick as a Victorian tourist attraction. Part of the original wall may still be seen. The Naval Museum in Spring St portrays New Zealand's naval history.

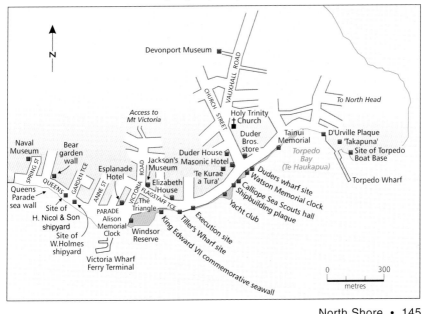

Access from Takarunga Rd, off Cheltenham Rd. Toilets, panoramic views, coastal and self-guided historic walks (pamphlets and tapes available from DoC). Bring a torch to explore the tunnels.

North Head is the eroded remains of a scoria cone overlying the eastern portions of a tuff ring. Scoria forms only the top of the cone and can be seen in an old quarry on the access road. Most of the tunnels were dug in the firmer, underlying ash beds (tuff). The bedded tuff is best seen along the coastal walk around the base of the headland.

North Head was traditionally known as Maungauika, 'the mountain of Uika', an ancestor who occupied it c.800 years ago. The name Takapuna is also used for the cone, although it traditionally applied specifically to a spring flowing from its base.

The cone's strategic location meant that it was an important coastal defence site from the earliest colonial period. Fears of a Russian invasion of the Pacific led to the construction of a muzzle loader fort (1885), and three 8-inch disappearing gun batteries (1886). They were supported by a minefield, searchlights, and a torpedo boat base at Torpedo Bay. When installed, the disappearing guns were the latest in military technology. After firing they recoiled underground to be reloaded and kept out of sight. The 8-inch gun that remains at the North Battery is the only intact and mounted example left in the world.

Between 1888 and 1914 some of North Head's buildings housed prisoners who excavated many of the tunnels that link the batteries and their service facilities. During The Second World War, two 4-inch gun batteries and a Fire Control Post were constructed and close defence guns were installed around the base of North Head. North Head was included as a reserve in the Hauraki Gulf Maritime Park in 1972.

Apart from the scattered pohutukawa on the lower cliffs, most of the woody vegetation consists of aggressive weeds such as tree privet, Chinese privet, rhamnus, woolly nightshade, brush wattle, bone-seed, Japanese spindle tree and poygala.

The unique sequence of military structures remaining on North Head span the entire development of Auckland's coastal defences, 1885–1962.

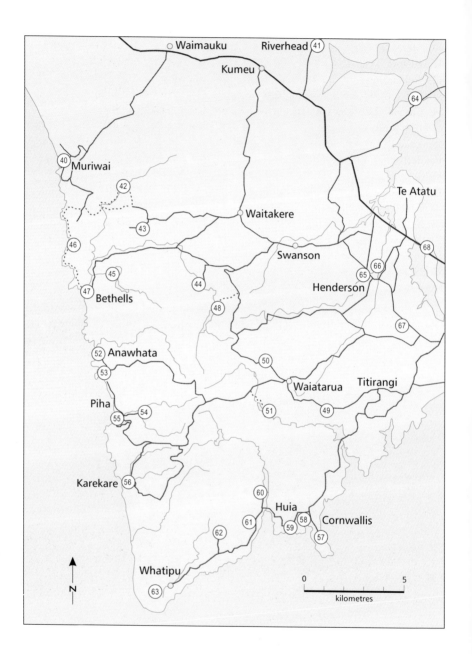

Waimauku Riverhead ⑪

Kumeu

⑭

⑩ Muriwai

⑫

Te Atatu

Waitakere

⑬

⑯

Swanson

⑥⑧

⑯

⑮

Henderson

⑮

Bethells

⑭

⑰

⑱

⑰

Anawhata

⑲

⑳

Waiatarua

Titirangi

Piha

⑭

⑲

Karekare ⑯

Huia

Cornwallis

⑯

⑯

⑯

Whatipu

N

0   5

kilometres

148 • West

West

Keyhole Rock from Anawhata Beach (52).

Page 147: Remains of Black Rock kauri dam, Piha Valley (54).

At end of Motutara Rd, 10.5 km from Waimauku. Surf patrol in summer, surfing, changing sheds, BBQ and picnic areas, store, gannet colony, bush walk, information booth, campground.

Motutara Domain, established in 1906, was enlarged over the years and became Muriwai Regional Park in 1969. The park is sited at the end of 48-km-long Muriwai Beach, which is backed by a series of sand dunes that have built up over the past two million years to form the South Kaipara barrier. The black sand grains are titanomagnetite, a magnetic iron oxide mineral eroded from volcanic ash layers in Taranaki and carried up the coast by currents.

Muriwai Beach was traditionally known as One Rangatira, 'the chiefly beach'. The wider park area was referred to collectively as Motutara ('island of seabirds'), a name which originates from the bird colony on the rock stack that adjoins Otakamiro Point. The name Muriwai traditionally applied only to wetland in the Okiritoto Stream Valley. Otakamiro ('the dwelling place of Takamiro') Pa is a reminder that the area was occupied by Maori for many centuries — from the early 1700s until the 20th century by Ngati Te Kahupara, a subtribal group of both Ngati Whatua and Kawerau descent.

A patch of regenerating forest may be seen on the Lookout Track entered from Motutara Rd. The track passes by windswept forest containing pohutukawa, karaka,

The pillow lava flow high in the cliffs above Maori Bay is one of the best examples in the world of lava that has been extruded onto the sea floor.

karo, taraire, kawakawa, houpara and large nikau palms. Panoramic views are obtained from the lookout over Muriwai Beach and Woodhill Forest, which was planted in pines from 1934 to stabilise the once-active dunes.

Muriwai Beach was renowned for the large shellfish known as toheroa. This delicacy was harvested by Maori for generations. It continued to be dug by the public until rapidly declining stocks led in 1976 to a total ban on its harvest. Flat Rock has remained a popular fishing spot for centuries, in spite of its dangerous and unpredictable seas.

Muriwai Regional Park is home to New Zealand's most accessible gannet colony.

Another resource of importance in pre-European times was basalt eroded from Maori Bay pillow lavas, used in the manufacture of weapons and implements. This internationally significant rock formation may be viewed from the carpark above Maori Bay, which occupies part of an old quarry, in use 1940–75.

Here and in the cliffs 1 km to the south (accessible at low tide) are the uplifted and eroded exposures of two spectacular, 17-million-year-old lava flows. They spewed out onto the sea floor on the lower submarine slopes of the ancient Waitakere Volcano (see p. 30). These flows are composed of hundreds of elongate, interconnecting lobes, 0.2–3 m in diameter. Seen in cross-section in the cliffs, they appear to be composed of a pile of discrete pillow-like forms (see p. 31). These branching, finger-like lobes are fed by larger lava tubes, 50 m or more in diameter (seen in the quarry faces).

Muriwai is now visited by a million visitors annually, with the main attraction being the 'Takapu Refuge', which is accessible by pathways over Otakamiro Point. Australasian gannets, or takapu, overflowed from nearby Oaia Island and began nesting on Motutara Island in 1975. The colony spilled over onto the mainland in 1979, at which time the refuge was formally established. The colony is generally deserted in autumn and early winter. The first birds begin nesting in late July and reach peak numbers by mid-November. Most gannet chicks fly at 15 weeks and migrate to the east and south coasts of Australia, returning to New Zealand to breed when three to seven years old. The colony contains 1000 birds and is still expanding. Between October and January, smaller white-fronted terns (tara) nest on cliff ledges below the gannets. New Zealand fur seals rest on Oaia Island but have not bred there yet.

Rough access to mill site off State Highway 28 at the western end of the Rangitopuni Stream Bridge, Riverhead. Gum Store and Museum in School Rd.

'River-head' was named because of its location at the head of the Waitemata River. It was traditionally known as Rangitopuni ('the day of the dog skin cloaks') after a peace secured there between Ngati Whatua and Te Kawerau in the 1700s. European settlement began in 1844, although the township was not surveyed until 1858.

Riverhead has an interesting industrial history, which is focused on the riverside south of the Rangitopuni Stream Bridge. The site was ideal for a mill as it had all-tide access and was adjacent to a permanent source of fresh water and motive power. Erasmus Brereton operated a kauri timber mill on the site 1845–56. It was replaced by the Waitemata Flour Mill operated by John Brigham and later John Lamb. This mill was the region's largest, producing vast quantities of flour and biscuits until it was relocated to Fort St, Auckland, in 1876. In the 1890s it became New Zealand's largest paper mill, producing vast quantities of newspaper and paper bags until 1914 (see p. 82).

Vestiges of the mill and its accompanying village remain today. On the mill site, the scow landing, foreshore breastworks, building debris and part of the old water race are visible. At the western end of Elliot St are four of the original mill-workers' cottages, and at its southern end is the historic Forrester's Arms Tavern (1876). Other buildings of interest are the Riverhead Public Hall (1915) and the Riverhead School (1903).

Riverhead was an important kauri gum-digging locality in the late 19th and early 20th centuries. In the 1920s it was noted for the production of 'Riverhead Gold' tobacco, and it has been an important exotic timber-milling centre since Riverhead State Forest was established in 1927. The district's history is reflected in the Kauri Gum Store and Museum (c.1860).

The as-yet undeveloped Riverhead Mill Foreshore Reserve. The mill complex was located below the large pine in the background.

Bush walks from the end of Horsman Rd, off Wairere Rd, 7 km from Waitakere township. Track down to Mokoroa Falls (1.5 hrs return). More primitive circuit track through Goldie Bush and back up Mokoroa Stream valley for experienced trampers (3–4 hrs round). This track links with the Te Henga Walkway (46) via Constable Rd.

Mokoroa Falls cascade over thick beds of 20-million-year-old volcanic sandstone. Their name originates from a fearsome dragon-like taniwha Te Mokoroa whose lair was beneath the falls.

David Goldie, timber merchant and Mayor of Auckland 1898–1901, acquired 'Goldie Bush' in c.1900. He established a small mill on the south-western edge of the block with Mr Rooke as manager. Wagon loads of timber were taken by bullock down the track that is now Wairere Rd to Waitakere Station. Following Rooke's death when a wagon load of timber rolled, the mill was resited near the Mokoroa Falls and operated by the Hunter Brothers. In 1920 the Kauri Timber Co. (KTC) acquired cutting rights over 35,000 acres in the district. Ebenezer Gibbons of the KTC built three timber dams in the Mokoroa catchment and flushed Goldie's logs down to the Waitakere River. The logs were tow-ed by steam launch to the head of Bethells

Water hurtles towards the Mokoroa Falls, seconds after the gate had been opened on the driving dam just upstream (1920s).

Swamp (then more like a lake) and transported over the KTC tramway to Waitakere Station. They were milled at Goldie's Oceanic Mill on Auckland's waterfront.

Goldie Bush was completely milled out, with even small saplings being cut for scaffolding poles and clothesline props. Following Goldie's death in 1926 the 190-ha property was gifted to the Auckland City Council. Today tall kanuka dominates with mamangi, or tree coprosma. Mamangi plays a similar ecological role to kanuka and its brownish yellow foliage stands out in the canopy. It is unusual in that the young plants have much smaller leaves than the adults. Dense kauri ricker stands with rimu and tanekaha are common. The grove of kowhai around the falls makes a golden display in September. Titoki are present just below the falls. Common native bird species such as native pigeon, tui, fantail, kingfisher, grey warbler and silver-eye can be seen beside the tracks.

The swamp may be viewed from Bethells Rd or Matuku Reserve entrance. The reserve is accessible from the northern side of the swamp, 1 km along Jonkers Rd from the intersection of Wairere and Horsman Rds.

Bethells Swamp from the lookout at Matuku Reserve entrance.

The 80-ha Bethells Swamp is one of the region's largest wetlands. During the Last Ice Age, the lower reaches of the Waitakere River and Mokoroa Stream flowed seaward through valleys that had been eroded well below modern sea level. When sea level rose to its present height, 6500 years ago, these lower reaches became arms of the sea, but they were soon cut off by the growth of a sand dune barrier across the mouth of the river in the vicinity of Te Henga Beach. This created an elongate lake, similar to Lake Wainamu (**45**) today. Sediment slowly began to accumulate and fill it in, forming a swamp.

In 1859 Bethells Swamp was described by the Austrian geologist Ferdinand von Hochstetter as a relatively deep river system teeming with wildlife.

Flax was harvested extensively from the wetland around the turn of the century and the riverbed was raised several metres by siltation after the construction of the Waitakere Dam (1910) upstream. Parts of the swamp around the junction with Mokoroa Stream were still open enough to be considered as a landing area for the Walsh Brothers seaplanes in 1914. Following the intensive milling of the catchment (1925–26) the river was subjected to massive siltation, creating the extensive wetland seen today.

The Waitakere River snakes its way through the swamp, marked in most places by a fringe of crack willow. Raupo, *Baumea articulata* and swamp millet form extensive semi-floating mats. Flax, cabbage trees, *Baumea rubiginosa* and willows are common along the swamp margins. The exotic bladderwort (*Utricularia gibba*) appears to be replacing the rather similar native species (*U. australis*); both have yellow flowers. The swamp is also the home for some 15 native bird species, including pukeko, bittern, fernbird, spotless crake and banded rail.

Access through Waitakere Golf Course at end of Falls Rd, 2 km off Te Henga Rd. BBQs and picnic areas, toilets, bush walks; Auckland City Walk (loop track 1 hr); longer, steeper walks to kauri ridges and beyond.

The best remaining kauri forest in the Waitakeres is in Cascade Kauri Park. The golf course area was cleared and farmed by the Sisam family in the 1870s. Most of the kauri forest in the area was milled by the Smythe Bros in the 1890s, but the Cascade kauri were left because of their inaccessibility. When the Kauri Timber Company announced plans to fell what was the last large virgin stand of kauri in the Waitakeres, the Auckland City Council moved to acquire the area as a public reserve. Cascade Kauri Park was purchased in 1925 at the then substantial cost of £28,000.

From the carpark and picnic areas mature kauri tower above on rocky ridges and bluffs. Emergent rimu and kahikatea protrude up from below and large heads of puriri, tawa and tanekaha are evident. Native pigeon, kingfisher, harrier, rosella and sulphur-crested cockatoo are

One of the large kauri seen on the Auckland City Walk.

frequently seen. Tui, tomtit, grey warbler, silver-eye and fantail are also present. Native long-tailed bats live near the stream.

Auckland City Walk is a relatively easy-grade, gravelled track that loops around through some of the best forest in the Waitakere Valley, including many huge kauri, large kahikatea, totara and pukatea with buttressed roots. Creeping African selaginella lines the track as it follows alongside the babbling Waitakere Stream for some way. The abundance of parataniwha, wheki, kiekie, nikau palms and mosses reflects the dampness of this area. A short side track leads up to the Cascade Falls, which are barely visible because they have eroded back into the bluffs along a joint. The towering bluffs and huge fallen boulders around the falls are made of erosion-resistant volcanic conglomerate that accumulated low on the submarine slopes of the Waitakere Volcano (see p. 30). From the third bridge, boulders over 2 m in diameter are evident in the Waitakere Stream, which is fed from the Waitakere Dam (**48**) and flows into Bethells Swamp (**43**). These rounded boulders reflect the power of this stream in flood.

Walking access from carpark beside bridge, 1 km from Bethells Beach. (1 hr return to lake).

Lake Wainamu fills a valley dammed by advancing sand dunes.

The access track follows Waiti Stream on an easy grade to the outlet of Lake Wainamu. On the dune margins grow spinifex, pingao, marram, pampas and a small amount of coastal toetoe. New Zealand pipits frequent this habitat.

From the lake outlet the track may be followed around the northern side of the lake to its head, where Wainamu Stream cascades over the Waitohi (baptismal waters) Falls, beside a pleasant picnic spot. The large jointed sedge, *Baumea articulata*, and raupo form a band around the lake together with lake clubrush, bolboschoenus, swamp millet, swamp willow weed and kiokio. Pied and little shags, kingfishers, ducks and black swans are seen on the lake.

Kauri forest around the headwaters of the lake was logged by the Kauri Timber Co., 1921–25. Five dams up the Wainamu Stream were used to flush the logs down to the lake. From the lake outlet the logs were transported along a horse-drawn tramway and dumped into the lower Waitakere River. They were towed to the head of the ponded river (now Bethells Swamp) by launch, and then transported by steam hauler and locomotive to Waitakere Station, and thence to the KTC Mill in Auckland. Today the lower Wainamu hills are mainly in kanuka and manuka, with more advanced regeneration of dense kauri ricker stands up the valley.

Lake Wainamu and nearby Lake Kawaupaku and Bethells Swamp (**43**) all occupy valleys dammed by the inland advance of sand dunes that accumulated behind Te Henga Beach over the last 6500 years. The Wainamu sand dune continues to advance into the lake but its supply of sand from the beach has been cut off by dune stabilisation projects.

In spite of its name Wainamu ('mosquito waters'), the lake was a favourite place in pre-European times. The earthworks of three pa overlook the lake, and the village of Ohutukawa was located under the pohutukawa grove on the lake's north-western shore.

Lake Wainamu Reserve was purchased by the Queen Elizabeth II National Trust in 1979 and is administered by ARC Regional Parks.

Access from Constable Rd, Muriwai; or from carpark just beyond Tasman View Rd, Bethells Beach. Approx. 9 km, 3–4 hrs each way (closed for lambing August–September).

From Te Henga, the track passes over the site of the former Maori village of Waiti and crosses Waitakere River via a wooden bridge. It then rises through regenerating coastal forest with some fine specimens of tawapou and a variety of divaricating shrubs. This section gives excellent views over Te Henga, the sand dunes impounding Lake Wainamu, the Waitakere River mouth and Ihumoana Island.

The track winds around O'Neill Bay, named after the first European family to settle in the district (1853). At its southern end are Erangi Pt and Kauwahaia Island. Their names commemorate a local tradition that dates back six centuries. Erangi, a young woman from the island pa of Ihumoana, had given birth to the child of a chieftain from the inland pa of Puketotara. Her people forbad her from meeting her lover and kept watch over her. In desperation Erangi strapped her baby to her back and swam north up the coast in order to proceed inland to Puketotara. She dived from the point which bears her name. Her long swim with her backburden is remembered in the names Kau-waha-ia and in her landing place on the rocky reef of Te Waha-roa.

From O'Neill Bay the walkway rises steeply to the top of Raetahinga Pt and the tableland area known as Waerengaroa. This section follows an old Maori pathway known traditionally as Te Ara Kanohi, literally 'the pathway of the eye'. This evocative name comes from the magnificent views that are available south to Manukau Heads and north to Oaia Island and Muriwai Beach.

The track proceeds around the top of the coastal cliffs, passing above Te Waharoa Reef and through the eroded pa of Te Wahatahi. It then passes under the old fortification known as Tirikohua through flax and regenerating pohutukawa forest to the impressive gut known as Te Tika. This area is the nesting and roosting place for terns and red-billed gulls. From here the walkway runs across farmland before rising steeply to the Constable Rd entrance/exit.

View south from Te Henga Walkway across O'Neill Bay, Kauwahaia Island, Erangi Pt and Ihumoana Island to Te Henga Beach beyond.

At end of Bethells Rd, about 45 mins drive from Auckland centre. Surf patrol in summer, surfing, changing sheds, toilets, beach walks.

The Te Henga area was the focal point of pre-European occupation in the Waitakere Ranges. The name Te Henga applies specifically to the beach's foredunes, whose shape was likened to the gunwale of a canoe. At the northern end of the beach is Ihumoana Is. ('the nose of the ocean'). The small bay between Ihumoana and high Erangi Pt is Waitakere ('the wave-swept rock'), the bay from which the wider district takes its name.

There are pa sites on Ihumoana Island, Kotau Pt (the small side headland on the south side of Erangi Pt), and Kauwahaia Island in O'Neill Bay, north of Erangi Pt (see **46**). The regenerating vegetation on Erangi Pt and the two adjacent islands is rather different. Erangi Pt vegetation is the tallest and most varied, with pohutukawa, tawapou, kowhai, houpara and karo, whereas Ihumoana is dominated by pohutukawa and houpara with some karo. To the north Kauwahaia Island is dominated by karo with houpara, but pohutukawa is strangely absent.

Cliffs at the mouth of the Waitakere River and forming adjacent Ihumoana Island and Erangi Pt are volcanic conglomerate. North of Erangi Pt is O'Neill Bay, the northern end of which is a volcanic crater blasted through the slightly older conglomerate rock. It was infilled with numerous flat-lying lava flows that can be seen in the high cliffs.

View north over Te Henga (Bethells Beach) with Erangi Pt and O'Neill Bay beyond.

The upper half of the amphitheatre-like cliffs and slopes behind O'Neill Bay are composed of much softer, orange-stained (limonite-rich) Pleistocene sandstone that accumulated as coastal sand dunes about half a million years ago. A thick, white band near the base of this sandstone in the middle of O'Neill Bay is rhyolite ash blown in from a large eruption in the Taupo-Rotorua area.

At the southern end of Te Henga Beach the rocky cliffs are mostly pillow lavas (undersea lava flows) overlying beds of volcanic conglomerate. Many of the pillows are separated by orangy brown deposits of fragmented volcanic glass formed as the molten lava was quenched when it came in contact with the cold ocean waters. A large cave has been eroded into the cliffs along several weak fracture planes and nearby is a dike of dark andesite intruding into the pillow lavas.

Goose barnacles attached to floating logs are frequently washed up on Auckland's west coast beaches.

Just 6500 years ago, as sea level rose to its present height after the end of the Last Ice Age, the Te Henga area would have been a large embayment on the west coast. Sand soon accumulated, filling the bay and forming sand dunes behind the beach.

New Zealand pipit can often be seen feeding among the sand dunes or along the beach. In winter flocks of white-fronted terns may also be present on the beach. A colony of spotted shags nests in winter on cliff-face ledges of Erangi Pt. Cliffs have provided protection for a large colony of grey-faced petrels, on Kauwahaia and Ihumoana Islands, where they dig nesting burrows in their soft Pleistocene sandstone caps.

Spinifex, marram and pingao dominate the dunes. Coastal toetoe and shrubs of tauhinu are on the more stable dunes and pampas grass dominates the hind-dunes. Violet shells, squid skeletons (*Spirula spirula*), Portuguese-men-of-war, by-the-wind-sailors and goose barnacles (attached to wood) are all found blown ashore.

The Bethells family has farmed the hills on the south side of Te Henga for more than a century, largely grazing sheep and cattle. For many years they ran an accommodation house that could sleep up to 60 guests.

Walk down sealed access road to Waitakere Dam from carpark on the Scenic Drive, approx. 1 km north of Mountain Rd Junction (1.5 hrs return). Scenic walk of moderately easy grade suitable for prams; toilets at dam with access to further tracks.

These days the Waitakere Falls are dry unless the dam above is overflowing.

Part way down the access road, a short track leads to a superb squat kauri (2.5 m diameter), whose lower branches support tank lilies (*Collospermum* and *Astelia*), *Pittosporum cornifolium* and puka. Small native ground orchids are visible beside the road in winter-spring. Kanuka with rimu, hinau, pigeonwood, lancewood and climbing rata vines dominate the regenerating roadside bush. Tomtit are present. Mature kauri can be seen across the reservoir from the dam; look north to see the forested Waitakere Valley and the Cascades.

The Waitakere Dam, completed in 1910, was the first of the six water reservoirs constructed in the Waitakeres. Materials and workers came in from Swanson Station on a horse-drawn tramway. Aggregate for the concrete dam was obtained from a quarry at the west end of the tramway tunnel under the Scenic Drive ridge. In 1927 the dam was raised in height to double the reservoir's capacity.

The dam was built on a solid foundation of hard volcanic conglomerate, just back from the lip of the once-spectacular Waitakere Falls. The erosion-resistant conglomerate band forms the top of the falls and the surrounding sheer bluffs. The falls were traditionally known as Awa Kotuku as their white plume was likened to the tail feathers of a kotuku or white heron. They were a major tourist attraction in the Victorian era.

From the dam, Waitakere Tramline Track follows the tramway and pipeline route around the face of an awesome amphitheatre with splendid views down into the forested Waitakere Valley below and back across to the falls. The track passes through a short tunnel and leads round to the old quarry site and locked gate to George's Tunnel (named after the original landowner), which passes under the Scenic Drive. Rougher bush tracks continue on from here but we recommend you now return along the route you came.

On Scenic Drive, 8 km from Titirangi. Major information centre for all the Waitakere Ranges, toilets, picnics, nature trail.

Auckland Centennial Memorial Park was established in 1940 to commemorate the centennial of the city's founding. Following its establishment, the park was augmented by donations of further land by many generous donors, such as Earle Vaile (699 acres), Sir William Goodfellow (175 acres), Sir Algernon Thomas (104 acres), Lady Rose Hellaby (**50**) and others. Park administration was transferred to the Auckland Regional Authority in 1964.

Arataki Nature Trail opened in 1974, with the large, new Visitor Centre opening in 1994. 'Arataki' — 'the instructional pathway' or nature trail — is across the road from the Visitor Centre. It outlines the process of natural regeneration and ends at a delightful grove of mature kauri.

Wooden observation decks provide a unique bird's-eye experience of the forest canopy as they weave among branches of kauri, rewarewa, kahikatea, New Zealand broom, ponga, nikau, lacebark and heads

The entrance to Arataki Visitor Centre features traditional Maori carvings which honour the history of the local tribe — Te Kawerau a Maki.

of rata vines. The decks give panoramic views of the lower Nihotupu Valley and Manukau Harbour. The harbour was an embayment on Auckland's west coast that has been impounded by the build-up of an elongate barrier of sand dunes (Awhitu Peninsula) over the last two million years. For about 80 percent of this time, the Manukau Harbour was a forested plain drained by several winding rivers. Only during the warm peaks between the succession of at least 20 ice ages has sea level been high enough to flood the plain and form the Manukau Harbour. The most recent dry period ended just 7–8000 years ago as sea level rose after the end of the Last Ice Age.

The Nihotupu Valley was farmland until the Lower Nihotupu Dam was completed in 1948. This was the first large controlled, rolled-fill, earth dam to be built in New Zealand. Evident below the dam is Big Muddy Creek, flanked by mangroves. Kanuka and mamaku tree ferns now cover the lower reservoir slopes. Rewarewa, kauri and rimu stand out in the foreground. A grove of nikau, mature kahikatea and puriri are evident below the uppermost deck.

The following short bush walks all have access off Scenic Drive, north of Arataki Visitor Centre. The Scenic Drive was constructed along the eastern ridge of the ranges, 1936–39.

Rangemore Track
Two entrances from Scenic Drive, full length 1.5 hrs return. Features a grove of young kauri, 10 mins in from west entrance.

Rose Hellaby House
The property was bequeathed to the people of Auckland by Miss Rose Hellaby in 1975. Part of the house is leased to the West Auckland Historical Society as a historical display centre (open weekend afternoons). The grounds are open daily and provide sweeping views of Auckland City and both the Waitemata and Manukau Harbours.

Parkinson Lookout
Grassy picnic areas in bushy surrounds. Easy 5-min. walk to lookout platform over the Henderson Valley and greater Auckland.

Large Kauri Walk
An easy 2-min. loop walk to see one of the largest kauri trees left in the Waitakeres.

Fairy Falls Track
A longer walk with some steep sections through regenerating forest with some large rimu specimens. To falls, 1.5–2 hrs return; loop track via falls to Mountain Rd and return up Old Coach Rd track, 2.5–3 hrs return. The Fairy Falls are a series of high cascades over sandstone and conglomerate, with the lips held up by two, resistant, columnar-jointed andesite dikes.

Spraggs Bush Walk
Picnic area, toilets. A 30-min. loop track, with gentle grades, passes a large kauri and an old cemetery. Ferns, mosses and liverworts abound in this wet forest. Katote, or Smiths tree fern, is common at this elevation. It stands out with its 'skirt' of frond mid-ribs.

Also worth visiting:
Pukematekeo Lookout at northern end of Scenic Drive.
Oratia Folk Museum (open Sundays) on West Coast Rd, Oratia, 0.5 km west of Parrs Cross Rd; housed in a quaint two-storeyed kauri cottage built by the Parker family in 1872, and surrounded by a Victorian garden.

Left: Fairy Falls are reached after an hour's bush walk from the Scenic Drive or Mountain Road.

Below: Location of short walks and stops on the Scenic Drive.

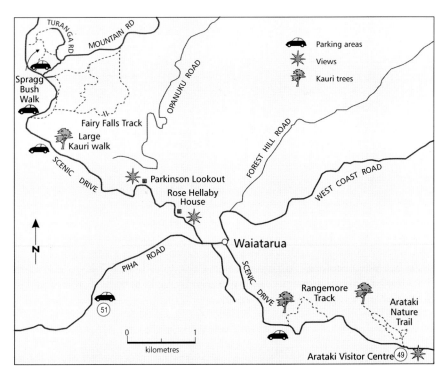

Walking access down gravel road to dam from gate on Piha Rd, 2 km from Scenic Drive (1.5 hrs return).

Luxuriant regenerating native forest clothes the hillsides right down to the edge of the Upper Nihotupu Reservoir and dam.

This walk is one of the most pleasant in the Waitakeres. The track passes a series of cascades and falls held up by thick volcanic sandstone and conglomerate beds. After crossing the Nihotupu Stream it descends to the head of the reservoir, where the Nihotupu Falls cascade over a hard andesite lava flow and into the lake. To the right of the falls is the overgrown quarry that supplied andesite aggregate for the dam. From here the road alongside the reservoir lake follows the former route of the tramway used to carry aggregate to the large crusher beside the dam.

Vegetation on wet banks is dominated by kiokio ferns, cudweed (*Anaphalis keriensis*) and parataniwha; small herbs of nertera and willow herb; and abundant mats of mosses and liverworts. This native cover is threatened by weeds such as selaginella, mist flower and Mexican daisy. Look up to see large northern tree rata and kauri trees silhouetted along the ridge tops. This track is ideal to see forest birds, including native pigeon and tomtit.

In 1902 the growing city of Auckland turned to the Waitakere Ranges as an additional source of water. A small timber dam was constructed on the site of the present Upper Nihotupu Dam and a pipe and tramline laid around the hillsides to Titirangi. The concrete Upper Nihotupu Dam was built (1915–23) on a solid base of volcanic conglomerate at the head of the deeply incised Nihotupu Gorge. Workers, supplies and cement came by barge to a wharf at Parau and thence by tramway and steep incline up the lower Nihotupu Valley to connect with the pipeline track.

The picnic and lookout area at the end of the road below the dam was the site of the workers' camp when the dam was built. The original pipeline route was shortened in the 1920s with 23 tunnels being driven through the spurs. This route is still in use and open to the public on special open days. Each tunnel carries the pipe and a narrow-gauge tramway for maintenance purposes.

Access down steep path (1 hr return) from end of Anawhata Rd, 10 km off Piha Rd. The west coast's most secluded beach, not safe for swimming.

The track down to Anawhata Beach leads through a gully of regenerating forest with numerous west coast kowhai (*Sophora microphylla* var. *fulvida*). This form with its small leaflets is restricted almost entirely to Auckland's west coast.

The beach is backed by a lagoon in the mouth of Anawhata Stream, frequented by Caspian terns, ducks, shags and other wetland birds. Flax, coastal toetoe, tauhinu, wire-vine and buffalo grass cover Parera Pt with northern parts of the beach backed by low spinifex-covered sand dunes.

Anawhata takes its name from the 'elevated rock shelters' in the surrounding bluffs, which were used by the Kawerau people while engaged in seasonal fishing activities.

Surrounding hills are clothed in young vegetation of wind-shorn kanuka, manuka, gorse and pampas grass. The cliffs, rock platforms and high inland knolls are composed of volcanic conglomerate that accumulated on the submarine slopes of the Waitakere Volcano (p. 30). In the cliffs at the northern end of the beach are several irregular, intrusive tongues of solidified andesite that squeezed their way into the conglomerates late in the volcano's history.

The conglomerate in the cliff south of Anawhata Beach opposite, Keyhole Rock, is tilted steeply next to the ancient wall of the Whites Beach crater (**53**). The crater is filled with flat-lying lava flows that form the high cliffs to the south. White spots high on the cliffs are the South African succulent, *Cotyledon orbiculata*. Lower down is the prostrate, west coast koromiko, *Hebe obtusata*.

Kauri in the Anawhata Valley was some of the last to be felled in the Ranges (1916–21) because of the difficulty of getting the logs out. Driving dams were used to flush the logs downstream to a holding dam in the gorge, about 1 km up from the beach. From here they were hauled up a tramway and over the Anawhata Rd ridge to North Piha, then south to the Piha Mill.

Surfing, changing sheds, toilets near North Piha surf club, picnic areas. Steep walk (Laird Thomson Track) from end of North Piha Beach over Te Waha Pt and down to Whites Beach (30 mins).

Laird Thomson Track starts 250 m along the beach from the end of North Piha Rd. Here the cliffs are made of volcanic conglomerate and a number of small caves have been eroded by storm waves along fractures in the rocks. Little blue penguins nest along this section of coastline and dogs are prohibited.

The track climbs steadily up from Kohunui Bay (so named because of its oft-present sea mist) through wind-shorn pohutukawa, with shrubs of houpara and kawakawa. Native herbs of New Zealand spinach, lobelia, parietaria, New Zealand celery, native chickweed, rengarenga and shore groundsel are present. At the junction on the crest of the ridge, ngaio and west coast kowhai are common. A short track to the left leads out to the coastal headland and the earthwork remains of Te Wahangu Pa.

The track straight ahead descends steeply through a grove of tawapou (**13**) and requires a clamber around the rocks at mid- or low tide to reach the beach. The track to the right is the high tide track to Whites Beach (named after Francis White, who purchased the area in 1861). It climbs up and through private property past several small holiday baches before descending as Rose Track to the northern end of Whites Beach.

The amphitheatre-like cliffs surrounding Whites Beach are made of lava flows that filled a volcanic crater which was blasted through the underlying conglomerate, 16 million years ago. It is one of many craters and vents that form a line along the present west coast (see p. 31). At sea level there are irregular-shaped intrusive bodies of dark, jointed andesite. These were tongues of magma that didn't erupt but cooled and solidified within the volcano. On the coastal cliffs is the attractive daisy *Celmisia major*.

Whites Beach (foreground) can be reached via a walking track over Te Waha Pt (middle) from North Piha Beach.

Access from the end of Glen Esk Rd, on right at the bottom of Piha Hill. BBQ and picnic area, toilets. Kitekite Track to falls is gravelled and an easy grade (round trip 1 hr). Piha Valley Track is flat to entrance of Piha Gorge (30 mins); steeper section leads to kauri dam remains (1.5–2 hrs to dam return).

The kauri forest in these valleys was felled in the 1910s and logs were flushed down the streams by a series of driving dams. The large Piha Mill (1910–21) stood nearby, on the site of the present Boys Brigade Camp, and mill-workers' houses peppered the hillsides. The mill sawed logs from the immediate area, and also those brought in by tramway from North Piha (**53**) and the Anawhata Valley (**52**). Sawn timber was taken out on a tramway that went up and over the Piha Hill to Karekare (**56**) and down the coast to the Whatipu Wharf (**63**). Most of the timber was sold to the New Zealand Railways Department, which purchased the Piha Mill in 1913.

Piha and Kitekite Valleys have eroded into volcanic conglomerate which often forms bluffs on the steep hillsides. Tall kanuka and large cabbage trees with nikau, ponga, mamaku, and kowhai dominate the lower flood plains. A

Kitekite Falls cascade over volcanic conglomerate which is intruded here by a thin dike of andesite. The deep pool at the foot of the falls is pleasant for summer swims.

few youthful northern tree rata are also present. Dense kauri ricker stands are common on the valley sides.

The middle reaches of the Piha Stream are deeply incised into the conglomerate, forming a narrow gorge with vertical and, in places, overhanging walls. More experienced and agile visitors can clamber up the stream bed through the lower half of the gorge. The remains of the Black Rock kauri dam can be seen beside the track where it crosses Piha Stream at the head of the gorge. In the 1910s, the gorge was blocked on several occasions by major log jams. Today several large logs from the logging days are still jammed in the gorge.

At the end of Piha Rd. Changing sheds and toilets, surf patrol in summer, surfing, store, campground, short steep tracks up Lion Rock (101 m) and Tasman Lookout Track (south end).

The cliffs and inland bluffs surrounding South Piha are made of weakly bedded volcanic conglomerate that accumulated on the submarine slopes of the Waitakere Volcano, 18–20 million years ago (see p. 30). From the south end of the beach, the walk around the rocks at low tide or over Tasman Lookout Track leads to The Gap. Here the conglomerates are intruded by several dikes of younger andesite lava. On the south side of The Gap itself the dark grey dike is quite irregular in form with several branches.

A regular 2-m-thick vertical dike with horizontal, columnar cooling joints intrudes Taitomo Island. The pounding waves have plucked out the hard, jointed andesite, creating the tidal tunnel which gives the island its name.

An old ring bolt in the cliffs opposite Taitomo Island dates back to an unsuccessful attempt in the 1870s to fell the local kauri forest, form log rafts in the shelter of Taitomo Island and tow them to Onehunga.

Lion Rock is made of the eroded contents of a volcanic neck with layers of scoria, ash and breccia that have slumped back into the vent. They have been intruded by a number of irregularly shaped andesite dikes, some of which possibly fed lava flows above. The track up windswept Lion Rock (1 hr return) is steep with numerous steps. It has bare patches interspersed with Kikuyu and pampas, flax, pohutukawa and, by the summit, a grove of karaka, kowhai, pohutukawa, rangiora, coastal karamu and tawapou.

Lion Rock was known traditionally as Te Piha after the wave pattern created by the rock. The important Kawerau pa on the rock was known as Whakaari because of its 'prominence'. Although some of the pa has eroded away, traces can still be seen. On the Lion's buttocks and right shoulder there are terraces and shell middens. The top of the head is terraced and has several pits. It was the tihi or last bastion of defence.

Lion Rock at Piha is the eroded remains of a 16-million-year-old volcanic neck and the site of Whakaari Pa.

Te Rua o Kaiwhare — The Lair of Kaiwhare

To the Te Kawerau tribe of Waitakere, The Blowhole at South Piha is known as Te Rua o Kaiwhare. It was one of the many lairs of the taniwha or sea monster known as Kaiwhare. Along with Paikea, this taniwha was the guardian spirit of the Waitakere coastline and the Manukau Harbour entrance. Kaiwhare also had lairs inside the Manukau Heads near Awhitu, as well as at Whatipu and Te Henga.

Unlike Paikea, who generally assisted humans on the ocean, Kaiwhare was renowned for causing flood tides and overturning canoes. As a result the local people always placated him before embarking on sea travel or fishing expeditions. They did so by placing food in a miniature house built on a small raft, which was set adrift on the outgoing tide. If there was no sign of the raft the next morning it showed that Kaiwhare was content and there would be plenty of fish. It was from this practice that the taniwha received his name, Kaiwhare, 'the house eater'.

After Kaiwhare began killing humans who were fishing, Te Kawerau and Ngati Kahukoka, who then occupied the Awhitu area, decided that he must be killed. In Kawerau tradition, Te Patunga o Kaiwhare — 'the killing of Kaiwhare' — was undertaken by a warrior known as Hakawau. He is said to have trapped the troublesome taniwha by placing a net over his lair (The Blowhole) at Piha and to have killed him using a patu paraoa (whalebone weapon). The writhing of Kaiwhare during his struggle is credited with creating the nearby rock shelf generally known as The Gap. It provides the southern opening to the bay known as Puaotetai — 'the foam of the sea' — a name that stems from the fact that sea foam builds up there during storms. Some say it is the work of Kaiwhare, who lives on to cause coastal erosion and the tidal surges of the Manukau Harbour entrance.

A view of Puaotetai Bay with Taitomo Island beyond.

Access from Piha Rd down Karekare Rd (sealed) or Lone Kauri Rd (gravel). BBQs, picnic areas, changing sheds, surfing, surf patrol in summer, beach and bush walks, rock fishing.

The route of the Piha Tramway can still be followed around the rocks at the southern end of Karekare Beach.

Tradition and archaeological evidence indicate that Karekare was intensively settled in pre-European times. The area offered rich and diverse sea and forest foods and the valley was favoured for growing kumara. The main village was located below Te Kakawhakaara Pa (on The Watchman), while there were other pa on Te Ahua Point and above Te Ahoaho (Karekare Falls). Wharengarahi, the large rock shelter above the lower end of Lone Kauri Rd, was palisaded and used as a refuge. Te Kaka Pa and the cave shelter were last occupied in 1826, when they were overrun by a musket-wielding Ngapuhi raiding party from Northland.

Karekare has witnessed two periods of kauri milling. The Karekau Sawmill (1881–86) operated on the flat between Lone Kauri Rd and Karekare Falls and employed up to 70 men. Logs were flushed down Company and Opal Pools Streams by driving dams and brought in by tramway from the Karekare Valley. Sawn timber went out by tramway around the point at the south end of Karekare Beach, through a tunnel north of Pararaha and down the coast to Whatipu Wharf. The mill was closed because of an economic decline, and small wood-turning and flax-milling enterprises followed.

In 1906, a smaller mill was established on the flat picnic area at the foot of Karekare Hill. It operated for four years sawing logs driven down from the head of the valley, before it was relocated to Piha. In the 1910s the celebrated Piha Tramway was laid over the hill from Piha, through the lower Karekare Valley, across the sand dunes and down the coastal route of the earlier Karekau tramway to Whatipu.

During the first half of the 20th century the lower Karekare Valley was farmed by the Farley family. Their homestead, named Winchelsea House after Mrs Farley's home town in the south of England, is still present tucked in behind The Watchman. The homestead and surrounding annexes were transformed into a popular guest house for weekend holidaymakers, who came for beach and bush walks, horse riding, tennis and croquet. Karekare Surf club, established in 1935, has been an important focus of Karekare activities in more recent years.

The cliffs and hills south and inland of Karekare are composed of layered volcanic conglomerate that accumulated on the submarine slopes of the growing Waitakere Volcano (see p. 30). The centre and northern parts of Karekare Beach were the site of a large explosion crater that was blasted out on the eastern flanks of the giant uplifted Waitakere Volcano about 16 million years ago. The crater was subsequently filled with broken-up lava flows and a dome of viscous, flow-banded dacite lava. The Watchman in the middle of Karekare Beach is the eroding remnant of the dacite dome. Dacite has more silica and is lighter coloured than the grey andesite that forms most of Waitakere Volcano. Part of the ancient crater wall can be seen in the cliffs forming Farley Point, at the north end of Karekare Beach.

Sheet-like dikes of columnar-jointed andesite can be seen intruding the older conglomerate in the cliffs at both ends of Karekare Beach. These dikes were possibly the underground conduits that fed andesite lava flows that were extruded into the crater.

During the Ice Ages when sea level was lower, Karekare Stream eroded its valley deep below the present beach and dune areas. When the sea rose to its present height 6500 years ago, the valley was flooded and a bay formed south of The Watchman. It subsequently filled with sand.

The largest taraire forest in the Waitakere Ranges can be seen along Taraire Track, which leads off from Karekare Falls. Along Horoeka Track (north Karekare) is a hybrid swarm of shrubs thought to be a cross between horoeka and houpara. The result is a most bizarre array of leaf forms. The vegetation on the hills behind Karekare is mainly windswept kanuka. At the northern end of the beach, pohutukawa are pressed against the cliffs together with flax. In the lee of the dunes it is surprising how large pohutukawa have grown.

Fur seals rest on Paratahi Island to the south, together with white-fronted terns and red-billed gulls that nest there. Taupata is the main plant cover.

View south over Karekare Beach with Whatipu Beach in the distance.

Take Huia Rd from Titirangi; main beach access via Pine Ave; wharf access off Cornwallis Rd.
Toilets, BBQs, short walks, safe swimming at high tide on Cornwallis Beach, fishing from wharf.

Cornwallis was traditionally known as Karanga-a-hape ('the call of Hape'). This evocative name arose when the Tainui ancestor Hape signalled the trapping of a taniwha visiting from the Hauraki Gulf. Karangahape was occupied for generations by the Waiohua and Kawerau tribes as a seasonal shellfish-gathering place, as is reflected in abundant shell middens. Another reminder of the long Maori occupation is the well-preserved Karangahape Pa located on a forest-covered headland near Cornwallis Wharf. The pathway from the area to Auckland provided the origin of the name of the Auckland thoroughfare Karangahape Rd.

In 1840 Karangahape was acquired by the New Zealand Manukau and Waitemata Co., who surveyed the 'model town' of 'Cornwallis', named in honour of its resident director Captain William Cornwallis Symonds. Over 100 Scottish settlers arrived, 1841–42. New Zealand's first steam-powered sawmill was erected near Mill Bay and a hotel established. The Cornwallis settlement was doomed to failure and was abandoned by 1843 after Symonds drowned, the mill closed and land titles were not secured.

The infertile Cornwallis property was farmed by the Kilgour family and later by John McLachlan, who was born at Cornwallis in 1842. He gifted the property to Auckland City in 1909 as a memorial to his mother and the settlers whose hopes had been dashed at Cornwallis 70 years earlier. The ACC planted 1.5 million pines as a commercial enterprise in 1923. The stunted pines still growing on the land are testament to the failure of this project. In 1926 the 200-m-long Cornwallis Wharf was constructed to provide ferry access to the reserve, which became popular with day trippers and fishers.

The remnant of Cornwallis Wharf, the last of the Manukau's original 16 ferry wharves, is being restored by the ARC.

Short flat walk from carpark beside bridge on Huia Rd, 500 m beyond Cornwallis Rd turnoff.

The track from the carpark to the beach (5 mins), alongside Kakamatua Stream, follows the route of a bush tramway used to bring kauri logs down to the Cornwallis Mill, which operated at the head of the inlet, 1860–78. Logs were also flushed down the stream by water released from four driving dams up the valley. Log booms and a low earth holding dam were constructed across the stream mouth beside the mill to catch the logs brought down by the drives. On one occasion nearly 1000 logs were washed into the Manukau Harbour when the booms and dam burst during a drive. To help prevent a recurrence, an overflow tunnel was put through a low spur on the west side of the dam. Parts of the dam and the collapsed tunnel are still visible on the opposite side of the stream from the track just before it reaches the beach.

A second wooden tramline was built on piles out across the Kakamatua Inlet to a wharf on the western point. It was used to transport sawn timber from the mill to berthed ships. The foundation holes of the wharf on the point are visible.

A stroll across the sand of Kakamatua Inlet at low tide is pleasant. The inlet is fringed with native bush, particularly kowhai, tanekaha, with kauri on the upper slopes and the occasional hinau, lancewood and rewarewa. On the flat, saltwater paspalum forms swards with clumps of sea rush, knobby sedge, cabbage trees and sometimes *Baumea articulata*.

The extensive tidal sand flats are inhabited by common cockles, pipi and wedge shells. Gulls, reef herons, white-faced herons, pied stilts, paradise shelducks, oystercatchers, kingfishers and swallows are often seen feeding on the flats.

The Cornwallis Sawmill (left) and settlement on the east side of the mouth of the Kakamatua Stream in 1867. Mill workers' houses are clustered around the mill.

Signposted off Huia Rd, between Cornwallis and Huia. Kaitarakihi Bay has BBQ and picnic area, toilet, safe swimming at high tide.

There are many ground orchids like Orthoceras novae-zeelandiae *in the gumlands around Kaitarakihi.*

In 1919 the area around Kaitarakihi Bay was donated to the people of Auckland by the Spragg family. Wesley Spragg erected the Spragg Monument on the high point east of the bay in 1920 to commemorate soldiers who lost their lives in the First World War, including his son.

Regenerating gumland scrub grows on the poor soils of Cornwallis and Kaitarakihi. The manuka scrub areas around Spragg Monument include club moss, umbrella fern, kumarahou, akepiro, *Dracophyllum sinclairii*, glossy karamu, toru, mingimingi, sundew, native sedges, ground orchids and two kinds of spiny Australian hakea shrubs.

Kaitarakihi Beach and picnic area is backed by regenerating native forest of kaihikatea, cabbage trees, nikau and flax, with kanuka, kauri and tanekaha on the slopes behind. Often washed up on the beach are slender, 2–3 cm long, tubular tusk shells that live partly buried in the sea-floor sand just offshore. This is one of the few places in New Zealand where they live in such shallow water and can be found on the beach.

The cliffs and shore platforms on either side of Kaitarakihi Beach are composed of volcanic sandstone and siltstone that accumulated around the foot of the growing submarine Waitakere Volcano about 19 million years ago (see p. 30). They contain beautiful examples of small faults, folds and trace fossils.

Closer to Huia, the Huia Point Lookout platform provides panoramic views across Huia Bay and New Zealand's second largest harbour — the Manukau. Straight across the bay are the awe-inspiring bluffs in the Karamatura Valley (**61**). They are made of volcanic conglomerate that accumulated on the submarine slopes of the Waitakere Volcano. The smaller conical peak at the western entrance to Huia Bay is Te Komoki, the top of which was a heavily defended pa in pre-European times.

Turn right at the Huia Stream Bridge, 1 km beyond Huia Store. Toilets, picnic areas, bush walks.
Walk from locked gate at Lower Huia Dam to Upper Huia Dam (3 hrs return).

Te Rau o Te Huia ('the plume of the huia bird') was a favourite occupation site for the Kawerau tribe. Shellfish were gathered from Huia Bay, taro and kumara were grown in the lower valley, and the catchment was harvested for its forest resources.

The valley was subjected to over 40 years of timber extraction. In the 1850s, a Nova Scotian, John Gibbons, acquired cutting rights. He and his sons used rolling roads, bullock teams, earth driving dams and a horse-drawn tramway to transport timber to the water-powered Huia Mill, which operated under various managers until 1889. The remains of its earth holding dam can still be seen near the Parau Track swing bridge. On nearby Twin Peaks Track is a cemetery containing graves of several mill workers and a child drowned in Huia Stream.

Huia Valley was farmed by the Higham and Page families, 1880–1920. Logs continued to be extracted until it was purchased by the ACC as a water-supply catchment in 1921. The ACC constructed the concrete gravity Upper Huia Dam, 1924–29. Materials and equipment were barged to the Huia Landing and then transported to the dam site via a narrow-gauge railway. It mostly followed the route of the present Upper Huia Dam Rd (along which you can now walk) through several large cuttings and two tunnels (one is now drowned beneath the Lower Huia Reservoir). Near the dam itself were two camps which housed 200 construction workers and their families. The Top Camp was a self-contained village which had its own hall, school and post office.

Dominating the lower valley is the Lower Huia Dam, constructed from rock quarried from the adjacent hillside and completed in 1971. The Huia Valley is clad in regenerating podocarp, kauri and broadleaf forest. The rare Hochstetter's frog is present and tomtit can sometimes be seen on its bush tracks.

A splendid pohutukawa with a 2-m-diameter trunk covered with twisted roots and clumps of tank lilies in its lower branches stands out in the domain by the coast.

During the day, visitors can drive to the top of the Lower Huia Dam to view the Reservoir and forested Huia Valley.

Located 2 km beyond Huia Store. Picnic areas, toilets, bush walks, campsites may be booked with ARC. Huia Museum (open Sunday afternoons).

Karamatura Valley and its high conglomerate bluffs, from Huia Point Lookout (59).

Karamatura Valley is clad in regenerating native forest dominated by kanuka on the valley floor. Along the 1-hr Loop Track kanuka gives way to abundant nikau with kahikatea, mahoe, rewarewa, pukatea and fine examples of northern tree rata. Landforms of interest in the upper valley are the six-tiered Karamatura Falls and the impressive volcanic conglomerate Wharenga Bluff.

The name Karamatura is a corruption of the Maori name Kaingamaturi. According to Kawerau tradition, a Waiohua woman fell in love with one of her Kawerau hosts during a summer fishing camp. She was asked to leave him behind when her people returned to their homes. In order to stay together the young lovers hid beneath a waterfall in the valley where they remained undiscovered for several days. When they emerged they had been temporarily deafened by the roar of the falls, which became known as Kainga-maturi, 'the dwelling place of the deaf'.

There have been three periods of kauri milling in the Karamatura. Adjacent to the main carpark and picnic area are the remains of an earth dam constructed by the Gibbons family in 1853. Water flowed from the dam along a 400-m water race to power the 8-m-diameter overshot waterwheel of the 'Niagara Mill', which operated on the foreshore until 1867. Logs were flushed to the mill using earth driving dams located in the upper catchment. They were also transported down a horse-drawn tramway route which is still discernible along the lower Karamatura track.

Kauri was again extracted from the Karamatura Valley and milled at the Manukau Timber Co. Mill, 1892–98. Its foundations are still visible in Hinge Bay, across the paddock behind the museum and south around the foreshore. In the early 1900s Thomas Barr rebuilt the old Niagara Mill dam and operated a small water-powered sawmill for nearly a decade.

The history of the area is portrayed in the Huia Museum. It features a remnant of the massive mast of the HMS *Orpheus,* wrecked on the Manukau Bar in 1863 (63).

Walking access from the end of steep, gravel Mt Donald McLean Rd, which branches off Whatipu Rd at the top of the hill above Little Huia. Easy-grade track to summit (30 mins return).

The summit of Mt Donald McLean (390 m) provides spectacular 360-degree views over the city, the southern Waitakere Ranges and Manukau Harbour. On a clear day you can see Mt Taranaki in the south across the Tasman Sea. The hill's traditional name is Te Rau o Te Huia from which the district takes its name. It was named Mt Donald McLean after a prominent colonial figure, who was head of the Native Land Purchase Dept in 1853 when the Waitakere Ranges were purchased by the Crown.

On the rocky outcrops is *Hebe bishopiana,* a low koromiko with purplish stems. It is the only higher plant restricted to the Waitakeres Ranges. Some of the more interesting trackside plants include:

The koromiko Hebe bishopiana *grows on the rocky outcrops of Mt Donald McLean.*

mountain flax with its pale green leaves and hanging capsules; *Alseuosmia macrophylla*, a shrub with pendulous fragrant flowers in August; *Corokia buddleioides*, a shrub with yellow star-like flowers in summer; Hall's totara, with thin bark; toatoa, growing adjacent to its smaller-'leaved' relative, tanekaha; and native passionfruit vine. The summit shrubland includes New Zealand broom, miro and ramarama with its blistered leaves.

This part of the Waitakere Ranges is composed largely of volcanic conglomerate that accumulated on the upper submarine flanks of the Waitakere Volcano about 18–19 million years ago. Characteristic landforms that have developed in these conglomerates are rounded domes and sheer bluffs of bare rock.

A thriving population of the large, carnivorous kauri snail lives in the Marama Valley on the Huia side of Mt Donald McLean. They were introduced to this area from Northland 50 years ago. Their dead shells are sometimes seen on Whatipu Rd or washed down to Little Huia Beach.

Another short walk in the vicinity is Manukau Bar View Track. It is signposted half way up the Whatipu Rd hill from Little Huia.

Road access from Huia at end of narrow, winding, gravel Whatipu Rd. Please drive with care. Toilets, lodge, camping, small store open in summer; rock fishing, surfcasting, beach, dune and bush walks, exposed sandy beach unsafe for swimming.

A 1-km-wide scrubby sand flat lies between the carpark at the end of the road and the Tasman Sea; 80 years ago the cars would have been on the beach. This rapid accretion of coastal sand flats and dunes mostly occurred during the 1930s and 1940s. This is just the latest phase of a longer term process, in which a huge volume of sand is slowly being moved northwards up the coast by currents and long-shore drift. A similar large sand flat was present off Awhitu Peninsula to the south until about 200 years ago, when it was eroded away. In the first half of the 19th century some of the offshore Manukau Bar was a dry, vegetated island but the sand has now moved north.

The old sea cliffs just north of Whatipu are made of volcanic conglomerate. Here visitors enjoy exploring the dry caves that were eroded by the sea along joint planes through the rock. The largest cave was used last century by the local timber-mill workers for socials and even had a wooden dance floor.

In the last 50 years the Whatipu sand flat and its mobile dunes have become stabilised. The scrub-and-grass-covered flats are home to rosella parrots, Californian quail, pheasants, swallows, harriers, various finches and other exotic species. Permanent freshwater ponds behind the dunes are frequented by white-faced herons, little shags, pied stilts and ducks. Mullet also live in the ponds. Less common inhabitants of these wetlands are bittern, spotless crake, fernbird and black swan.

Most of the Whatipu sand flat was formed during the 1930s and 1940s.

The largest expanse of pingao in the region is found at Whatipu, where it occurs with spinifex on the outer mobile dunes. In the damp dune flats are the most extensive salt meadows in the region. They are dominated by small native herbs of *Carex pumila*, *Myriophyllum votchii*, *Triglochin striata*, *Lilaeopsis novae-zelandiae*, *Isolepis cernua* and less commonly by *Limosella lineata*, lobelia and *Eleocharis neozelandica*.

In the 1910s the sea broke against the cliffs just north of Whatipu and the Piha Tramway was built on trestles across the mouths of the Whatipu Caves. Since then a 1-km-wide sand flat has grown out in front of the cliffs.

Pre-European fortified pa occupy four of the highest points around the mouth of the Whatipu Valley, in which kumara would have been cultivated.

A plaque on Paratutai Island, on the Whatipu side of Manukau Harbour entrance, marks New Zealand's worst maritime disaster. The British navy's corvette HMS *Orpheus* ran aground and sank on the Manukau Bar offshore on 7 February 1863. The *Orpheus*'s captain ignored signals from the signalman on Paratutai, telling him that he was on the wrong course. Survivors reached shore at Whatipu, in two small boats, including the ship's cutter, which landed beside Cutter Rock, today surrounded by vegetated sand flats. Some 189 officers and crew were drowned.

A kauri timber mill was established up the Whatipu Valley by Robert Gibbons in 1867. Remains of its earth holding dam can be seen on Kura Track about 1 km upstream of the road bridge. Sawn timber was taken down the valley by tramway to a wharf in the shelter of Paratutai. The wharf site, with its cliff overhang, is now a favourite fishing spot. Another mill (1870–81) was built by William Foote in the lower Pararaha Valley to the north. It too had a tramway down the coast to the Whatipu Wharf. Both mills closed in the 1880s, but the wharf remained the terminus for an extended tramway from a mill at Karekare (1881–86).

Following the closure of Whatipu Mill, the Gibbons family farmed the valley for many years and ran a boarding house. Their family home, with its steep gable roof, attic and wide verandah, is now part of Whatipu Lodge beside the carpark.

After a 20-year break, the coastal tramway was relaid and extended to become the well-known Piha Tramway, which brought sawn kauri timber down to Whatipu Wharf, 1907–21 (**54**, **56**). Some of the tramway route can be followed around the foot of the cliffs by Whatipu caves and Windy Pt and across the sand flats to Pararaha Pt and on through a tunnel to Karekare.

Access signposted off Upper Harbour Drive, Hobsonville. Toilets, licensed restaurant, tearooms, cinema (open Wed.–Sun., 11 am–4 pm).

'Juliet', a 1908 Briton, the only example in New Zealand.

Monterey Park is set in 10 ha of grounds at Clark Point, Hobsonville, which was settled by the Clark family of pottery fame in 1854. Fine views over a mangrove-fringed arm of the upper Waitemata Harbour can be gained from the carpark. The grounds are dotted with old Monterey pines which give the facility its name. Smaller maritime pines are present closer to the carpark.

The focal point of the property is one of New Zealand's finest motor museums, which chronicles the nation's motoring history. The museum displays a wide range of beautifully restored vintage, veteran and classic motor vehicles. They range from the more common classics, such as the Ford Prefect and the first Toyota model sold in New Zealand, to the more exotic. Such vehicles include a rare De Lorean as featured in the movie *Back to the Future*, a Lambourghini, a massive 1922 Packard Twin Six, and a rare example of an SS Sports Tourer, the forerunner of the Jaguar. Also on display is New Zealand's oldest four-cylindered car, a 1905 14 hp Star Tourer; and a 1929 Chevrolet, which was the 1200th vehicle assembled at the General Motors plant in Petone.

Several cars which are either unrestored or under restoration are also on display to provide a benchmark for the restored vehicles. Beside the museum is the restoration workshop where the vehicle restoration process may be observed during weekends.

The museum also displays vintage motorbikes, a wide range of vintage car accessories, licence plates and signs which tell of the nation's evolving motoring history. It also displays stationary engines, once so vital to agriculture, and a variety of vintage milking machines. An audio-visual presentation outlining the history of sheep farming in New Zealand is available by arrangement.

Signposted on Great North Rd immediately north of Henderson Township.

The Corban Winery Estate of 9.5 ha contains several historic buildings set in spacious grounds and gardens. It is the remaining part of the Mt Lebanon Vineyard and Winery that was established in 1902 by Assid Abraham Corban, who arrived in New Zealand from Lebanon in 1892.

The Mt Lebanon Winery selling depot (1913).

The Henderson property continued to be the headquarters of Corbans Wines Ltd until the Corban family sold its interests in 1977. The property is now owned by Waitakere City Council and operated by the Corban Estate Trust Board as a civic, recreational and tourist amenity. Corbans Wines Ltd lease a number of the historic buildings on the property. These include the original winery and cellar, built 1903–07, which is operated as offices and a wine shop. The largest historic building is the impressive 17-room Edwardian-style Corban Homestead, built in 1923.

Of particular interest is the original 'Selling Depot' (1913), which stands at the entrance to the complex as a unique reminder of the prohibition debate which divided New Zealand in the early 20th century. In 1909 the Eden electorate, within which most of the Corban property was located, became a 'no licence' district. This meant that the Corban family could no longer sell wine from their existing winery. They soon realised, however, that the railway which bordered their property was the electorate boundary, and that the eastern side of it was a 'wet' area. A small roadside section was purchased and wine sales were resumed from the Selling Depot.

Other vineyards of historic interest in the Henderson area are Pleasant Valley (1898), Henderson Valley Rd; and Babich's Vineyard (1916), signposted from the corner of Swanson and Metcalfe Rds.

Access from Ratanui St. Entrance to 40-min trail from Cranwell Park carpark.

In the midst of a busy urban centre is one of the region's oldest industrial archaeo-logical sites — the 'Dundee Sawmills' established by Thomas Henderson and John Macfarlane in 1849. Better known as 'Henderson's Mill', this enterprise was the focal point around which the town of Henderson developed. Over the next two decades the mill processed an estimated 45 million superfeet of kauri.

The mill was carefully sited at the tidal head of the Henderson Creek near the junction of two major tributaries flowing from the Waitakere Ranges. It was originally powered by a 5-m waterwheel and later by a steam engine. Waitakere City has recently installed a replica of the waterwheel on the old dam site. Immediately above the dam site is the original mill manager's house restored in 1994 to commemorate Henderson's centenary.

The heritage trail follows Opanuku Stream opposite the mill and waterwheel site, to the small point where sawn timber was loaded onto cutters and punts. They transported the timber directly to Auckland, or to the firm's 'Circular Saw Line' sailing ships for export around the world.

The trail continues around 'Cranwell Park', named after the district's first commercial orcharding family. The pear trees are remnants of Robert Cranwell's orchard. The park was originally the 'Delta Farm', which supplied the mill with food. At the confluence of the Opanuku and Oratia Streams is the 'Delta Point Landing' used by local residents as the main means of communication with Auckland until the arrival of the railway in 1880. From the landing the trail follows Oratia Stream to Tui Glen Wharf (1924), the focal point of Auckland's first motor camp. It then crosses Oratia Stream Bridge to Falls Park, the site of the relocated Falls Hotel (1856), constructed using kauri from the mill. Between the two road bridges is the 'Memorial to the Pioneer Winemaker' erected by the winemaking families of the district.

Foundation holes of Henderson's Mill dam in the stream bed just above Ratanui St bridge. The restored Mill Manager's house is behind.

Access from Great North Rd, Glen Eden. The 'Friends of Waikumete' take guided tours on the first Sunday of every month.

Waikumete (124 ha) is the second largest cemetery in the Southern Hemisphere and the final resting place for over 60,000 people. It reflects the successes and tragedies of the history of the Auckland region over the last century, containing memorials to heroes and villains, paupers and millionaires. It was opened in 1886 as a replacement for the overcrowded Grafton Cemetery. The site was chosen at Waikumete, as Glen Eden was then known, because it was located well beyond the city limits and beside the Auckland-Helensville Railway. Some coffins came out on horse-drawn wagons, although most came on funeral trains in box cars marked with a white cross. Funeral services were held at the graveside or in the restored Faith in the Oaks Chapel (1886).

The old cemetery was laid out by denomination and includes: Anglican, Wesleyan, Presbyterian, Non-Conformist, Roman Catholic and Hebrew sections. It also contains a children's section and a large soldiers cemetery focused around an obelisk commemorating the dead of both world wars. A large lawn cemetery has been formed to the north of the old cemetery and a Maori urupa has recently been opened.

Remnants of short manuka with associated native grasses, sedges, ferns, ground orchids and kumerahou, termed gumland vegetation, still exist on these poor soils. Rimu, totara, tanekaha, kahikatea, oaks, gums and other trees were planted in late 19th and early 20th centuries. Over the years, large numbers of garden plants have been planted on and around the graves and many are now growing wild. When they blossom in spring and early summer they provide the finest display of wildflowers to be found in New Zealand. A particular feature are African and Mediterranean species whose bulbs, rhizomes and corms thrive in the cemetery's poor clay soils. Narcissus and snowflake bring colour to the cemetery in winter. The main display is in spring from freesias, sparaxis, babianas, watsonias, tritonias and ixias, which are all members of the iris family. A small Wild Flower Sanctuary is being managed near the old chapel to protect these flowers.

Wild babiana (foreground) and sparaxis in full bloom in Waikumete Cemetery.

At the end of Rosebank Peninsula on the harbour side of the North-western Motorway. Clearly seen by passengers travelling on the motorway or from Te Atatu Peninsula. Because of the fragile salt meadow and salt marsh communities, access is not encouraged.

500 ha of mostly intertidal ecosystems between Whau Creek and Waterview (surrounding Pollen and Traherne Islands) are fully protected in the Motu Manawa-Pollen Island Marine Reserve, established in 1996. Motu Manawa means mangrove island.

Pollen Island is a narrow, low, vegetated bank protecting an extensive area, between it and the motorway, of high-tidal mangrove forest, salt meadow and salt marsh flats. These ecosystems are established in a thin veneer of sandy mud deposited over a terrace of stiff clay and peat that had accumulated in a swamp or lake over the last two million years.

At higher tidal levels the mangroves become smaller, eventually giving way to extensive glasswort salt meadow, peppered with mud snails and numerous mud crab burrows. Other low, mat-forming plants present in the salt meadows are sea primrose, selliera and sea blite. In turn this passes into reedy salt marsh, dominated by sea rush (*Juncus maritimus*) and oioi (*Leptocarpus similis*), occupying areas that are only inundated on spring high tides.

Mobile shell spits on the seaward sides of Pollen and Traherne Islands provide shelter for the establishment of new mangrove forest. These vast deposits of cockle shells were used for park pathways by ACC from the 1920s. For this a small tramway was built out to the north end of Pollen Island.

The tidal mud flats extending out into the harbour are favourite feeding grounds for migratory wading birds — godwit, knot, pied oystercatcher and wrybill — which also use Pollen Island to roost at high tide. New Zealand dotterel, fernbird and banded rail breed on the higher parts of the narrow island. Here sea rush, oioi and salt marsh ribbonwood are the main vegetation, with flax and *Olearia solandri* forming taller clumps. Manuka, mapou and karamu are present in the best developed shrubland at the north end.

The most extensive area of low mangrove forest and glasswort salt meadow in the Waitemata Harbour occurs in the shelter of Pollen Island, beside the North-western Motorway.

Central

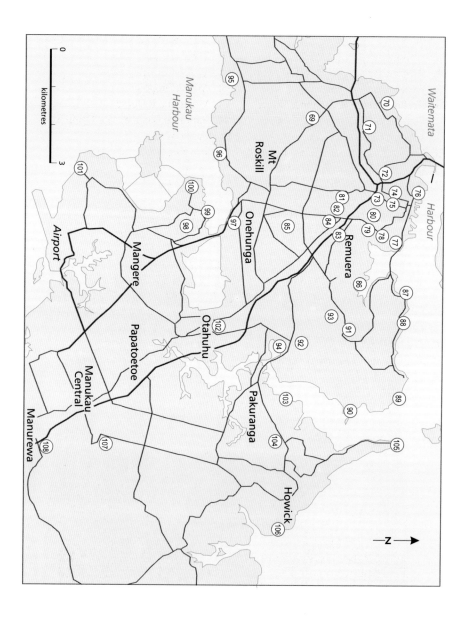

Central

69. Mt Albert
70. Te Tokaroa (Meola) Reef Lava Flow
71. Western Springs and MOTAT
72. Western Park & Ponsonby Road
73. Grafton Bridge & Symonds Street Cemetery
74. Albert Park
75. University Precinct Heritage Walk
76. Maritime Museum & Port Area
77. Judges Bay
78. Parnell Heritage Walk
79. Auckland City's Historic Houses
80. Auckland Domain & War Memorial Museum
81. Mt Eden
82. Withiel Drive Lava Field Forest
83. Mt Hobson
84. Mt St John
85. One Tree Hill
86. Orakei Basin
87. Kelly Tarlton's & Tamaki Drive
88. Mission Bay
89. Achilles Point & Karaka Bay Coast
90. Tahuna Torea
91. St John's College
92. Mt Wellington
93. Waiatarua Reserve
94. Panmure Basin & Van Dammes Lagoon
95. Blockhouse Bay Reserve
96. Waikowhai Coast
97. Onehunga Blockhouse
98. Mangere Mountain
99. Kiwi Esplanade Lava Flows
100. Ambury Regional Farm Park
101. Ihumatao Fossil Forests
102. Mt Richmond
103. Farm Cove Ignimbrite
104. Howick Colonial Village
105. Musick Point & Coast
106. Awaroa Walkway
107. Murphys Bush
108. Regional Botanic Gardens & Totara Park

Autumn in Symonds Street Cemetery.

Page 185: Clocktower of Auckland University Old Arts Building.

Vehicle access from Summit Drive, off Mt Albert Rd. Playing fields, toilets.

Mt Albert's best-known Maori name is Owairaka ('the dwelling place of Wairaka'). Tainui sources, however, apply the names Te Wai o Raka ('the drinking waters of Rakataura') and Te Ahi Ka a Raka ('the long burning fire of Rakataura'), to the mountain and its environs. Rakataura was the leading tohunga on the Tainui canoe.

Mt Albert is the remains of a large scoria cone that has had the top third removed by quarrying. 1.5 million cubic metres of scoria was removed between 1860 and 1959 to provide material for roads, railway-line ballast and for the North-western Motorway construction. The floors of these quarries have been rehabilitated as grassed playing fields around the top of the mountain.

During its eruption, about 30,000 years ago, large volumes of lava flowed out from around the base of Mt Albert to form extensive flows to the west, north and east. The toe of the northern flow can be seen forming the Waterview coastline adjacent to the North-western Motorway.

Although the cone is generously planted in trees they lack the age and stature of the plantings on many of the other Auckland cones. Apart from numerous gums, trees on the outer flanks of the cone are mainly puriri and pohutukawa. A great mixture of trees are planted around the playing fields — most are exotic and include flowering cherry, various gums, poplar, willow, olive, coral tree, coast banksia and silky oak. For a change there are no English oaks. The largest trees are in a group planting by the soccer field carpark and include a large macrocarpa, several holm oaks and pohutukawa.

Aerial view of Mt Albert shows flat playing fields where quarries once bit deeply into the upper parts of the scoria cone.

Access through Meola Reef Reserve, Meola Rd opp. Sir Keith Park Memorial Airfield. Easier access to the end of the reef across the tidal sand flats from the end of Garnet Rd, Westmere.

Te Tokaroa ('the long reef') was also known as Te Ara Whakapekapeka a Ruarangi ('the perplexing pathway of Ruarangi'), a renowned ancestor who was trapped while being pursued by his enemies along the reef.

The reef extends two-thirds of the way across the harbour towards Birkenhead. About 20,000 years ago, fluid lava flowed down a narrow stream valley from its source in Three Kings volcano. At the time, the world was gripped by the cold of the Last Ice Age. Sea level was lower than at present and the Waitemata Harbour was a forested river valley. The flow came down the Motions Creek tributary and stopped when it reached the Waitemata River. As the molten lava cooled to solid basalt rock, it contracted forming sets of vertical, hexagonal joints, which are still clearly visible on top of parts of the reef.

The reef used to have a dense growth of the shelly tube worm *Pomatoceros.* Since its arrival in New Zealand in the 1960s, the Pacific oyster has largely displaced the tube worms. Today these oysters form an extensive covering of sharp shells over most of the tidal parts of the reef.

Near the end of the reef at low tide is a rich array of seaweeds, sea squirts and brightly coloured sponges. Many of these are usually only seen by scuba divers in subtidal gardens, but here the murky waters of the upper harbour so reduce the sunlight

penetration that they can grow around low tide mark.

Exposed at spring low tides on the sand flats to the east are the largest patches of sea grass (*Zostera*) currently living in the harbour. Extensive inter-tidal sea-grass flats used to be common, but they died off from fungal attack 40–50 years ago.

At the landward end of Te Tokaroa reef, there is an unusual occurrence of salt marsh, salt meadow and mangroves growing on the solid rock substrate.

Accessible off Great North Rd and from Motions Rd, next to Auckland Zoo (open daily). Easy walks, playground, toilets, picnic tables, Museum of Transport, Technology and Social History (MOTAT, open daily).

Canada geese, black swans and other birds gather for a free lunch beside the Western Springs lake.

Western Springs are natural freshwater springs that feed an extensive lake. The water comes to the surface through cracks in a basalt lava flow, which came down Motions Creek valley from Three Kings volcano 20,000 years ago (**70**). Rain water flows underground following the old stream course but now percolates through cracks in the lower parts of the flow.

The springs were traditionally known as Waiorea, after an eel caught near their outlet. In 1877 the springs were impounded by an earth dam, creating an artificial lake. For the next 30 years this was the source of Auckland's first reticulated bulk water supply. Water was pumped by a large steam-powered beam engine to reservoirs at Ponsonby, Khyber Pass and Mt Eden. The original pumphouse and beam engine (one of only three in working order in the world) remain as the focal point of MOTAT, which presents a fascinating record of the nation's rich technological and social history. Vintage electric trams link MOTAT with Auckland Zoo and the Sir Keith Park Memorial aviation, rail and military history display.

The lake and surrounding wetlands support a variety of waterfowl. Common are mallards and native grey ducks, feral geese, black swans and Australian coots, all of which frequently have young families on the lake. Our endemic diving duck, New Zealand scaup, is present in low numbers and more recently Canada geese have established. Pukeko and the occasional white-faced heron frequent the swampy fringes, pied and a few little shags nest in the willows. Shags feed on eels in the lake.

A wide range of native and exotic shrubs and trees are planted around the lake. Close to the zoo is Australian toona, kaffir plums and a Chinese raisin tree (*Hovenia dulcis*) named after its edible fruit stalks. The adjacent small pond is ringed by North American swamp cypresses which possess characteristic knobby roots (knees). Autumn colours are exhibited by pin oaks (red), liquidambers (yellow-red), claret ashes (purple), poplars and willows (yellow).

Access from Ponsonby Rd near Hepburn St or from end of Beresford St. Short walks, picnic tables, toilets, playground, fitness trail.

Western Park, originally known as 'City Park', was established in 1873 on what was then the western edge of the city. After a public design competition it was decided to plant the gully as Auckland's first large public arboretum. Trees were donated by the renowned tree collectors Sir George Grey, Judge Thomas Gillies and George Owens among others. A number of the original trees were removed from the lower part of the park when the Auckland Girls Grammar School playing fields were extended in 1950.

Western Park is Auckland's oldest large public arboretum.

The extensive original plantings include several natives but are dominated by a remarkable group of exotic trees. These include Queensland kauri, stone pine (flat-topped) from the Mediterranean, Canary Island pine, Cooks pine (possibly New Zealand's tallest) from New Caledonia, camphor tree (one of the finest in the region), Bhutan cypress, Mexican cypress, Mediterranean cypress (one of the largest in the region), numerous Moreton Bay figs, Port Jackson Bay figs, redwoods, London planes, Norfolk pines, weeping lillipilli (one of the region's finest) from East Australia — particularly attractive in spring with pink and yellow new foliage — common elms, English oaks and a 36-m-tall radiata pine.

A trip to Western Park may be combined with a walk along historic Ponsonby Rd. From the Karangahape Rd end, buildings of particular interest in Ponsonby Rd are the former Newton Police Station (1906) and beside it the Unitarian Church (1901); Allendale, one of Auckland's finest late Victorian houses (1892); the former Grey Lynn Fire Station (1889) (50 m down Williamson Ave); and St John's Methodist Church (1882). Near the northern end of Ponsonby Rd is Renall St, which provides an excellent example of the Victorian and Edwardian houses that dominate Ponsonby. Opposite the northern end of Ponsonby Rd is a fine group of Edwardian buildings dominated by the Ponsonby Post Office (1911) and the Leys Institute and Library (1905). A brochure outlining a longer 'Ponsonby Heritage Walk' can be obtained from the Library or ACC.

At the eastern end of Karangahape Rd. Woodland and historic walks.

Sparaxis flowering in spring in Symonds St Jewish cemetery.

Symonds St Cemetery was established in 1842 on the then rural outskirts of Auckland. It was sited on the western side of the stream valley known traditionally as 'Waiparuru' because of its damp and gloomy aspect. The valley became known as 'Grafton Gully' (after Governor Fitzroy's grandfather, the Duke of Grafton) and the cemetery was named after the road which bisected it.

The cemetery was developed in the sentimental picturesque style favoured by the Victorians. An informal woodland garden among the graves was traversed by winding gravel walks, and featured oaks, elms, Norfolk pines, Moreton Bay fig and Italian cypress, underplanted with Victorian shrubs, bulbs, roses and perennials. Native trees such as kauri were planted, and native species spread up from the gully bottom. Beautiful native forest was destroyed to make way for the motorway in 1966. Today a tiny remnant survives upstream of the bridge with puriri, rewarewa, kohekohe, taraire, mahoe, pigeonwood and tree ferns.

The cemetery was laid out in five denominational burial grounds, which contain a remarkable collection of 19th-century funereal art forms, including wooden and iron railings, statues, headstones, obelisks and sarcophagus, crafted from such materials as Sydney sandstone, and marble from Italy and South Africa. These memorials provide a valuable commentary on the history of colonial Auckland. They mark the last resting place of thousands of ordinary citizens and many figures prominent in colonial society. They include: Governor William Hobson, missionary William Fairburn, the eccentric Baron Charles de Thierry, philanthropist James Dilworth, and Captain Henry Mercer, killed at the Battle of Rangiriri (1863). Memorials in the Anglican and Roman Catholic sections commemorate the reinterment of the remains of 4100 people exhumed during the construction of the adjoining motorway.

The eastern section of the cemetery is dominated by Grafton Bridge, an internationally recognised historic concrete structure. When completed in 1910, it incorporated the longest three-hinged, single span, reinforced concrete arch in the world. At the western end of the bridge is the region's oldest tram and omnibus shelter, also built in 1910.

Access from Princes St, Wellesley St East or Victoria St East. Short walks, toilets, formal gardens.

Albert Park is located on a ridge mantled by ash erupted about 100,000 years ago from a now-quarried volcano, located at the junction of Victoria St East and Bowen St. The park was the site of the Maori village of Rangipuke, and later of the 9-ha 'Albert Barracks'. The Barracks housed 900 imperial troops until their withdrawal from the colony in 1870, at which time the land was set aside as a public reserve. Auckland City Council developed the park from 1882 using the competition-winning design of architect James Slater.

Albert Park has a formal layout with walks and gardens radiating out from an elaborate Victorian fountain (1882) and statues including: Queen Victoria (1897), the South African War Memorial (1902) and Governor George Grey (1904). Other interesting structures include: a restored barracks' well, the Park Keepers Cottage (1882), a band rotunda (1901), and 'Russian Scare' muzzle-loading guns (1897). At the top of the Kitchener St steps is one of the few functioning gas lamps left in the city, and at the centre of the park is a meteorological station established in 1909. A floral clock commemorates the 1953 visit of Queen Elizabeth II.

The park contains a fine collection of historic exotic trees, many of which were donated by Governor Grey. They include an Argentinian ombu, cork oaks, towering Washingtonia palms, and 12 oaks which commemorate the visit of the US Great White Fleet (1908), Moreton Bay figs with low spreading limbs, a deciduous fig (*Ficus superba*) from north-eastern Australia, a chestnut oak with large hairy-scaled acorn cups, and trees of heaven near Bowen Ave.

Near the Victoria St steps is the entrance to a series of tunnels and public air-raid shelters excavated under the park during the Second World War. On the south-west edge of the park is the Auckland City Art Gallery (1887), an imposing French Renaissance-style building which houses one of the best collections of New Zealand art.

Albert Park is one of New Zealand's best-preserved Victorian parks.

Two-hour walk beginning at Albert Park (**74**).

Remains of the Albert Barracks Wall, constructed by Maori stonemasons after the '1845 War' in Northland, can be seen in the University grounds. The University Old Arts Building made of limestone from Mt Somers, Canterbury, stands behind (left).

The focal point of one of the city's most interesting historic precincts is Auckland University's first purpose-built facility, the Old Arts Building (1926). This elegant limestone building was designed in the Gothic tradition by two young Melbourne architects, Lippincott and Bilson. Its landmark tower was based on Wren's 'Tom Tower', Oxford. An interesting collection of labelled native trees surrounds the building.

Princes St features a fine group of 1870s Victorian merchant houses. No 27 was replaced in 1934, although its stables remain as the Frank Sargeson Centre for writers. On Bowen Ave corner is one of New Zealand's oldest concrete buildings, the former Jewish Synagogue (1885). Designed by Edward Bartley, it incorporates a mixture of Gothic and Romanesque styles and fine interior decorative features. Home to Auckland's Hebrew community for 83 years, it has been beautifully restored and reused as a bank.

The Northern Club (1867), the city's oldest private club, was constructed on the site of Auckland's first hotel. Designed by James Wrigley, it features a street facade inspired by Italian palazzi. Nearby the facades of the Grand Hotel (1889) and the Freemasons Hall (1881) have been incorporated in new buildings. Beside them are two impressive 1870s buildings. At the end of Princes St a pohutukawa grove marks Emily Place Reserve. A monument to Reverend John Churton, Garrison Chaplain stands on the site of St Pauls Church (1841), demolished when Point Britomart was finally removed c.1880.

Old Government House (1856) is Auckland's largest wooden building. It was the Vice-Regal residence for 113 years, replacing the first Government House, destroyed by fire in 1848. Designed by Government Architect William Mason in a classical Georgian style, it was criticised by contemporaries as pretentious and ill-proportioned. The building has been the University Staff Commonroom since 1969. Its grounds contain historic trees planted by governors and royalty. Of note are Auckland's oldest grove of oaks (1844–45), offspring of the 'Royal Oak' Shropshire, the largest kaffir boom in New Zealand, and an impressive redwood, Californian big tree and Norfolk pine.

The High Court (1867) is one of Auckland's finest colonial buildings. The red brick 'decorated gothic' building features castellated towers, tall chimney pots, and stone portrait heads and gargoyles carved by Prussian immigrant Anton Teutenburg. Its interior features some of New Zealand's best carved panelling. Behind it, two pohutukawa trees mark the former entrance to New Zealand's Parliament House (1854–65).

Courtville Apartments, one of the country's best Edwardian apartment blocks, feature prominent bay windows and balconies, and early art deco interior design elements. Corner Courtville (1919) includes New Zealand's oldest electric lift. Below the beautiful University Marae in Alten Road is no 23, the last remaining Albert Barracks Officer's Cottage. St Andrews is Auckland's oldest Presbyterian church. Its rectangular bluestone nave was built 1847–50 while the classical portico and tower were added in 1882.

At 12–18 Symonds St are three of Auckland's oldest concrete houses restored for University use. Opposite is the former Choral Hall (1871). Numbers 8 and 10 Grafton Rd are unusual houses designed by Charles Le Neve Arnold c.1903. No 9 Grafton Rd is an unusual wedge-shaped store (c.1885), once tuck shop for Auckland Grammar School.

Auckland's oldest street planting (1877) of plane trees and elms leads to one of Auckland's most impressive stone churches — St Pauls (1895). It incorporates memorials to Governor Hobson, Major General Pitt and crew members of the *Wairarapa* drowned in 1894. Opposite are 'Queen Anne' style Terrace Houses, featuring Dutch gables and cast-iron railings, built by prominent businessman John Endean for his children (c.1905). Nearby is the AIT Marae and the former Auckland Technical College (1909).

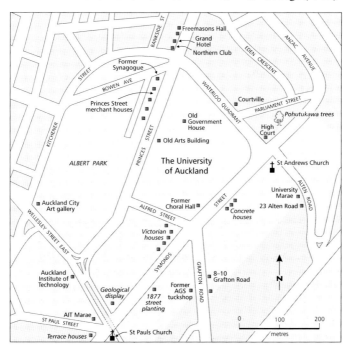

New Zealand Maritime Museum, west end of Quay St (open daily).

The New Zealand Maritime Museum, Hobson Wharf, portrays New Zealand's maritime heritage and the voyaging traditions of the Pacific. Its entrance incorporates the former Launchman's Building (1920), once home to the small launch companies serving the Waitemata from the 1920s. The museum marina features traditional Polynesian craft, sailing vessels, and the floating steam crane *Rapaki*. The scow *Ted Ashby* and the steam launch *Puke* carry visitors on short inner-harbour trips.

The historic Viaduct Lift Bridge (1932) with the New Zealand Maritime Museum and the (privately owned) steam tug, the William C. Daldy beyond (left).

The museum galleries, augmented by soundscapes and videos, provide a thematic account of New Zealand's maritime heritage. Among the highlights are: the Hawaiki Gallery of Pacific voyaging canoes, 19th-century immigrants' steerage quarters, the Hall of Yachting, and functioning workshops.

The adjacent port area, reclaimed 1859–80, includes many historic buildings and structures. West of the museum is the Viaduct Basin, home of Auckland's fishing fleet since 1932. The Viaduct Lift Bridge is one of only two such bridges in the world. The former Auckland Harbour Board Workshops at 1 Hobson St (1930) now house restaurants. The nearby 'Tepid Baths' (1914) are Auckland's oldest heated indoor pools.

East of the museum is Princes Wharf, terminal for the world's great passenger liners since 1924. Between Princes Wharf and the Ferry Terminal are the Launch Shelters (c.1914), used by launch passengers prior to the introduction of motorised transport.

The port precinct to the east is dominated by the magnificent Edwardian Baroque Ferry Building (1912) constructed of brick, Sydney Sandstone and Coromandel Granite. Close by are other places that reflect Auckland's maritime heritage. The AHB 'Red Fence' (1913) is one of the best examples of wrought iron work in the country. Marsden Wharf is of interest as the site of the *Rainbow Warrior* bombing (1985). No 2 Quay St, for many years the Wharf Police Station, was built (1904) as the Auckland Office for the Colonial Sugar Refining Co (**30**). Nos 16–20 Quay St, built as W.A. Ryan's marine engineering workshop (1906), features a fine polychromatic brick facade. Nos 22–24 Quay St (1898) was Head Office of the Northern Steamship Co, which operated New Zealand's largest fleet of coastal steamers for 80 years.

Access down Judges Bay Rd off Gladstone Rd; Parnell Rose Gardens.

Judges Bay was named after two prominent colonial judicial figures — Sir William Martin and William Swainson. It was a favourite campsite for Maori bringing produce to Auckland, 1840–63. They often attended services at a stone chapel erected above the bay by Bishop Selwyn. It collapsed in 1847, as it incorporated poor-quality mortar, and was replaced in 1857 by the present St Stephen's Chapel, a beautiful little building designed by Frederick Thatcher. The chapel specifically incorporated the plan of a Greek cross for the signing of the constitution of the New Zealand Church of England. Beside the chapel is a graveyard which is the resting place of many historic figures.

Judges Bay was a popular rowing and yachting venue until cut off from the harbour by the construction of Tamaki Drive (1931–32). The 'Parnell Salt Water Baths' have been a popular recreational venue since 1914. Above the cliffs is Point Resolution Park. It has few visible archaeological features, although it was the site of ancient Tararua Pa, a military blockhouse (1860), and the 'Russian Scare' gun fort — Fort Resolution.

Above the western end of Judges Bay is Dove Meyer Robinson Park, which includes the Parnell Rose Gardens. The park contains many fine trees including a huge pohutukawa planted by Robert Gillies c.1855. One of the most majestic trees in Auckland, a lemon-scented gum, was once prominent in the park until it was blown over in 1988 by Cyclone Bola. Two of its progeny planted near the Korean War Memorial are now over 8 m tall. Other interesting trees include a large Norfolk Island hibiscus, a two-headed bunya bunya, Moreton Bay figs, male and female Bermuda junipers, a dragon tree, and two butia palms behind the restaurant. Nearly 4500 named roses are in formal beds, and the Nancy Steen cottage garden, with an emphasis on old-fashioned roses and white flowers, should not be missed.

Behind the Parnell Baths and its carpark are old sea cliffs formed of Waitemata Sandstone. Within these is a 5m-thick bed (top of cliff) of Parnell Grit that flowed into the Waitemata Basin as a submarine lahar from the Waitakere Volcano about 20 million years ago. This is where the Parnell Grit beds were first recognised and named in 1881.

An easy urban walk begun at any point. Pamphlets available from the ACC or Ewelme (79).

Claybrook — one of Auckland's oldest houses.

Parnell was Auckland's first suburb (1841) and has been the Anglican diocesan headquarters since 1842. It features a group of ecclesiastical buildings designed in the Gothic Revival style favoured by Bishop Selwyn. At their centre is 'Bishopscourt', a complex of wooden buildings designed by the noted colonial architect Frederick Thatcher. Other buildings include: the library (1861), the steepled octagonal belfry (1862), and the Bishop's house (1863).

Neligan House (12 St Stephen's Ave), now the Anglican Trust Board Office, is a grand brick house (1908–10) incorporating a private chapel. It was designed by Bamford and Pierce in the Arts and Craft style for Bishop Neligan as the new 'Bishopscourt'. Across the road is a spectacular dragon tree (planted c. 1898), which is now almost extinct in its native Canary Islands.

The Deanery (17 St Stephen's Ave) was one of the first buildings (1857) designed by Frederick Thatcher. It incorporates Rangitoto basalt stonework with dressed stone quoins and openings by Benjamin Strange, and a board-and-batten upper storey. The Deanery was briefly Bishop Selwyn's residence and a hospital during the Land Wars.

St Mary's in Holy Trinity Cathedral designed in the Gothic Revival tradition by Christchurch architect Benjamin Mountford, is regarded as one of finest wooden churches in the world. It has a magnificent interior featuring kauri lining and framing timbers. Built 1886–97, it was relocated amid great controversy from the other side of Parnell Rd in 1982, to sit beside the new cathedral. The oaks on its original site were grown from acorns presented to Selwyn by Queen Victoria.

'Claybrook' (6 Claybrook Rd) was built for architect Sampson Kempthorne around a prefabricated core thought to have been brought to New Zealand c. 1842. Three brick Edwardian terrace houses can be seen at 469–473 Parnell Rd. On the footpath nearby is the region's only 1860s horse-hitching post. Walkers may detour south to visit Kinder House and Ewelme Cottage, Ayr St (**79**); or the restored Blind Institute Jubilee Building (545 Parnell Rd), designed in Gothic Revival style by Auckland architect Edward Bartley.

There are many historic buildings in or adjacent to the Parnell Rd Shops. On the St

Stephen's Ave-Parnell Rd corner is the former Kemp's Department Store. When built (1885) it was regarded as the city's finest retail store and fashion emporium. The former Parnell Library and Lecture Hall (390 Parnell Rd) was designed in the neo-classical style by M.K. Draffin (co-designer of Auckland Museum) in 1924. In Birdwood Cres. is Knox Presbyterian Church (1899), designed by R.W. de Montalk.

Hulme Court (350 Parnell Rd) is the oldest Auckland building on its original site. This elegant regency-style plastered basalt house was built for Sir Frederick Whitaker, Attorney General and Premier, in 1843. It was later the home of Auckland's military commander, Colonel Hulme, temporarily Government House, and the home of Bishop Selwyn.

Whitby Lodge (330 Parnell Rd), 1874, is one of the few remaining Auckland houses

constructed of Mt Eden basalt. Opposite is the colonial village developed around the fine victorian house 'Myrtleton', which features a rooftop belvedere. A landmark Norfolk pine, planted in 1864, grows at 320 Parnell Rd. St John the Baptist (242 Parnell Rd) is Auckland's oldest Roman Catholic church. Consecrated by Bishop Pompallier in 1861, it was enlarged in 1897 when the adjoining convent was built.

Passing Denby St, once the home of famous aviatrix Jean Batten, one reaches the former Heard's Confectionary Factory. A short detour down Tilden St leads to the Stone Mason's House (1863), built by colonial Auckland's best-known stonemason, Benjamin Strange, for his own use. Walkers may wish to quench their thirst at Exchange Hotel (c. 1880), or the Windsor Castle Hotel (1884), which has been licensed since 1847.

Just beyond Heather St are the Mayfair Apartments designed by Gummer and Ford and built in 1929. In Cracroft St are Auckland's best examples of semi-detached Edwardian terrace houses. 46 Parnell Rd is 'The Old Coffee House' (1929), built in the neo-Georgian style as a shop and coffee packing house for J. Royce & Co.

Many other architectural delights are to be found in the side streets off Parnell Rd.

Opening times may be obtained from the New Zealand Historic Places Trust, Auckland.

Ewelme Cottage

14 Ayr St, Parnell.

Built in 1863–64 for Rev. Vicesimus Lush (1817–82), who was the first Vicar of Howick. For many years Lush travelled by horse to hold services in the remote outer settlements of South Auckland. Ewelme was constructed so that his wife Blanche and family could be near the educational and religious facilities of Parnell. It was named after the village in Oxfordshire where Blanche had lived during her youth. The large kauri cottage, which is influenced by the Georgian style, was designed by Lush, who had studied architecture at Cambridge University. Although it was extended by Blanche soon after her husband's death, it has remained largely unchanged since that time.

Ewelme was occupied by the Lush family until 1968, when it was purchased by the Auckland City Council and leased to the New Zealand Historic Places Trust. A feature of the cottage is its interior, which makes use of even the smallest space. Ewelme retains much of its original furnishing and an important collection of over 800 books. They include works by John Milton, who was an ancestor of both Reverend Vicesimus and Blanche Lush. The restored garden is dominated by a magnificent oak planted in 1864.

Kinder House

2 Ayr St, Parnell. Open to the public daily.

This elegant two-storeyed house was the first of three stone houses in Parnell to be designed by well-known colonial architect Frederick Thatcher. It was commissioned by Bishop Selwyn to house Dr John Kinder, the first headmaster of Auckland Grammar School. Kinder was one of colonial New Zealand's best-known photographers and painters. Examples of his work are displayed in the house, which is furnished in period style. The grounds are planted as a Victorian garden featuring old-fashioned roses.

Kinder House was built in 1857 by stonemason Benjamin Strange using basalt collected from the foreshore of Rangitoto Island. The walls are constructed of random rubble held together with mortar and the facings are of large squared basalt blocks.

Highwic

40 Gillies Ave, Newmarket; opp. Gillies Ave exit from Southern Motorway.
Highwic is one of New Zealand's finest Gothic Revival timber houses. It was constructed from 1862 on a small Newmarket farm by Alfred and Eliza Buckland, who were among colonial Auckland's most substantial landowners. Buckland and his second wife Matilda engaged Auckland architect James Baber to enlarge the house in its original style. Named after the Devonshire village of 'Highweek', it features vertical board-and-batten weatherboards, ornate parapets and bargeboards, diamond pane casement windows and a slate roof. The interior contains dramatic contrasts in style between the plain colonial kitchen and servants' quarters, and the ornate kauri-panelled ballroom, dining room and billiard room. Highwic was home to Alfred Buckland's 21 children and remained in the family until its acquisition by the ACC and New Zealand Historic Places Trust in 1978. The spacious gardens contain a number of historic trees including a pair of Norfolk pines, weeping lillipilli, brush cherry, camphor tree, Kentia palms, Australian fan palm (*Livistona australis*), nikau and king fern.

Alberton

100 Mt Albert Rd, Mt Albert.
This unique two-storeyed timber building began as an elegant farmhouse in 1863 and developed into a remarkable 18-roomed mansion. Alberton was built (1832–90) by Allan Kerr Taylor, one of colonial Auckland's most promi-nent citizens. The house was once the focal point for a large estate, and was famed for its balls, musical evenings, garden and archery parties and hunts.

Alberton's imposing towers and verandahs designed by Mathew Henderson to reflect Allan Kerr Taylor's Indian military background.

Allan and Sophia Kerr Taylor brought up 10 children at Alberton. Sophia was a renowned entertainer and a staunch advocate of women's suffrage. After her husband's death she ran the estate for 40 years. Her three unmarried daughters managed the property for a further 40 years until Alberton was left to the New Zealand Historic Places Trust in 1972. The interior provides a remarkable example of Victorian social stratification, with its grand family and entertainment rooms contrasting with the spartan servants' quarters in the attics. Alberton is set in gardens featuring fine old trees, original garden ornaments and a fountain. An Australian fig (*Ficus coronata*), which is very rare in New Zealand, is represented by tall male and female shrubs.

Vehicle and pedestrian access from Stanley St, Park Rd, Carlton Gore Rd, George St and Domain Drive. Large formal gardens, duck ponds, tea house, picnics, walks, Winter Gardens and Fernery (open daily 10 am–4 pm), Auckland Museum (open daily 10 am–5 pm). Pamphlet available from ACC.

The 81-ha Auckland Domain (established in 1845) sprawls over one of the oldest volcanoes in the Auckland field. The volcano has a classic 'castle and moat' layout with a small central scoria cone inside a large, shallow explosion crater with surrounding tuff ring. The museum is built on top of one side of the tuff ring and Auckland Hospital is built on the other. The sports fields are the floor of the wide crater, which was a lake at first, but over thousands of years it filled with sediment and plant remains to become a swamp. In European times the swampy floor has been drained to form playing fields.

The Domain's duck ponds are freshwater springs, derived from ground water draining the crater. The springs provided Auckland's first piped water supply in 1866. Spring water together with overflow from the original crater lake has gradually eroded away the soft tuff ring on its northern side. Here a small stream cascades over numerous falls through a forested glade of native trees and English oaks towards the Stanley St tennis courts, which only a few hundred years ago was the coast of the Waitemata Harbour.

Tree planting began in the Domain in 1864. Gum Hill, once the site of an 1860 blockhouse, features a mass 1920s planting of eucalypts including over 12 species. Impressive groves of tall-trunked English oaks grow on the scoria cone and tuff ring. The most interesting group of trees are north-west of the duck ponds on the site of the

The circular Domain Volcano explosion crater is now occupied by sports fields which surround Pukekaroro, the small central scoria cone partly covered in oak trees. The Winter Gardens and Fernery are located on the side of the cone and Auckland Hospital (bottom right) sits on part of the tuff ring.

Acclimatisation Society Gardens established in 1867. They include impressive examples of Queensland kauri, radiata pine, Californian big tree, Norfolk pine, Moreton Bay fig, pin oak, Canary Island palm, and a thicket of an unusual bamboo (*Bambusa balcooa*).

The Winter Gardens include a Cool House (1921), a Tropical House (1929), and the Fernery established in an old quarry on the side of the scoria cone in 1930. Plants in the Cool House are changed regularly; the Tropical House plants are more permanent. By the lily pond, which separates the glasshouses, there are many unusual exotic vines to admire on the overhead pergolas. The most attractive is *Thunbergia mysorensis*, with its yellow and red hanging strands of upright flowers.

A fine example of a Queensland kauri (Agathis robusta) *growing in the Domain.*

Nearly 20 bird species can be seen in the park. The many mallard ducks from the duck ponds feast on the acorns in the autumn while escaping the duck shooters.

Auckland War Memorial Museum is appropriately sited on Pukekawa, 'hill of bitter memories', referring to the blood shed in ancient tribal battles. The museum was built in two halves — the front (opened in 1929) and back (opened in 1960) were constructed as memorials to all those citizens of the Auckland Province who lost their lives in the First and Second World Wars. The names of all 12,000 are inscribed on the walls of the two Halls of Memory on the top floor. Its neoclassical facade, with octastyle portico influenced by the Parthenon in Athens, is constructed of reinforced concrete faced with Portland stone and bronze detailing. Names above the windows commemorate battles from the First World War in the front building and from the Second World War around the back. During the Second World War the Domain lawns were covered in American Barracks, 1942–44.

Other structures of particular historic interest include the Domain Grandstand (1899), one of New Zealand's oldest sporting structures, and two buildings remaining from the 1913–14 Auckland Exhibition attended by 870,000 people. They include the Band Rotunda, and the Tea Kiosk constructed as an ideal home.

The scoria cone named Pukekaroro ('hill of the black-backed gull') retains the remnant earthworks of a former Maori pa. On its top a totara tree is enclosed by traditional carvings and a manuka palisade. This tree was planted by Princess Te Puea Herangi during Auckland's centennial celebrations (1940) on the site of a house occupied by the Tainui chief Potatau Te Wherowhero in the 1840s.

Vehicle access off Mt Eden Rd; pedestrian access from Clive Rd and Owens Rd (steep path); panoramic views from the top (196 m).

Mt Eden was named by William Hobson in honour of his naval superior George Eden, Lord Auckland. Its Maori name is Maungawhau ('hill of the whau tree'). It is one of the highest scoria cones in Auckland, its elongate shape consisting of three overlapping cones which erupted in close succession about 19,000 years ago. The two older, northern cones have had their craters filled with scoria ejected by lava fountaining from the 50-m-deep, slightly later, southern crater.

Viscous lava flowed out in all directions from around the base of the cone and built up a 60-m-thick pedestal of overlapping flows. Several large quarries in these flows were operated for many years near Mt Eden Prison and produced dressed stone for some of Auckland's older stone buildings (**78**) and most of the basalt kerb stones that line the city streets. Several other quarries were dug into the flanks of Mt Eden's scoria cone prior to the 1920s. One of these has been rehabilitated as Eden Gardens, which is open to the public and well known for its camellias and rhododendrons.

In pre-European times, Maungawhau had particular significance as its crater was known as the 'foodbowl of Mataaho', the deity responsible for volcanic activity (see p. 71). It was intensively occupied and heavily defended, as can be seen from the mountain's extensive earthworks. These cover most of the summit, except where buried water reservoirs were constructed in 1912 and 1930.

Planted trees are common over most of the mountain except the upper slopes and crater. The southern slopes are mainly young totara (6–8 m tall) with a group of smaller rimu among them. Elsewhere there are groups of pohutukawa, Kermadec pohutukawa, totara, holm oak (some fine specimens) and Tasmanian blackwood (east side). Other mature natives include puriri, karaka, titoki, rewarewa and northern tree rata. Over 25 native woody species are present including, most appropriately, whau. Other exotics include a Moreton Bay fig, English oaks and plane trees.

Mt Eden scoria cone with its deep, steep-sided crater and prominent terracing from its use as a pre-European pa.

On north side of Withiel Drive, between Mountain Rd and Gillies Ave, Mt Eden.

Small Withiel Thomas Reserve preserves the best remnant of Auckland's original forested lava fields. The rocky surface on these 19,000-year-old basalt flows from Mt Eden is an example of what many parts of the isthmus were like when the first humans arrived about a thousand years ago. Most of Auckland's forests were burned in pre-European times and the rocky volcanic soils used extensively for gardening. Early European settlers established pastoral farms and most of the rocks were cleared and used in stone walls between paddocks. As suburbia spread, many parts of these walls were left between sections and the rocks from others were reused for retaining walls and fill.

The forest canopy is dominated by mangeao, titoki, puka, mahoe and houpara. A few large, multi-trunked pohutukawa are also present. Kawakawa and karamu are the main shrubs and on the rocks a native pepper, (*Peperomia urvilleana*), is present. Puka stands out from the mainly smooth-barked trees with its rough bark. In the upper parts of the reserve are individual tall planted trees of northern tree rata, rimu, totara and the Australian Illawarra pine. Sadly, the succulent South American wandering Jew is invading parts of the forest.

The forest area now protected in Withiel Thomas Reserve was jealously guarded by Professor A.P.W. Thomas for 50 years. During that period he constructed the paths and retaining walls that loop through the reserve.

Another example of remnant lava field forest can be seen by driving down the narrow portion of Almorah Rd between Gilgit and Mangawhau Rds, behind Mercy Hospital. Large trees are common in this suburb, encouraging the abundance of tui and the occasional presence of native pigeon in the area.

Puka trees, which normally begin life as perching plants (epiphytes), grow directly on the well-drained basalt rocks in Withiel Thomas Reserve, as they also do on the Rangitoto lava.

Main pedestrian access off Remuera Rd with paths to the top, secondary walking access from Dilworth and Mt Hobson Rds. Spectacular views.

Mt Hobson (143 m) is a moderately large scoria cone built by lava fountaining from a central crater. The crater has been breached by a small lava flow which rafted away the south-western side of the cone. The lava flowed both north and south in the vicinity of the present-day Southern Motorway.

The ancient Maori name for the hill is Ohinerangi, 'the dwelling place of Hinerangi'. Its later Maori name Remuera, a corruption of Remu-wera, 'the burnt hem of a garment', arose in the 1700s when a young Hauraki woman was killed and eaten by the Waiohua inhabitants of the pa. Like all of the other cones of Auckland, Mt Hobson was a defended pa in pre-European times. Many of the terraces, ditch defences, storage pits and middens from this period are still clearly visible around the cone's crest, except in the north-west where a large, flat-topped reservoir (1935) is buried. Its western slopes, seen from the Newmarket Viaduct, are thought to have been extensive hillside kumara gardens.

The vegetation of most of the cone is grazed pasture but stands of planted trees are present, especially on the north side. English oaks and pohutukawa are the most common trees. Two of the more impressive trees are a squat macrocarpa with a trunk diameter greater than 3 m and a holm oak with a tall trunk almost 2 m in diameter. At the top of the north-west fenceline is a medium-sized Japanese black pine (*Pinus thunbergii*) with dense foliage and needles in pairs. Other trees include both exotic and native: plane trees, holly, Port Jackson fig, Norfolk pine, elms, cherry laurels, totara, puriri, karaka and recently planted mangeao. Hawthorn is present on the south side.

The grassed slopes on the north side above Remuera Rd turn golden in early spring with the flowering of masses of daffodils, planted 'to commemorate all those who gave their lives in the Second World War'.

Mt Hobson is a prominent Auckland scoria cone with a breached, horseshoe-shaped crater. The flat north-western crest of the cone is the grassed top of a large buried water reservoir.

Pedestrian access up graded paths to the top from Market, Mt St John and Belvedere Rds, Epsom.

Mt St John (156 m) is a simple, well-preserved scoria cone formed about 22,000 years ago by lava fountaining from a single, bowl-shaped crater.

Its Maori name, Te Kopuke, means 'the prominent mound'. The crest of the cone has numerous food-storage pits, terraces and ditch defences from the pre-European pa that once presided over a renowned gardening area. The hill was named Mt St John after Colonel St John, who commanded a British Regiment in the New Zealand Wars of the 1860s. A reservoir (1957) is buried beneath the eastern rim of the crater and the earthworks restored over the top of it. The concrete base of a Second World War anti-aircraft gun battery can also be seen.

The vegetation is mostly grazed pasture, but planted trees cover most of the northern slopes and scattered trees are frequent in the crater. The largest trees are three tall radiata pines with trunks over a metre in diameter. Pohutukawa is the most common tree. Other trees include exotic olives, acmenas and *Photinia serrulata* from China, and native puriri, karaka, totara and rewarewa. Perhaps the most interesting tree is a large American water oak (*Quercus nigra*), one of only two known in the region. It has a trunk diameter of 1.3 m and grows in a fenced area in the north-east corner. Swallows, skylarks, starlings and tui are common.

The rim of Mt St John scoria cone still retains many of the storage pits, terraces and ditches from its use as a pre-European pa.

Vehicle access from Greenlane Rd West and Manukau Rd, pedestrian access also off Campbell Rd; road to obelisk with views from top; large farmed and landscaped park, numerous walks, picnic and BBQ areas, playground and Observatory (near Manukau Rd entrance), toilets, kiosk, restaurant. Information pamphlets available from Huia Lodge Visitor Centre.

One Tree Hill's Maori name is Maungakiekie meaning 'hill of the kiekie vine'. The hill is a scoria cone built by lava fountaining from its three craters about 20,000 years ago. The highest part (183 m) is made of scoria that fountained out of the adjacent crater as frothy lava and built up on its north-eastern side during a period of south-westerly winds. The other two craters are horse-shoe shaped, having been breached by lava flows that carried away the scoria ramparts on their downhill sides.

Huge volumes of fluid lava flowed out in all directions from around the base of the central scoria cone. It built up a rubbly lava-flow field covering 20 square kilometres that extends southwards to the Onehunga foreshore.

Maungakiekie is the most extensively terraced of all of Auckland's volcanic cones and one of the most extensive pre-European archaeological site complexes in New Zealand. It includes extensive house-site and garden terraces, and numerous groups of food-storage pits. The mountain lay at the centre of Nga Maara o Tahuri — the expansive cultivations of Tahuri, a Waiohua ancestress.

One Tree Hill's scoria cone was built by fire-fountaining from its three craters. One crater is complete but two have been breached to the south-west and south-east (right of photo) by lava flows. Earthworks from pre-European occupation are prominent over the entire cone.

Maungakiekie is an extensive pa, sometimes claimed to have been the largest prehistoric fort in the world. Its four summits were all heavily defended by ditches and wooden palisades. On its peak was the 'tihi', the most sacred and heavily defended part of the complex. It was named Te Totara i Ahua after the sacred lone totara that grew there until the 1850s.

Many of the original olive trees planted in the 1860s by Sir John Logan Campbell still survive in Cornwall Park.

Thomas Henry purchased Maungakiekie from the Maori in 1845 and developed it as the 400-ha 'Mt Prospect' estate. Governor Grey set aside the hilltop and the south-western slopes as a reserve in 1848 and this became One Tree Hill Domain. The rest was purchased by Brown and Campbell in 1853 and owned solely by Sir John Logan Campbell from 1873. He gifted the park (named in honour of the visiting Duke and Dutchess of Cornwall) to the public in 1901. Campbell's original home, Acacia Cottage (1841), Auckland's oldest house, was moved here in 1920. Opposite it is the restored Huia Lodge Visitor Centre, built as a caretaker's cottage in 1903.

In the 1860s Campbell began tree planting. On the summit he planted a group of pines to shelter native species. A lone pine remains as one of Auckland's best-known landmarks. From Greenlane Rd to the kiosk area, there is an avenue of immense pines, Moreton Bay figs, macrocarpas, puriri and poplars. This was going to be the entrance-way to Campbell's new home, but in the late 1870s he decided to build elsewhere. He also planted an olive grove in the 1860s with the intention of starting an oil industry. Campbell was buried on the summit of Maungakiekie in 1912. The 21-m obelisk beside his grave was bequeathed by him as a memorial to the Maori people of 1840. It was finally completed in 1948 and unveiled by the Maori King, Koroki.

The eucalyptus arboretum, south-west of the roundabout, was planted in the 1930s. Originally 36 species were planted in lines of five; today all the species survive, but several rows are reduced to a single tree. A few of these gums are unusual in New Zealand and some are fine specimens, such as the bastard tallowwood (*E. planchoniana*) with ribbed fruit, pit-barked spotted gums (*E. maculata*) and karri (*E. diversicolor*). Below the arboretum are plantations of native trees, including kauri, rimu and totara.

Over 230 woody plant species grow on One Tree Hill. One of the finest trees is a beautifully formed specimen Algerian oak (*Quercus canariensis*), west of Pohutukawa Drive, with a trunk diameter of 1.4 m. Small flocks of brightly coloured eastern rosellas are a frequent sight in the park.

Vehicle access off Orakei Rd, pedestrian access off Upland Rd and Lucerne Rd.

Orakei Basin is a large, shallow explosion crater which erupted on the side of Purewa Creek valley about 25,000 years ago. Ejected ash and debris built up a tuff ring around three sides, but on the northern side the ash was plastered onto the steep slopes of Purewa Valley. In wet weather these water-saturated ash deposits are prone to slumping. Thus these unstable Kepa Rd slopes are not developed and are in grazed pasture.

Purewa Creek breached the tuff ring, and the crater became a tidal lagoon with the rising sea levels at the end of the Last Ice Age. Construction of the railway line embankment through the crater in the 1920s created a shallow, artificial salt-water lake. The water is periodically exchanged by the opening of control gates under the railway line. Original mangrove forest was cleared so the basin could be used for model-boat sailing, although today water skiing is the predominant use.

Since it was ponded, a 20–30 cm thick layer of mud and decomposing seaweed has built up over the original shelly sand floor. Most of the cockles and pipi are now gone, replaced by millions of the introduced small Asian mussel, which thrives in dense thickets in the mud. Near the margins of the basin, large sharp shells of introduced Pacific oyster stick up. The nutrient-rich environment promotes the growth of a thick, intertwining mass of seaweeds that spread out over the muddy floor. A patch of introduced cord grass (*Spartina*) grows at the water's edge beside the boat ramp.

There is a pleasant walk around the southern perimeter through tree privet, hybrid coral trees and weeping willows to the water ski club. Pied and little shags fish in the basin and roost on a fallen macrocarpa jutting out over the water on the southern shore. Occasionally white-fronted terns visit. The earthworks and shell middens of a prehistoric village can be seen along the western crest of the tuff ring.

Orakei Basin is an explosion crater with surrounding tuff ring.

Kelly Tarlton's Antarctic Encounter and Underwater World, Orakei Wharf, Tamaki Drive.

Kelly Tarlton's displays Antarctic wildlife and New Zealand marine life, including penguins, sharks, rays, and shoals of fish. They are viewed through transparent underground tunnels built in the holding tanks of Auckland's first sewage pumping station (1909).

Tamaki Drive was constructed 1931–32 as a road link to the eastern suburbs. Planted pohutu-

View across Okahu Bay to Kelly Tarlton's Antarctic Encounter and Underwater World. Adjacent is Orakei Wharf (1983), a favourite recreational fishing spot.

kawa line the route. Many appear to flower 'out of season' but these are actually Kermadec pohutukawa with small, roundish leaves. By Akarana Yacht Club several of the pohutukawa-like trees possess acorns in late summer. These are actually evergreen holm oaks from the Mediterranean — a planting mistake? The cliffs backing onto Tamaki Drive are made of bedded Waitemata Sandstone strata clothed in places with pohutukawa.

A few decades ago the cliffs east of Kelly Tarlton's used to feature predominantly native vegetation. Today they are covered with the weedy South African shrub bone-seed, which is a mass of yellow daisy flowers in winter.

A number of historic structures can be seen between Mechanics Bay and Orakei Wharf. TEAL Park, Mechanics Bay, commemorates the seaplanes that served Auckland in the 1930s–50s. The concrete structure offshore is the Compass Dolphin, constructed (c.1920) for sailing vessels and steamers to reset their compasses after being in dry dock. To the north-east is Bean Rock Lighthouse (1871), New Zealand's sole surviving wooden-tower lighthouse. The rock itself was named after P.C.D. Bean, master of the mission vessel *Herald*.

On the Hobson Bay foreshore are the Auckland Harbour Board Dinghy Lockers, built as part of the Okahu Bay Boat Harbour (1939), constructed to replace the Mechanics Bay moorings removed with the introduction of flying boats. The development included the Okahu Bay haulout area and the protective wooden-piled wave screen. Near Hobson Bay Bridge are the distinctive Whakatakataka Bay Boat Sheds (c.1930).

Okahu Bay, meaning 'the dwelling place of Kahumatamomoe', was the site of a Ngati Whatua village until it was relocated by the ACC in the 1950s. Above Okahu Bay stands the finely carved Ngati Whatua meeting house Tumutumuwhenua.

Access from Tamaki Drive. Changing sheds, safe swimming, playground.

The Melanesian Mission House is the only remnant of an Anglican missionary training school that operated at Mission Bay, 1859–67.

Mission Bay has been a popular recreational area since Tamaki Drive was constructed, 1931–32. Over the years the beach has washed away and periodically been replenished with sand brought in from elsewhere. The largest and most recent of these endeavours was in 1995–96, when 30,000 cu m of sand dredged from 40 m depth off Pakiri was barged, then trucked to the beach. With it came vast numbers of unusual and pretty shells, some of which are seldom washed up on beaches.

The reserve contains two interesting structures — the Davis Memorial Fountain (1950) and the Melanesian Mission House, which now operates as a restaurant. This historic building is the only remaining structure from St Andrews College, the Anglican missionary training school from which the bay takes its name. It was founded in 1858 as an adjunct to St John's College (**91**), and was sited beside the sea so that its Melanesian students would feel more at home.

The building was designed by architect Reader Wood as the college's dining room and kitchen, and constructed in 1859 by colonial Auckland's finest stonemason, Benjamin Strange (**78**). It incorporates basalt rubble from the Rangitoto foreshore with dressed quoins and openings. Some basalt blocks still have oyster shells attached. The stone wall behind it is part of a shelter wall constructed to protect the college quadrangle from the prevailing westerly winds.

The mission transferred to Norfolk Island in 1867. The college was then used briefly as a Naval training school, as the Kohimarama Industrial School, and as the Walsh Bros New Zealand Flying School, 1915–24. The dilapidated building was restored as a Melanesian Museum in 1928. It again fell into disrepair before it was once more restored by the New Zealand Historic Places Trust in 1974.

By the Mission House are tall Norfolk pines, Canary Island pines and two tall Tasmanian blue gums. Pohutukawa provide the park with the most shade.

Walk around the foreshore, 2 hrs either side of low tide. Access down steps to Ladies Bay off Cliff Rd; down steps at end of Waitara Rd by Glover Park; down a zig-zag path to Karaka Bay from end of Peacock St; or from end of Glendowie St. Leaflet available from ACC.

The coastline between Ladies Bay (named after Lady Grey, wife of Sir George) and Glendowie, on the west side of the mouth of the Tamaki Estuary, consists of small beaches separated by intertidal sandstone platforms. In summer the beaches are frequented by nudists.

Waitemata Sandstone (see p. 26) is well exposed in the base of the cliffs and in the intertidal rocks. Features include a variety of trace fossils and occasional layers of black woody material that was carried into the Waitemata Basin during storms. A 20-m-thick bed of Parnell Grit (see p. 28) forms the base of the cliffs at the northern end of Karaka Bay.

On 4 March 1940 local iwi signed the Treaty of Waitangi at Karaka Bay. Splendid pohutukawa tower over a small 'drinking fountain' which marks this event.

On the foreshore below Glover Park are blocks of basaltic tuff and

Sandstone reefs and small sandy beaches backed by pohutukawa-clad cliffs form the Achilles Pt coastline, east of St Heliers.

breccia that have fallen from the clifftop. These come from the eroding eastern side of the Glover Park tuff ring. Here the beach has numerous dark grey pebbles of basalt and greywacke that have eroded out of the fallen blocks. Pieces of greywacke were ripped from deep in the throat of the Glover Park volcano and thrown out with the ash and basalt. The old concrete St Heliers water tower stands on the opposite, western rim of the tuff ring.

If the tide is high, you can still view the coast from the Achilles Point lookout on Cliff Rd. Here you also get a panoramic view of the Waitemata Harbour, Rangitoto, Motutapu and Motukorea Islands. Achilles Pt commemorates the pivotal role of HMS *Achilles* in the Battle of the River Plate in 1939. Achilles Point was originally named Te Pane o Horoiwi ('the head of Horoiwi') by a crew member of the Tainui canoe.

Main entrance at end of West Tamaki Rd; walking access from junction of Riddell Rd and Roberta Ave, or down steps from Vista Cres. Flat bush and beach walks. Leaflet available from ACC.

Tahuna Torea means 'the sand spit frequented by the oystercatcher'. The spit has grown up in just the last few thousand years. Cockle shells and sand are carried up the estuary by incoming tidal currents and seaward by outgoing tidal currents, resulting in the accumulation of the spit in this location. The narrow seaward end stretches almost right across to Bucklands Beach at low tide. The landward end encloses a triangular area of fresh- and salt-water ponds, bush areas and mangrove swamps. The area by the base of the cliffs was once farmed and a few hawthorn trees probably still mark an old fence line.

Around 1970, a group of local residents formed the Tamaki Estuary Protection Society. They saved Tahuna Torea from being turned into a marina or rubbish tip and won Auckland City Council's support for its enhancement as a wilderness area. They created bush tracks through the regenerating tea tree scrub (supplemented by native tree plantings) to lookouts over the spit and wetlands. Native birds frequenting this area include fantail, silver-eye, grey warbler, tui and morepork. Mallard, grey duck, pukeko, white-faced heron, swallows, kingfishers, pied and little shags feed in and around the freshwater and brackish pools.

The track to the sandy beach runs beside a tidal pond containing embankments that were used by the pre-European Maori to trap fish when the tide receded. Here the saltmarsh contains glasswort flats with sea rush, fringed by saltmarsh ribbonwood with its interlacing branches. In the more tidal ponds, sea primrose and mangroves abound.

The most common wading birds are the South Island pied oystercatcher (autumn and winter) and godwit (summer). Together with pied stilts, knots and turnstones, waders can be seen seasonally on the shelly coastal fringe and spit at high tide, or feeding well out on the mudflats at low tide.

The South African shrub bone-seed, is an aggressive weed above high tide on open areas of the spit.

Tahuna Torea sand and shell spit juts out into the Tamaki Estuary.

202–210 St John's Rd, Meadowbank. The college is a functioning theological institution; buildings should not be entered without permission.

The Anglican Theological Training College of St John The Evangelist was transferred from Waimate North to its present site at 'Purewa' in 1844. It was planned by Bishop Selwyn and developed by his Domestic Chaplain Rev. William Cotton.

The College retains a nationally significant group of buildings that date from the 1840s. The most impressive is New Zealand's second oldest church, the tiny Chapel of St John The Evangelist (1847), which was designed by Frederick Thatcher in the Gothic Revival style favoured by Bishop Selwyn. Its magnificent interior features exposed timbers, the nation's oldest stained-glass windows, and memorials that reflect the church history of New Zealand. Behind the chapel is a cemetery containing the graves of many notable colonial clergymen and the infant daughter of Bishop Selwyn. To the west is the original stone-walled college kitchen (1845), named the 'Waitoa Room' in honour of Rota Waitoa, the first Maori to be ordained. Beside it is the College Dining Hall (1849), which is still used for its original purpose.

St John's trained its early students not only in theology, but also in the practical skills required by clergymen in that period. Reverend Cotton, known as 'Bee' because of his passion for apiary, established practical courses for college students in that discipline, as well as gardening, orcharding and forestry. Under his supervision the grounds of the college were planted with a wide variety of native and exotic trees. Some of the original plantings (1844–47) still remain near the college buildings, in a small gully behind them, and on adjoining properties. They include: kauri, totara, impressive macrocarpas, oaks (holm and English) and Italian alder. Other large trees include camphor, redwood, Norfolk pine, bunya bunya and plane tree.

The Chapel of St John The Evangelist, St John's College.

Vehicle access to the top off Mountain Rd from Panmure roundabout. Pleasant walk around rim of crater with spectacular views.

Mt Wellington's steep-sided crater with the huge aggregate quarry in the basalt lava flows beyond.

Mt Wellington is Auckland's second youngest volcano, erupting about 9000 years ago. It consists of a 100-m-high scoria cone produced by lava fountaining from the three vents in the 60-m-deep crater. One of these has been filled by a water reservoir (1960) with its flat top camouflaged by a grass field. Lava poured from around the base of the cone forming an extensive lava-flow field. The thickest parts to the west of the mountain have been quarried for aggregate and road metal for Auckland city. Mt Wellington Quarry is the largest aggregate quarry in New Zealand. One tongue of lava from Mt Wellington flowed 6 km south-west through Penrose to the Manukau Harbour shoreline at Southdown.

The steep southern side of Mt Wellington, now clothed in pine trees, was quarried for over 100 years until 1967, and two smaller scoria cones (Purchas Hill) between Mt Wellington and Tamaki Campus have been removed by quarrying.

The mountain was named by colonial surveyor Felton Mathew in honour of the Duke of Wellington. Its Maori name Maungarei is translated as 'the watchful mountain'; or as 'the mountain of Reipae', a Tainui ancestress who travelled to Northland in the form of a bird (8). Maungarei is an impressive archaeological site. Its flanks are covered in terraced house sites and food-storage pits (see p. 76). The crater rim has three strong points each defended by transverse ditches.

The cone is covered by Kikuyu grass with a few pines. Where bare scoria occurs a tiny annual fern, *Annogramma leptophylla*, may be found. Mt Wellington is a major New Zealand stronghold for this threatened species. Other native ferns present include: *Cheilanthes distans*, *Pellaea* species, rasp fern, necklace fern, hound's tongue fern, shield fern, leather fern, shining spleenwort and hanging spleenwort.

On the eastern side of Mt Wellington is Winifred Huggins Woodland (at the end of Fraser Rd). It was started in 1969 to mark Winifred's contribution to the Auckland Tree Society. It contains a mixture of exotic deciduous and evergreen trees.

Well-marked entrances off Grand Drive, Abbotts Way and Towle Place. Flat gravel paths and board walks, playground and toilets near Abbotts Way and Grand Drive junction. Leaflet available from ACC.

This low-lying basin was once a shallow lake formed by the damming of a valley by a lava flow from Mt Wellington (**92**). The valley used to drain east to the Tamaki River. The lake so formed was traditionally known as Waiatarua ('the waters of reflection') and later named Lake St John. In 1929 a tunnel was dug under Remuera Rd ridge and amid much public opposition the 22-ha lake was drained into Orakei Basin. An important habitat

Boardwalks and viewing platforms meander through the constructed wetlands of Waiatarua Reserve.

with many uncommon native wetland plants was lost. Silt and pollution from the Waiatarua catchment is blamed for some of the smell and mud problems now experienced in Orakei Basin. To address these problems shallow siltation ponds have been installed in the swampy floor of former Lake Waiatarua.

Waiatarua Reserve was acquired by the ACC in 1918 under an arrangement with Mr R. Abbott, who gifted much of it to the citizens of Auckland. The inner (bird sanctuary) area is fenced off and surrounded by rough grazed pasture with areas of rushes. The earliest artificial wetlands were constructed in the centre of the reserve in 1987 and surrounded with native plantings of manuka, kanuka, cabbage trees, karamu, tarata and flax. Other plantings include kahikatea, totara, kowhai, *Coprosma* species, toetoe, *Carex* species and some inappropriate species such as *Olearia solandri*. In early spring the cabbage trees make a spectacular, sweet-scented flowering. This community planting project is coordinated by the ACC. Further peripheral ponds are to be constructed.

The planted bush areas are home to increasing numbers of fantail, tui and grey warblers. Wetland inhabitants include abundant pukeko, white-faced heron, little shag, mallard and grey ducks. The drier areas are utilised by spur-winged plovers, pheasants, quail and also pukeko. Grass carp were introduced into the reserve's waterways in 1994 to eat the waterweeds that are clogging the ponds.

Panmure Basin — access from Lagoon Drive, Ireland Rd (high-tide boat ramp), Peterson Rd (model railway) and Watene Rd. Pleasant 45-min walk on sealed path around basin perimeter. Van Dammes Lagoon — access off Mt Wellington Highway.

Panmure Basin was traditionally known as Te Kai a Hiku, 'the eating place of the guardian taniwha Moko-ika-hiku-waru', from whom the name Mokoia came. On its southern shores was the sacred spring Waipuna o Rangiatea, named by the Tainui crew after a spring in east Polynesia.

The basin is an explosion crater formed by a series of eruptions about 27,000 years ago. It is encircled by a low tuff ring that is now mostly covered in houses, shops and the Waipuna Hotel complex. Layers of bedded ash (tuff) can be seen around the basin shores and in the cliffs on either side of the outlet channel.

Initially the crater filled with fresh water creating a lake. Seepage eroded through the north-eastern corner of the tuff ring and rising sea level after the Last Ice Age caused the sea to invade the crater, which then became a tidal lagoon. The patches of mangroves that dot the shoreline are remnants of a once more extensive mangrove forest margin. The footbridge over the outlet provides ideal viewing of a large pied shag colony. Close-up views of the nests can be seen from the path behind the colony. Little and black shags also frequent the area with white-faced herons, gulls and kingfishers.

Van Dammes Lagoon is a small landscaped reserve between Ireland Rd and Mt Wellington Highway. A pleasant loop track encircles a lake and swamp ponded behind a dam built in the 1860s for the Ireland Bros tannery (1860s–1923). In the 1930s the property was purchased by Theodore Van Damme, who set about beautifying it. He planted trees and stocked the ponds with goldfish, carp and water lilies. After his death, the site reverted to wasteland until it passed into public ownership in 1975. Since then it has been greatly tidied and Van Damme's vision restored. Original plantings include walnut, swamp cypress, camphor and Canary Island palm. A large Peruvian 3-m-tall canna (*Canna iridiflora*) with rose-pink flowers grows in the swamp.

Van Dammes Lagoon, to the west of Panmure Basin, is one of Auckland's best-kept secrets.

Access from Endeavour St or the end of Blockhouse Bay Rd. Toilets, playground, coastal walk.

This attractive seaside reserve is dominated by large pohutukawa, and pines planted by Charles Paice c.1889. The adjoining coastline is clothed in modified, regenerating coastal forest. The area's traditional name Te Whau originates from the locally present whau tree. Dark mats of a red alga, *Gracilaria chilensis*, often cover the mud flats. Waders are common on the intertidal flats, with high numbers of white-faced herons perhaps being due to numerous nesting sites (pine trees) along the coast.

Within the reserve, shell middens, faint terracing and karaka groves indicate a former Maori village. On the south-western headland are the heavily eroded remains of Te Whau Pa, which commanded the Whau River-Manukau Harbour canoe portage. It was also a traditional tribal boundary marker between the Kawerau and Waiohua tribes.

Te Whau Bay was used as a camping spot by early European travellers journeying down the Manukau or crossing the portage. In 1860 the Government built a wooden blockhouse above the bay, hence its present name. It was manned until 1863 by colonial militia and detachments of the Imperial Army's 57th and 65th regiments. They camped behind the bay, patrolled the clifftops, and kept a lookout from the point.

In the Edwardian era, Blockhouse Bay became a popular holiday spot for city dwellers. They caught the train or tram to Avondale, and then walked or travelled by dray, and later motor bus, to the bay. A bach community developed from c.1900. Several examples of early baches can still be seen in Blockhouse Bay Rd. The reserve had a community fish smokehouse and a beach store from 1912. During the 1930s depression unemployed workers built the reserve's stone seawalls and paths.

Te Ara o Tiriwa ('the pathway of Tiriwa') Walkway (see p. 84) extends in both directions along the adjoining coastline. It is possible to do a short loop walk, which gives extensive harbour views, by returning along Taunton Tce.

View across Blockhouse Bay to Te Whau Pt.

Access down Waikowhai Rd off Hillsborough Rd to Waikowhai Park. Boat ramp, playground, coastal walks.

Pleasant Wesley Bay, east of Faulkner Bay, is backed by regenerating coastal forest.

The sea cliffs along the northern side of the Manukau Harbour are composed of bedded Waitemata Sandstone strata. The points on either side of Faulkner Bay (carpark) are made of a thick, erosion-resistant bed of Parnell Grit. It consists of small volcanic particles that flowed down into the basin as a submarine slurry from the Waitakere Volcano (see p. 28) to the west. Within this Parnell Grit are numerous fossil lumps of bryozoa (sea mosses), 2–3 cm across, and rare, usually broken, fossil bivalves and gastropods.

Thrown up on the beach in Wesley Bay, one bay east of the carpark, are numerous, dark grey, fossilised mud crabs and tubular burrows. These erode out of subtidal deposits offshore and are probably less than 10,000 years old. The crabs and burrows were fossilised by a process that turns them into phosphate and cements sand grains together.

In the last decade or two, the shoreline has been invaded by introduced Pacific oysters with razor-sharp shells that stick up from the rocks. Many grow one on top of the other and collect thick deposits of mud around them. In places the dead oyster shells are accumulating in deep drifts at the back of the beaches.

Waikowhai, meaning 'bay of the kowhai trees', was part of a large block of land owned last century by the Wesleyan Mission at Three Kings. The coastal parkland was obtained by the ACC for the people of Auckland in 1911. The access road down to the beach zigzags down the face of a large refuse tip that was closed in the 1960s and has been landscaped. Advanced regenerating forest surrounds this site.

A strip of forest extends along much of this part of the north Manukau Harbour coastline and includes excellent pohutukawa forest. From the road abundant canopy trees of kowhai and kohekohe are evident. Rewarewa, karaka, kahikatea, mapou and mahoe are all common. Good views can be obtained across the forest, and to the west a pied shag colony is evident in pohutukawa trees on the coast.

Jellicoe Park, Onehunga. Access from Park Gardens Rd off Quadrant Rd. Toilets, picnics, public swimming pool.

Onehunga Blockhouse was constructed by the Colonial Government in 1860 as one of a series of 10 block-houses designed to protect Auckland from an attack by the Waikato tribes. It was strategically sited on a ridge that provided unobstructed views over the Manukau Harbour, the Mangere Crossing and the Otahuhu Portage.

Onehunga Blockhouse is Auckland's only remaining intact defensive structure from the New Zealand Wars of the 1860s, and the only brick blockhouse in New Zealand.

The building, which is cruciform in shape, was constructed using bricks made on the site of what is now Harrahs Sky City Casino in the central city. The 280-mm-thick brick walls, heavy steel-plate doors, and steel-shuttered windows were all designed to deter attackers. Barrels of water and wet sacking were stored in the building in case of an outbreak of fire during an attack.

The blockhouse was garrisoned (1860–63) by Auckland Militia, who were accommodated in tents surrounding the building. One room of the blockhouse was used as a Guard Room for the Duty Detachment, while the other was used as a Militia Office and Store.

After 1863 the Onehunga Blockhouse was used variously as a school and as a private home. From 1889 until 1892 it was used as the Council Chambers by the Onehunga Borough Council which elected Elizabeth Yates as the British Empire's first woman Mayor in 1893.

The blockhouse was restored by the New Zealand Historic Places Trust (1962–66) and is used today by local organisations as a meeting place. Nearby are two other heritage buildings: Laishley House, the original Onehunga Congregational Manse (1859), and a replica Fencible Cottage and Museum. The latter is furnished in colonial style and contains material associated with the history of Onehunga.

Jellicoe Park is an ideal place to begin the Onehunga Historic Walk outlined in a pamphlet available from the Onehunga Public Library. Also worth a visit is the Auckland Railway Enthusiasts Society Museum in the region's oldest railway station at 38 Alfred St, Onehunga.

Access from Domain Rd, off Coronation Rd. Easy walk up grassed roadway to summit.

The small hill in the centre of Mangere Mountain crater is an extruded plug of viscous lava (called a tholoid). It is surrounded by several gas explosion craters.

Mangere Mountain is a large, well-preserved scoria cone produced by lava fountaining from its huge crater about 18,000 years ago. The crater is breached to the east by lava flows, which carried away the scoria ramparts in the vicinity of the present soccer fields (the site of a former quarry). A deep, secondary crater occurs in the northern rim of Mangere Mountain's scoria cone and was the site of further lava fountaining. Lava flowed from around the base of most of the volcano, forming an extensive lava-flow field covering 5 sq km.

From the top of Mangere Mountain there are excellent views across the Manukau Harbour and Auckland Isthmus. To the west is Puketutu Island, a volcano composed of lava flows capped by small scoria cones. Just below Mangere Mountain in the south-west is Mangere Lagoon explosion crater with the flattened remains of a small scoria cone in the middle. The circular explosion crater has been used as sludge ponds for Auckland's sewage treatment since the 1960s. North of this is Ambury Park (**100**).

The mountain is grazed pasture with groups of planted trees, mainly pohutukawa, puriri, macrocarpa and Norfolk pines.

The name Mangere originates from Nga Hau Mangere, the 'lazy breezes' observed by Taikehu of the Tainui canoe when he landed below the mountain six centuries ago. The cone, one of Auckland's most impressive archaeological sites, is essentially an extensive 'townscape' lying at the centre of a once wider garden landscape. The mountain, which was occupied until c.1836, has numerous house terraces and food-storage pits, a mound garden, and several defensive positions.

In nearby Church St, Mangere Bridge, is St James, Auckland's oldest stone Selwyn church.

See also: Kiwi Esplanade lava flows (**99**), Ambury Park (**100**).

In foreshore rocks alongside Kiwi Esplanade, Mangere Bridge; especially well displayed opposite the junction with Boyd and House Avenues. Visible between mid- and low tide.

During Mangere Mountain's eruptions 18,000 years ago, large volumes of fluid lava flowed from around the base of its scoria cone. It spread out as an extensive sheet of overlapping lava flows on the gentle slopes of the Manukau River valley, which at that time was dry land and forested (because sea level was much lower during the Last Ice Age).

Most of the lava from Mangere Mountain was particularly hot and fluid and would have flowed rapidly off down slope at speeds of up to 10 km/hour. The surface of these red-hot flows chilled quickly forming a black, smooth or ropy skin. As the lava continued to flow this skin wrinkled up into small curved ridges, like the skin on a pot of boiling fudge or toffee. These wrinkled surfaces are typical of hot, fluid lava flows called pahoehoe — a Hawaiian term.

The best examples of wrinkled, pahoehoe features in the Auckland volcanic field can be seen in the basalt lava flows from Mangere Mountain that form the intertidal rocks adjacent to Kiwi Esplanade. For most of their existence the surfaces of these flows had been protected from weathering and erosion by a thick covering of volcanic ash that had erupted from Mangere volcano after the lava flows.

Following the end of the Last Ice Age, sea level rose to its present height about 6500 years ago and only in the last thousand or so years has wave erosion along the Kiwi Esplanade coast removed the soft ash covering and exhumed the unweathered lava flow surfaces beneath.

In autumn and winter the grassed strip between Kiwi Esplanade and the sea is frequented at high tide by thousands of South Island pied oystercatchers.

See also: Takapuna Reef fossil forest (**34**) and Rangitoto Island volcano (**132**).

Ropy (toffee-like) pahoehoe surfaces on lava-flow tongues in the foreshore rocks beside Kiwi Esplanade, Mangere Bridge.

Access from the western ends of Kiwi Esplanade or Ambury Rd, Mangere Bridge. Toilets, picnic areas, farm park walks.

Needle tussock and yellow lichens (Xanthoria) *grow on a basalt outcrop on the Ambury Park coastline.*

In pre-European times, Ambury Park was part of the stonefield gardening landscape associated with Mangere Mountain. It takes its name from the Ambury Milk Co, which operated the property as a town milk supply farm, 1893–1965. The land was purchased by the ARA, 1965–73, as a buffer for the adjoining Mangere Wastewater Treatment Plant.

The park sits on ash-covered lava flows from Mangere Mountain. When it erupted 18,000 years ago, at the peak of the Last Ice Age, the flows spread out across the gentle, forested slopes of the Manukau Valley. The toes of these flows, north and west of Ambury Park, were drowned as sea level rose to its present height, 6500 years ago, and mud has since accumulated over them. Bare lava flow surfaces can be seen along the shoreline.

Most of the shrubs and trees are planted shelter belts, although there are occasional original pohutukawa, karo and taupata. The coastal fringe supports small salt meadows of glasswort and sea primrose, and on the rocky islets flax, karo and boxthorn grow.

Ambury Park is popular with bird watchers, primarily for the migrant waders that roost in their thousands around its coastal fringes and on the islands in the adjacent oxidation pond, when their feeding grounds are immersed at high tide. The Arctic waders, particularly godwit and knot, are present in significant numbers between October and March. In autumn and winter, South Island migrants are common, particularly pied oystercatcher and wrybill. A reflection of the richness of this coastal habitat is that over 86 species of birds have been recorded here including royal spoonbills and cattle egrets.

Also commonly seen around the rocky coastal fringe and small shelly beaches are pied, black and little shags and white-faced herons. Feeding on and around the grazed paddocks are pukeko, spur-winged plover, swallow, various ducks, finches, myna, starling and skylark.

Ambury Park is a working farm with periodic public open days.

Access from end of Renton Rd, off Ihumatao Rd, Mangere. Public access to the coast is also obtainable from the end of Ihumatao Rd. Visit between mid and low tide.

At the end of Renton Rd are the fossilised remains of two forests. The older forest consists of large stumps in growth position and fallen trunks of an ancient kauri forest. They were buried and preserved in a peat swamp c.100,000 years ago. Today the overlying soft rocks and peat are eroding away, exposing the fossil kauri forest in the foreshore.

The wood of the fossil kauri stumps and logs is nearly as fresh and hard as modern wood, probably as it has remained waterlogged since burial. Small lumps of kauri gum can be found in the peat and also in splits in some of the stumps. Growth rings in some of the 2–3-m diameter stumps show that these kauri were hundreds of years old when they died. The forest may have been killed by the natural ponding of this area which created the peat swamp in which the remains were preserved.

About 30,000 years ago, a younger forest was growing on the black peat when it was overwhelmed and preserved beneath the first ash showers from nearby Maungataketake Volcano (Elletts Mountain). Fossilised leaves in the ash indicate that this forest was more varied than the first and was dominated by rimu, miro, hinau, kauri and tanekaha.

The remains of this forest are only seen in the low cliffs. Two upright trees that were killed and buried by volcanic ash can be seen in the cliffs 20–50 m west of the steps. The lower layers of soft grey-brown ash (called tuff) also contain fallen logs and branches, many of which have rotted away leaving hollow moulds.

The cliffs to the west are clothed in pohutukawa and associated native bush, which is rare for most of this coast. Kingfishers nest in the cliffs and wading birds are common on the extensive tidal flats.

The large fossilised stumps and fallen trunks of an ancient kauri forest can be seen in the foreshore at Ihumatao.

Vehicle access off Great South Rd and Atkinson Ave. Playing fields, pleasant walks up formed roadway to summit reservoir or informally around grassed tops and craters.

Mt Richmond consists of the partly quarried remains of several small scoria cones formed by lava fountaining from a number of craters. The cones sit in the middle of a 1-km-diameter explosion crater with surrounding low tuff ring. The bowling club and soccer pitch are sited on the previously swampy floor of the explosion crater between the cones and the tuff ring.

In places it is difficult to recognise the original shape of the scoria cones and tuff ring because substantial parts have been removed. The sites of four scoria pits lie within Mt Richmond Domain and can easily be confused with the two small circular craters in the middle of the complex.

All of the scoria cones were extensively modified with surface earthworks for occupation sites and defensive pa in pre-European times, and there are several very large kumara storage pits. Particularly impressive is the high, steep-sided defensive position at the eastern end of the complex. The mountain was of strategic importance as it commanded the main Waitemata-Manukau canoe portage. Its Maori name Otahuhu is translated as 'the dwelling place of Tahuhu', and as the 'ridgepole' of Tainui. The latter is a reference to the portage of the Tainui canoe in the 14th century.

Mt Richmond Domain was gazetted in 1890. Planted trees are common over most of the cone in rough grazed pasture. Most of the species are exotic, but the familiar natives of pohutukawa, puriri, totara, karaka and titoki are also present. Exotic evergreen trees include Port Jackson fig, holm oaks, olives which are becoming wild, gum trees, macrocarpas, holly, Norfolk pine and Chinese fir. Deciduous trees include elms, plane trees, Lombardy and necklace poplars, liquidamber, horse chestnut, English and pin oaks, common beeches, paulownia and hawthorn.

Large Moreton Bay fig trees from east Australia, with their spreading, above-the-ground-roots, are common in Mt Richmond Domain. One is pictured here on a terrace.

Access along concrete walking path off Fisher Parade and short side streets.

Most Pakuranga residents who use the walkway along the banks of the Tamaki Estuary at Farm Cove are oblivious to the white cliffs they pass. Yet this 3-m-thick deposit of rhyolitic ash provides graphic evidence of a huge eruption in the Taupo-Rotorua area several hundred thousand years ago. Charred vegetation beneath the ash shows that the ignimbrite flow which deposited it was still hot when it arrived.

Scattered through many parts of Auckland city are similar, usually thinner deposits erupted from the large caldera volcanoes in the centre of the North Island. These deposits indicate that on a number of occasions in the last few hundred thousand years the isthmus has received the tail end of hot ignimbrite flows. These flows would have swept down the Waikato Valley at enormous speed and across the Manukau lowlands to blanket Auckland within an hour of being erupted.

The low white cliffs beside the Tamaki estuary at Farm Cove are the deposit from an ignimbrite flow that reached Auckland from the Taupo area several hundred thousand years ago.

Large eruptions from these caldera volcanoes throw pumice and ash 50 km or more into the atmosphere. Huge quantities may be erupted in a matter of minutes and denser parts of the eruption column collapse, blasting superheated clouds of gas, ash and pumice outwards across the ground, like horizontal snow avalanches. These are hot ignimbrite flows. They travel away from the vent at speeds of up to 1000 km per hour and may have sufficient momentum to flow up and over mountain ranges.

Hot ignimbrite flows sweep outwards and deposit thick sheets of pumice and ash over large areas near the vent with thinner veneers further away. A few have travelled as far as Auckland city. South-east winds during times of eruption have periodically carried white rhyolitic ash from the Taupo-Rotorua volcanoes to mantle the Auckland landscape.

Lloyd Ellsmore Park, Bell Rd, Pakuranga. Open 7 days a week. Living museum days 3rd Sunday of the month. Toilets, picnics, Bell House Restaurant.

Open day at the Howick Colonial Village.

Howick Colonial Village is one of New Zealand's finest 'living' local history museums. It portrays the Maori and European history of Howick-Pakuranga and surrounding districts. The village is based on the Fencible settlement of Howick (1847–80) and includes 24 buildings which have mostly been relocated from the surrounding district. It has authentic Victorian streetscapes and features a village green and a pond complete with ducks and geese. The village's gardens contain Victorian flower and vegetable species, and old varieties of fruit trees such as loquats, quinces, persimmons and medlars.

The village was created around 'Bell House', which stood nearby when it was built for Fencible Officer Captain Charles Smith in 1852. Genuine fencible cottages include 'Henry Brindle's Cottage', a single unit constructed c.1854; and the McDermott Cottage, a double unit constructed for two privates and their families in the same period. Larger houses include the Maraetai Homestead built for Thomas Eckford in 1850, on what is now Omana Regional Park (**110**), and the McLaughlin Homestead built for William McLaughlin at Puhinui in 1861. Colonel De Quincey's Cottage, built for the son of the famous English essayist in 1863, houses Maori and Fencible settlement artefacts and displays. In the unrestored Carter Cottage visitors can view original Victorian whitewashed walls, wallpapers, pitsawn framing timber and hand-split kauri roof shingles.

The village also features non-residential buildings typically found in a Victorian village. Examples are the Pakuranga School (1880), the original Howick Methodist Church (1852), Howick Courthouse, thought to be New Zealand's oldest administrative building (1851), White's Store and the reconstructed Wagstaff's Forge. The village flour mill is a replica of the mill built in 1855, in what is now the Regional Botanic Gardens (**108**), for one of New Zealand's best-known millers, John Bycroft. Farm buildings include several barns, the Somerville cowshed and creamery built in the 1860s near Howick, and a coach house, which was the forerunner to the modern garage.

Coast accessible by walking around Musick Pt at low tide, from the northern end of Bucklands and Eastern Beaches or down a steep path from Clovelly Rd. A drive or walk out along the top of Musick Pt through Howick Golf Course ends at a carpark by the Musick Pt radio station.

Musick Pt is composed of Waitemata Sandstones (see p. 26) that are clearly seen in the surrounding cliffs and shore platforms.

Concretions are well developed within some of the beds, particularly along the west side. These are much harder blobs of sandstone that have been cemented by the growth of crystalline quartz or calcite that precipitated out of the passing ground water while the rocks were deeply buried. Some concretions are individual spheres or ovoids, 30–50 cm across. Others have grown together to form crazy oblong or sausage shapes.

The Musick Pt cliffs support many fine pohutukawa, with karo and houpara. The Mediterranean shrub rhamnus is wild here and rampant on the adjacent islands. Several groves of tainui trees (*Pomaderris apetala*), up to 8 m tall, are growing at the end of Musick Pt. Local Maori tradition states that they were brought here from Polynesia in the ancestral Tainui canoe. Tainui is considered native to both Australia and New Zealand where it is found from Kawhia to Mokau.

Musick Pt and the radio station were named in memory of Capt Edwin G. Musick, the well-known Pan American Airways flying-boat pilot killed when his plane crashed at Samoa in 1938. A pleasant walk around the old station leads to the end of the point which gives magnificent views over Tamaki Strait and the inner Gulf islands.

The Maori name for the point is Te Naupata after the shiny leafed coastal shrub naupata or taupata (*Coprosma repens*), which grows there. The main defensive ditch and other earthworks of the Ngai Tai pa of Waiarohia are still visible on the point.

In the cliffs about 1 km north of Eastern Beach is the spectacular Eastern Beach Anticline (upfold) of Waitemata Sandstone strata. Its outwardly tilted layers can be traced back into the shore platform to give a better appreciation of its three-dimensional shape.

Shelly Park to Musick Pt via Cockle Bay, Howick Beach, Mellons Bay and Eastern Beach (4–5 hours or in sections). Walkway and Howick historic walk pamphlets available from Manukau City or Howick Historical Village (104) are essential. The Awaroa Walkway follows the shoreline, however alternative inland routes are available at high tide.

At Howick Beach the Awaroa Walkway passes the site of the old Howick Wharf.

The Shelly Park-Cockle Bay section of the walkway begins at the sandspit boat haulout area. Here many waders can be seen. In late summer masses of knots and godwits gather prior to their Arctic migration. The inland route follows a shell-covered path rising to a memorial seat giving extensive views. A historic settlers cottage once occupied by the Broomfield family can be seen nearby. This section of the walkway follows local roads and emerges at the historic Windross Restaurant (1898), Cockle Bay. At the eastern end of the beach an ancient pohutukawa is associated with the Ngai Tai ancestor Manawatere (**110**), who was said to have marked it with red ochre after skimming over the sea from Hawaiki.

The inland part of the Cockle Bay-Howick Beach section follows local roads and footpaths. It passes several Second World War gun emplacements, and follows a concrete footpath through the defensive ditch of the now-destroyed Tuwakamana Pa. The coastal route is along the Waitemata Sandstone shore platforms above which shags and kingfishers nest. Several more gun emplacements can be seen at Howick Beach, and a plaque marks the site of the old Howick Wharf (1895). A self-guided walk through historic Howick, founded as a military Fencible settlement (1847), can be taken at this point. Mellons Bay, named after Fencible William Mellon, can be reached either via the shore platform or local roads.

On the Mellons Bay-Eastern Beach section the inland route gives extensive views from MacLeans Reserve. The tidal route follows the sandy beach and shore platform past a wild rock pigeon colony. The Eastern Beach-Musick Pt section follows sandy Eastern Beach, which is a popular swimming spot and ends at Musick Pt (**105**).

Access from Murphys Rd, between Ormiston and Redoubt Rds, 4km from Manukau City motorway turnoff. Picnic areas, toilets, flat bush walks.

Murphys Bush Reserve, established by Manukau City Council in 1981, is an advanced regenerating kahikatea forest encircled by a grass margin. The bush was named after Mr Conway Murphy and his family, who owned and preserved it for a century. Most of the trees are slender, nearly reaching 20 m and usually less than 50 cm diameter. Kahikatea dominates the canopy with

Murphys Bush is wonderful dense kahikatea forest on rural flat land, east of Manukau City centre.

rimu, puriri, kohekohe and totara scattered through it. Matai is less common. In a wet stream gully near the carpark is a broadleaf canopy of puriri, taraire, tawa and pukatea.

Like most New Zealand podocarps, kahikatea has male and female cones on separate trees. As the fruit matures in autumn the stalk swells, becomes fleshy and colours to red (or yellow). In a good fruiting year the foliage can be completely hidden by the abundance of fruit, which is a welcome sight to fruit-eating birds such as native pigeon, tui and silver-eye. In winter the ground becomes swampy in places, which is ideal habitat for kahikatea.

There are few trees between the canopy and the dense shrub layer, a reflection of past stock damage before the area was fenced out by the Murphys some 30 years ago. Nikau palms dominate this shrub layer, together with the narrow, small-leaved coprosma *C. areolata*. Other small-leaved shrubs include *Coprosma spathulata*, *Melicope simplex* and *Melicytus micranthus*. Ponga, pigeonwood, hangehange, mapou and lancewood are also common. Various ground ferns are present, including thread fern searching for a trunk to climb. Nikau seedlings and occasional tussocks of the large sedge *Gahnia xanthocarpa* are present. Climbers include knobby stems of supplejack, native passionfruit, kiekie and New Zealand jasmine. Weeds are remarkably scarce.

The usual bush birds are present including native pigeons, even though large-fruiting tree species are in low numbers in the reserve. Neighbouring bush areas would supplement the pigeons' diet.

Flat Bush School located near the reserve entrance operated 1877–1929. It has been restored for community use.

Access to Botanic Gardens from Hill Rd, adjacent to Southern Motorway at Manurewa (open 7 days, 7.30 am to dusk). Visitor centre, library (11 am–3 pm), kiosk, garden rambles first Sunday of the month (March–December). Access to Totara Park via Wairere Rd, off Hill Rd, Manurewa. BBQs, playground, bush walks, swimming pool (November–March).

The site of the Botanic Gardens was purchased by the ARA in 1968 from the Nathan Estate and the gardens opened in 1982. The 65-ha property slopes gently northwards to the Puhinui Stream and ends with a south-facing escarpment covered in regenerating bush. The remainder of the gardens are mostly developed with some grazed pasture and small relic stands of majestic totara. Several small water courses flow through the gardens, and two lakes and a wetland have been added. The site of an 1855 flour mill can be seen near the north-western boundary (**104**). Beyond the Rose Display Trial Garden are several concrete pads that remain from the large US military camp located there, 1943–45.

About 30,000 plants are displayed representing 8,000 different species, including specialist plantings of natives, herbs, magnolias, camellias, salvias and numerous roses. Rose of the Year is judged in November followed by a Sunday rose festival.

Manukau City purchased the remainder of the Nathan Estate and developed Totara Park. The main valley contains the best tall flood plain forest remaining in South Auckland. It is dominated by totara, kahikatea, rimu, tanekaha and the best matai in the region. Loop tracks through the bush (10–40 mins) provide views of the understorey of tawa, taraire, tangles of supplejack vines and abundant nikau palms. This forest is contiguous with the Botanic Garden bush, making it one of the largest forest remnants in Manukau. Walking tracks connect the two. Other trees present are pukatea, karaka, titoki, kowhai and the regionally rare kaikomako. Kohekohe dominates much of the steeper slopes with tawa, taraire, puriri and tree ferns. The younger forest on the ridge tops is mainly kanuka and totara. Kauri is scarce.

Some 21 birds are known to nest in the two areas, including native pigeon, tui, morepork, fantail, grey-warbler, silver-eye, kingfisher, pukeko and paradise shelduck.

The rock garden at the Botanic Gardens has a succulent theme and is especially rich in aloes and agaves. The tall Aloe bainesii *stands out (centre).*

South

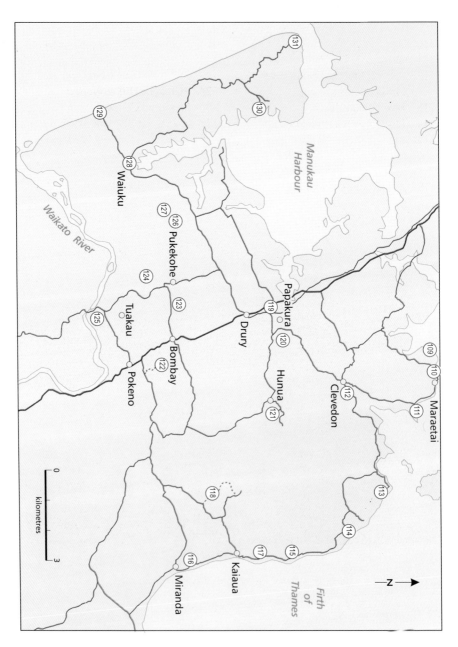

South

Awhitu Regional Park.

Page 233: Waha-rau, the ever-changing stream mouth.

Access to beach down steps from the corner of Hawke Cres and Puriri Rd, then walk across sand flats to Motukaraka at mid- to low tide.

Motukaraka Island viewed from Beachlands.

Motukaraka Island and the adjacent Beachlands area are composed of Waitemata Sandstones that can be seen in the cliffs and intertidal reefs. On Motukaraka the beds are almost horizontal and are cut by several small faults. The cliffs and shore platform around the Hawke Cres steps are made of breccia, lignite and rhyolitic sandstone that fills a former valley (c. 1–2 million years old) cut into Waitemata Sandstone. Preserved with the lignite layers are large logs that were buried in this old swampy valley. The flat top of Motukaraka and the adjacent mainland is an uplifted terrace that was eroded intertidally from the soft Waitemata Sandstones a few hundred thousand years ago.

The sand flats on the way out to the island support significant beds of cockles, pipi and wedge shells. The sandstone reefs are colonised by acorn barnacles, clusters of small black mussels, clumps of sharp Pacific oysters, tube worms and extensive carpets of Neptune's necklace seaweed. Oystercatchers, godwits, stilts, herons, terns, gulls and kingfishers feed on the tidal flats.

Large pohutukawa top Motukaraka's cliffs, together with other native trees and shrubs, including karaka, after which the island is named. Motukaraka was one of the few places in the region where the rare, red-flowered kakabeak shrub was found growing naturally in the 19th century. Karaka was once common, but a large fire in the 1950s destroyed most of the island's forest, reducing it to rank pasture and weeds. A local community project hopes to restore the vegetation.

The island was intensively occupied by the Hauraki tribes in association with seasonal fishing activities, as indicated by the thick layers of midden exposed at the clifftop beside the access track. Motukaraka also provided a natural refuge, although local tradition records that it was successfully attacked on several occasions. In the early 18th century an attacking force from lower Northland scaled the cliffs using kauri saplings and stormed the pa at dawn.

Access off Whitford–Maraetai Rd, 1 km west of Maraetai. Changing sheds, picnic areas, BBQs, walks, best swimming beach 800 m east of park, summer campsites.

Omana was for generations a dwelling place of Ngai Tai, who occupied the impressive ring-ditch pa from which the park takes its name — O-Manawatere ('the dwelling place of Manawatere'). Ngai Tai tradition records that this ancestor travelled from th Pacific homeland not by canoe, but by 'gliding over the waves'.

The well-preserved ring-ditch pa, O-Manawatere, sits on the edge of the cliffs in Omana Regional Park.

The property was part of William Fairbun's 'Maraetai Mission Station' (1837–42), and one of the region's first farms. It was cut for timber, dug for kauri gum, and even prospected for gold and silver. From 1849 to 1970 the property was farmed by successive owners until being purchased for a regional park.

A 2-hr perimeter walk follows the pohutukawa-lined clifftops with views across to Waiheke Island and up the harbour. Two boardwalks cross mangrove-filled arms of Te Puru Creek, containing patches of oioi. In one arm, raupo is present in an unusual association with mangroves.

Near the main road, walkers may take the inland track to observe farm animals and common introduced bird species, or continue around the edge of the park through regenerating coastal forest dominated by kanuka, tanekaha, kahikatea, rewarewa, kohekohe and titoki. Here native birds such as fantail, grey warbler, tui and native pigeon may be seen.

Omana Park is composed entirely of Waitemata Sandstone, which can be seen in the low cliffs and extensive intertidal rock platforms. Greywacke forms the hills and coastline to the east and is 20–30 m down, beneath the sandstones at Omana. The tops of several 22–million-year-old greywacke stacks, once buried by overlying basal Waitemata rocks, are being exhumed and stick up near low-tide level off Omana Beach.

The intertidal sandstone reefs at Omana Beach have a variety of marine organisms, such as acorn barnacles, small black mussels, sharp-shelled Pacific oysters, Neptune's necklace seaweed, tube worms, chitons, snails and sea anenomes. Gulls, oystercatchers, pied shags and kingfishers are common on the foreshore and cliffs.

Road access off Maraetai-Clevedon Rd, 500 m inland from Duders Beach. Toilet, farm walks — trig loop (1.5 hrs); to pa on point (2 hrs return). Spectacular views from high points. Nearby Duders Beach has safe swimming at high tide, changing sheds, toilets, picnic area.

The most impressive walk in Duder Regional Park is to the tip of Whakakaiwhara Peninsula.

The park has an unusual human history in that it concerns just one tribal group — Ngai Tai, and one European family — the Duders. Whakakaiwhara Peninsula, on which the park is located, was visited by the Tainui canoe in the 14th century. Its crew went ashore and harvested its forest foods, hence the name Whaka-kai-whara meaning 'to eat the bracts of the kiekie vine'. The Ngai Tai occupation is reflected in the number of archaeological sites, most notably Whakakaiwhara Pa, which was associated with seasonal shark fishing and commanded the strategically important Wairoa River mouth.

The peninsula's kauri was logged in the 1850s. Thomas Duder, a survivor of the wreck of HMS *Buffalo* (1840), purchased the 243-ha property from Ngai Tai in 1866. His descendants farmed the property until it became a regional park in 1995. They continue to farm the surrounding land and occupy the historic Duder homestead, 'Rozel'.

Whakakaiwhara Peninsula has been carved by erosion out of greywacke rocks. Fresh exposures can be seen in the intertidal rocky fringe, but they are deeply weathered to clays on the hills.

Most of the park is exotic pasture. Several coastal forest remnants, dominated by taraire, kanuka and tawa, are scattered around the park, with the largest fenced off in the central valley. A few large kauri trees are present within the grazed paddocks beside the walks. Kahikatea, puriri (some very large), kowhai and even a few matai are also present. Resident native bush birds include silver-eye, native pigeon, morepork, tui, fantail, grey warbler and kingfisher. Small flocks of colourful rosellas are common.

Extensive salt marsh, mangroves and shell banks exist (mainly outside the park) to the south where variable oystercatcher and New Zealand dotterel nest. Pukeko, white-faced herons, pied oystercatchers, pied stilts, godwits, gulls and shags frequent all intertidal areas.

Signposted off Clevedon-Kawakawa Bay Rd, 1 km east of Clevedon.

European settlement in the Clevedon area began with the arrival of several Scottish families, 1852–54. The first to settle were Duncan and Marian McNicol from the Isle of Arran. They initially lived in a raupo whare on the property they named 'Glen Albyn', with their nearest Pakeha neighbours being at Papakura. The McNicol family occupied a small cottage until the present two-storey kauri house was built in 1878.

McNicol Homestead (1878), constructed from kauri sawn by Duncan McNicol.

The homestead was donated to Manukau City by Mr B. Ross in 1980 and restored by the Clevedon Historical Society as a district museum. It contains a pioneer kitchen, a settler's bedroom, a sports and trophies room and a military room. This latter display provides a reminder of the battles fought in the area between Maori and the militia in 1863. An item of particular interest is infant Archie McNicol's cap pierced by a bullet during an attack on the nearby Settlers' Stockade (see p. 84) in September 1863.

At the rear of the homestead there is a farm-workers' cottage and a display of old tools and farm implements. In front of the house is a rare example of a 'haha' or stockproof ditch that allows uninterrupted views from the garden.

Clevedon has a number of other sites of historic interest. Near the McNicol Homestead turnoff is the landing reserve where the early settlers disembarked, 1852–63. It contains a stone cairn dedicated to them during centennial celebrations in 1952.

In North Rd, Clevedon, is All Souls Church built for Bishop Selwyn in 1861. It has been altered sympathetically over the years and retains its original Selwyn-style design features. Many local pioneer settlers are buried in the adjoining graveyard.

The roadside forest remnant by the Clevedon Polo Ground contains a flood plain forest type now scarce in the region, consisting of kahikatea, totara, matai, kowhai, pukatea, kaikomako and ribbonwood.

Fifteen minutes south-east of Clevedon on the Kawakawa Bay Rd is Te Tokotoru Tapu Maori Church (1910). Built in meeting-house form, its entrance porch features traditional Maori carvings.

Walking track access (20 mins to beach) from end of Kawakawa Bay Coast Rd, 4 km past Kawakawa Bay. Safe swimming, backpack camping (book with ARC Parks), toilet.

The track to Tawhitokino Beach starts around the rocky foreshore from the carpark (avoid high tide) and then ascends steeply over Papanui Point and down to the north end of Tawhitokino Beach. Regenerating forest on Papanui Point is dominated by tanekaha and kanuka, and a native bamboo-like sedge (*Gahnia lacera*) forms waist-high ground cover. Tanekaha is an unusual conifer because it lacks leaves. The celery-like 'leaves' are actually flattened stems which 'bear' the small cones.

Sandy Tawhitokino Beach is backed by pohutukawa that provide welcome shade in summer. Tanekaha and kanuka, with occasional kowhai, form the main vegetation behind the pohutukawa. At the east end of the beach (20 mins walk), a greywacke reef runs out from Te Kaiahorawaru Point. Shags perch and kingfishers hunt among the rocks and pools at both ends of the beach. The intertidal rocks are covered in Pacific oysters, flea mussels, tube worms, starfish and various algae. Waders feed on the tidal flats.

Tawhitokino was one of the ancestral homes of the Ngati Paoa tribe. Their long occupation is reflected in foreshore middens and kumara pits, as well as Te Papanui and Te Kai a Horawaru — the headland pa located at each end of the beach. Tawhitokino was purchased and milled by Jack Ashby from the 1870s. Mr R. Cashmore later built a timber mill beside the main stream and used three driving dams to 'float' logs down to the mill. The remains of the mill boom can be seen at the stream mouth. Here a small grassy flat is now an attractive backpackers' camping spot complete with toilet.

The area was dug for kauri gum in the early 1900s and then cleared as part of an extensive pastoral grazing run. Papanui Pt and the 4 ha of reserve behind Tawhitokino Beach comprise Auckland's smallest regional park. It has never been officially opened

Tawhitokino Beach.

Park access from Derry Rd, south of Orere Point on East Coast Rd. Toilets, picnic area, BBQs, walks, swimming, camping.

Tapapakanga is a 121-ha coastal farm park, opened in 1995, and located on the western shores of the Firth of Thames. A dominant feature of the park is the winding Tapapakanga Stream, which cuts through terraced alluvial flats and a small gorge to a sandy beach lined with pohutukawa. Here, and on the extensive rock platforms below the main headlands, a number of coastal bird species can generally be seen.

The park includes a signposted circular walk which gives panoramic views of the Firth and the Coromandel Peninsula and passes through several areas of regenerating coastal forest. The walk also passes an excellent example of a prehistoric stonefield garden and through two Maori pa sites. These provide a graphic reminder that

One of the two pou that stand at the entrance to Tapapakanga Regional Park.

Tapapakanga was an important dwelling place for the Marutuahu tribes, Ngati Whanaunga in particular, for many centuries.

The Maori occupation of the land is commemorated by two pou or carved posts standing at the park entrance. An unusual feature of these carvings is the inclusion of a representation of a European, James Ashby. He settled on the land in 1899 and enjoyed a lifelong friendship with the local chief Tukumana Taiwiwi Te Taniwha. James and his wife Rebecca built the existing kauri homestead in 1900 and raised 14 children on the property, most of which remained in the Ashby family ownership until 1990.

Large spreading pohutukawa are a feature of the park's coastline. Many of the steeper slopes are now fenced from stock, and tea tree has been planted. One of the better bush remnants is at the north-western end where there are fine canopy trees of puriri, taraire, rewarewa, mahoe, tawa, tanekaha and tarata. The understorey is now regenerating rapidly, having been fenced off from grazing. *Olearia albida*, a tree daisy up to 6 m tall, is common along this part of the coast, although it is uncommon elsewhere in the Auckland region. Its sweet-scented flower heads appear around autumn.

On East Coast Rd, 8.5 km north of Kaiaua and 21 km south of Kawakawa Bay. Toilets, picnics, bush walks, Waharau Outdoor Education Camp.

Waharau Regional Park is a narrow slice of land extending from the gravelly shore of the Firth of Thames up into the eastern foothills of the Hunua Ranges.

On the southern edge of the park is the sandy bay known as Waihihi. It was a landing place of the Tainui canoe in the 14th century. According to local tradition the area was renowned for its aute (paper mulberry) grove and for its karaka groves, one of which still grows on the foreshore. From the 17th century Waharau was occupied by the Ngati Puku subtribe of Ngati Whanaunga. They still maintain an urupa or burial ground within the park.

Waharau was one of the larger Maori settlements on the coast in the late 1800s and was a summer residence of the Maori King. This tradition is maintained in the Tainui tribe's campground.

In early European times this area provided kauri spars for Europe's navies. In the 1860s kauri and hard beech were felled to supply timber to the gold-rush towns and mines in the Coromandel Ranges, across the Firth. Much of the remaining forest on the eastern Hunua hills was cleared around the turn of the century to establish farms. The poor soils and steepness of the country, among other factors, resulted in the abandonment

Waha-rau, 'the everchanging stream mouth'.

A track through regenerating tanekaha and kauri on the lower slopes of Waharau Regional Park. Beside the track, the ground is covered with reindeer and coral lichens (Cladina confusa *and* Cladia retipora).

of many farms in the 1930s and their gradual reversion to forest, a process which continues today in Waharau Park.

The park was purchased by the ARA, 1970–73, to provide vehicular access to the Hunua water catchment land. It was subsequently developed as a regional park and opened by the Maori Queen in 1979.

Four loop walks of increasing steepness and length (0.5–5 hrs) provide a taste of the regenerating forest and panoramic views across the Firth. The lower slopes are mostly covered in tea tree that provides a nursery for the vigorous regeneration. Species diversity is very high, and on the ground club mosses (*Lycopodium*), filmy ferns, ground orchids, clumps of mosses and liverworts, lichens (some like lumps of coral) are common and give the bush a 'goblin-like' appearance.

Higher parts of the park have a regenerating mixed kauri and hard beech forest on the ridges with abundant tanekaha, rewarewa, hinau and towai. The adjacent gullies are clothed in tawa forest with scattered large emergent rimu, northern rata, kahikatea and totara. Common forest birds are silver-eye, tui, fantail, grey warbler and native pigeon.

The flat between the road and the sea is made of greywacke gravel and alluvial silt that has accumulated as a small delta around the mouth of the Waharau Stream in the 6500 years since sea level rose to its present height (see p. 21). Patches of large puriri, kowhai and karaka are the only remnants of the original coastal forest still growing on this flat. Large flocks of spotted shags often roost on the rocky reefs just to the north.

On either side of East Coast Rd along the western side of the Firth of Thames. Miranda Naturalist Trust information centre, 2 km north of Miranda — displays, toilets, bird watching (especially at high tide). Miranda hot pools.

Near Miranda, shell spit fingers advance during storms into a sheltered muddy enclave, which has been colonised by mangroves.

The 1–2 km wide coastal plain north of Miranda has progressively built out from the old cliff-line over the last 4000 years. The plain is somewhat unusual for it has grown seawards by the addition of a succession of shell and sand ridges, called cheniers.

A ridge of sand period-ically develops on the offshore intertidal mud at an angle to the beach. As it moves towards shore, the ridge accumulates the shells of dead cockles that live in vast numbers in the mudflats. The ridge attaches itself to the shore at its northern end, while the southern end slowly advances southwards and shorewards. Mud builds up in behind the shell ridge and this embayed tidal flat is eventually colonised by mangroves and salt marsh. The shell ridge continues to advance landwards over these habitats mainly during storm events. A modern example of this process can be seen along the coast between Miranda and the Naturalist Trust centre to the north.

The mangrove and salt marsh embayment gradually fills with sediment and becomes ephemeral freshwater ponds and eventually land. A succession of 13 shell ridges is recognisable in the Miranda chenier plain. The oldest ridges at the back are several metres higher than those near the modern shore. Studies of the plain indicate that 3600 years ago sea level was 80 cm higher than present and that it gradually fell until 1200 years ago, after which it has remained relatively constant at close to its present height.

The Miranda hot springs are located several kilometres south of Miranda along the line of a major fault. West of the fault the Hunua Ranges' greywackes have been pushed up and to the east the Firth of Thames has subsided, all in the last few million years. The fault provides a conduit up which deep subterranean water, which is naturally hot, can rapidly rise to the surface. The original hot springs are now tapped to provide the public hot pools.

Miranda was named after the steam corvette HMS *Miranda,* which landed British troops there in November 1863.

The intertidal mud flats of the Miranda Coast support rich cockle beds with fewer pipi, oysters and whelks. Polychaete worms, shrimps, sea slaters (isopods) and sea hoppers (amphipods) are abundant and are an attractive food resource for thousands of wading sea birds.

The embayed tidal mud flats are inhabited by burrowing trough shells (*Mactra ovata*) and the sediment-eating mud snail (*Amphibola crenata*). The salt marsh is colonised by sea rush and shore ribbonwood. Glasswort and sea primrose dominate the salt meadow, and on the more inland flats bachelor's button and bolboschoenus are also present. The dry shell banks have a sparse cover mainly of weeds, including the attractive blue-flowering *Echium plantagineum*.

Miranda is an ornithologist's haven, as it offers one of the most accessible areas in New Zealand to see large numbers of migratory wading birds. A public hide is available for bird watching, with best viewing at high tide when the birds roost along the shoreline. October to March is when the majority of Arctic migrant waders are present. Most abundant are bar-tailed godwit (10–15,000) and lesser knot (7–10,000). There are fewer Eastern curlew, turnstone, sandpiper and red-necked stint (world's smallest wader). Several rarer species of Arctic vagrants are usually present; a few overwinter in New Zealand.

Many of the indigenous wading birds are migrants from the South Island present at Miranda in late summer through winter, outside their breeding season. The most common of these are South Island pied oystercatcher (18,000), wrybill (5000), pied stilt (6–10,000) and banded dotterel (c.150). The wrybill is an endemic New Zealand wader that is unique in the world in having a bill that twists sideways for probing under rocks or shells for food. A small number remain during summer. The other endemic New Zealand wader, New Zealand dotterel, frequently nests at Miranda. Other sea birds present include variable oystercatcher, white-faced heron, spur-winged plover, and various species of gulls, terns, shags and ducks. Total bird numbers at Miranda are fairly consistent due to seasonal replacement of one set of migrants by the other.

The sky darkens as thousands of bar-tailed godwits and knots (New Zealand's commonest migrant wading birds) take to the air along the Miranda coastline.

On either side of East Coast Rd between Wharekawa and Kaiaua, 4–5 km north of Kaiaua. At Whakatiwai Regional Park a track extends inland over pasture up an old logging road to link with Waharau (5 hrs) and Mangatangi (7.5 hrs).

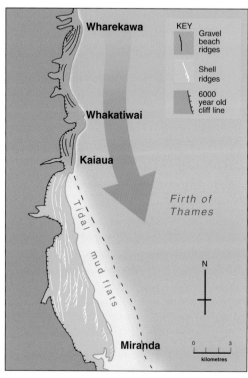

KEY
- Gravel beach ridges
- Shell ridges
- 6000 year old cliff line

Wharekawa

Whakatiwai

Kaiaua

Firth of Thames

Tidal mud flats

Miranda

N

0   3
kilometres

Map showing the distribution of gravel, shell and sand ridges that have accreted onto the west shore of the Firth of Thames in the last 4000 years to form the internationally famous coastal plain between Wharekawa and Miranda.

The coastal plain between Kaiaua and Wharekawa has built up in front of the old cliff-line by the addition of a series of gravel beaches over the last 4000 years.

Greywacke cobbles and pebbles, eroded from the uplifted Hunua Ranges, are carried down streams to the coast. Southwards-moving longshore drift shifts the stones down the coast where they build up as a storm ridge along the back of the beach. Moving southwards from Whakatiwai to Kaiaua the pebbles get progressively smaller and eventually the ridges become sand and shell cheniers of the Miranda chenier plain (**116**). The combination of an actively growing gravel and shell chenier plain as seen along this coast from Wharekawa to Miranda is unique in the world and attracts international attention.

Close study of the gravel ridges around Whakatiwai suggests that sea level has fallen approximately 1 m over the last 4000 years, as the oldest gravel ridges are that much higher than the modern ones. Quarrying of the gravel ridges for aggregate has destroyed large sections of the record. Today the best place to see several unmodified, stranded, gravel ridges is around the narrow Whakatiwai Regional Park.

Little of the original vegetation remains on the coastal plain, as it is almost entirely farmed. The gravel ridges support isolated patches of kowhai forest (one in the Regional Park), pockets of cabbage trees and isolated tanekaha.

Vining Walkway (5–6 hrs to trig and return) crosses private farmland (closed August–September for lambing). Access off Kaiaua Rd, 6 km from Mangatangi. Road access to Mangatangi Reservoir from Workman Rd, off Kaiaua Rd, 9.5 km from Mangatangi. Visitor Centre (open daily).

The walkway crosses grazed paddocks (40 mins, follow orange markers) to reach Vining Scenic Reserve, where the track follows a narrow ridge up to Mangatangi trig (487 m). The walkway and reserve are named after the Vining family, who settled on the land in 1872. Initially the track passes through regenerating forest of tanekaha and kanuka with occasional kauri, rewarewa and towai. In forest gaps on ridge-tops attractive mats of mosses and lichens are common, often associated with filmy ferns, ground orchids, comb fern and an erect clubmoss. Off the ridge there is a dense cover of young tree ferns. There are good views of adjacent forested ridges with emergent northern rata, kauri, tanekaha and hard beech.

Further up there is a dense belt of pure beech, which are the first large trees encountered on the ridge. Above this the

Mangatangi Reservoir from Workman Rd.

ridge becomes flatter and the forest changes to a mixture of tawa, quintinia, hinau, rewarewa, rimu, miro, Hall's totara, kohekohe and pukatea. Climbers are common with rata vines, supplejack, kiekie and a fern (mangemange). Crown fern, bush rice grass, *Blechnum fraseri* and parataniwha form a dense ground cover. Forest birds include tomtit and morepork. Panoramic views are obtained from the open summit. From here you can continue east down the steep forested Ring Track to Workman Rd below Mangatangi Dam (2 hrs) or return by the same route.

Mangatangi Dam, commissioned in 1977, is New Zealand's largest water-supply dam and second largest earth dam. Its 169-ha lake impounds 37 million cu m of water and has an average daily yield of 101,100 cu m. Mangatangi Valley and most of the surrounding land was milled for kauri over a 50-year period from 1870. Logs were floated to booms on the Vining property, transported to Kaiaua by traction engine, and then towed by steam tug to Auckland for milling. Today, some of the region's finest regenerating pole kauri stands grow on the south side of Workman Rd, and are visible from the dam.

Access from Great South Rd, Beach Rd and Southern Park, just south of Papakura centre. Gravel paths provide a level stroll of 15–30 mins.

Grove of towering taraire and pukatea, Kirks Bush, Papakura.

Kirks Bush (5.5 ha) is known locally as 'Papakura's living treasure', which it is. The bush is named after brothers John and James Kirk, who owned it 1884–1919. When the bush was threatened with subdivision in 1921 a public campaign was mounted to preserve it. It was purchased by public subscription and a government grant in 1922. Kirks Bush has been administered as a scenic reserve since 1926 and has had a full-time custodian since 1959.

Tracks pass through a spectacular grove of towering 20-m-tall taraire and pukatea. Although both species are smooth-barked, pukatea stands out with its buttressed roots. The canopy height is rather even, and the dense tree trunks are mainly 40–60 cm in diameter. Other common canopy trees include tawa, puriri, karaka and kohekohe, with occasional rewarewa and rimu.

On the bush fringes are scattered large specimens of kowhai, kahikatea, totara and kauri, some of which were planted. Apart from pukatea and kowhai, all the canopy species have fleshy fruit which attract native pigeons to the forest.

Look for the occasional furrowed roots of puka. It starts life as an epiphyte high in the canopy and then puts roots down to the ground, but does not overpower its host.

The lower parts of many tree trunks are clothed with the climbing fragrant fern and rata vines. The largest common epiphytes are the tank lilies, *Collospermum hastatum*.

In many places the forest is rather open with little undergrowth. Oddly, ground ferns are scarce and the main ground cover is the fallen leathery taraire leaves which decay slowly. Apart from seedlings and saplings of canopy species, hangehange, ponga, and young nikau form the main undergrowth.

The health of Kirks Bush is reflected by the low number of weeds, which is surprising for a small suburban reserve and is a credit to the local friends who maintain it.

Accessible off Red Hill Rd, Papakura; extensive views from the top (5-min walk). A bush reserve is present 400 m down Red Hill Rd, on its southern side.

Red Hill is the extensively eroded remains of a 1-million-year-old basalt volcano. The magma is believed to have come up the Drury Fault, which forms the straight boundary between the uplifted greywacke rocks of the Hunua Ranges to the east and the Manukau lowlands to the west. Several other volcanoes to the south, including the Bombay Hills, erupted along the line of the Drury Fault, 1.5–0.5 million years ago.

Scoria and ash thrown out by Red Hill volcano buried parts of the existing topography and for a time dammed the mouth of Hunua Gorge. Lava flowed west from the vent and now underlies parts of Papakura. Red Hill gets its name from the red volcanic soils on its slopes.

The Maori name for Red Hill is Pukekiwiriki, meaning 'the hill of the little kiwi'. Its flat summit, surrounded on three sides by cliffs, provided an ideal position for the construction of the pa known as Paritaiuru. Its gently sloping northern side

The track to the top of Red Hill (Pukekiwiriki) climbs up stairs cut in layers of bedded volcanic ash.

was defended by a 3-m-deep ditch and 2-m-high bank (still present) that would have been topped by palisades. The remains of a number of storage pits are still visible within the pa.

Paritaiuru Pa is associated in tradition with Marama, a chieftainess on the Tainui canoe. It was occupied by her descendants Nga Marama, and by the tribes of the Waiohua confederation. The village of Te Aparangi on the lower slopes of Red Hill was occupied until July 1863, when it was taken by British troops after a short engagement.

Remnant stands of native forest on Red Hill are dominated by taraire with large specimens of puriri, rewarewa, nikau and tanekaha. Carmine rata vine climbs over Red Hill's cliffs with taurepo shrubs (New Zealand's only member of the gloxinia family), a maidenhair fern (*Adiantum diaphanum*), a tiny filmy fern (*Trichomanes endlicherianum*) and the succulent native pepper (*Peperomia urvilliana*).

Broadleaf forest of puriri, kohekohe and taraire dominate the rather steep scenic reserve along the road. Here there is a 10-min loop track and a branch track down to a gully with abundant supplejack vines, parataniwha and a giant buttressed kohekohe.

Hunua Falls are at the end of Falls Rd, signposted from Hunua. Picnic area, toilets, bush walks. Cosseys Reservoir is at the end of Massey Rd, signposted off Falls Rd.

The Hunua Ranges are a large upfaulted block of greywacke cut by the north-south trending Wairoa Fault. The Wairoa River, which flows over the Hunua Falls, runs along the route of this fault. Greywacke rocks east of the fault have been pushed up higher than those on the west.

About 1.3 million years ago, magma came up the fault-line fracture and erupted to form the Hunua Falls volcano. Lava rose in the volcano's throat and solidified to form a plug of solid grey basalt. The Wairoa River has subsequently eroded away the whole northern side of the volcano and the falls are held up by the hard basalt in its core. The cliffs east of the falls are composed of volcanic ash and scoria, containing several large, fusiform volcanic bombs.

In Victorian times the 'Wairoa Falls' were an extremely popular weekend tourist attraction for Aucklanders. Visitors travelled by steamer to Wairoa South (Clevedon) and took day trips up to the falls.

Visible from the carpark are tall kanuka forest across the river and the rigid silhouettes of tanekaha along the eastern ridge crest. Cross the foot bridge and proceed to a platform in a grove of tawa for a good view of the falls and plunge pool. The dampness is reflected in the abundance of tangled green threads of a moss (*Papillaria*) hanging from the branches of titoki. Along the stream margin are many semi-aquatic plants, both native and exotic. One is a tiny native herb, *Crassula hunua*, named after the ranges, although it also grows elsewhere.

Cosseys Reservoir can be reached by car or via a 1-hr bush walk from the falls carpark. The reservoir, named after the valley's first European owner, Solomon Cossey, was the first of the Hunua water-supply catchments to be developed when a run-of-stream supply was tapped in 1953. Water was fed to the city via 5.6 km of tunnel and

aqueduct, and 24 km of pipeline. The reservoir was commissioned in 1956.

The Hunua Falls cascade over the hard basalt plug of an eroded volcano.

Southern access from end of McMillan Rd via Irish Rd off SH2. Northern access from end of Puketutu Rd, take Beaver Rd exit off SH1. Three hrs end to end or 3 hrs return to summit of Mt William from either end. Crosses private land (closed August–September for lambing).

From the north the track crosses grazed farmland. A side track leads to the highest point on the walkway, Puketutu ('the elevated hilltop') before reaching Mt William trig (369 m) and Mt William Scenic Reserve. Views from both high points extend from the Firth of Thames across to the west coast.

Follow the walkway from McMillan Road for 10 mins over pasture to the start of a 2-hr loop track through splendid forest (scenic reserve). A small

Mt William Walkway passes through open kauri-tanekaha-hard beech forest.

pre-European occupation site consisting of pits and terraces can be seen near the track where the walkway enters the reserve.

The right-hand track begins in the valley bottom where pukatea and taraire dominate. Other broadleaf trees include tawa, rewarewa, puriri, karaka and kohekohe. Occasional tall podocarps are totara, rimu, kahikatea and matai. Understorey plants such as pigeonwood, mahoe, nikau palm, tree ferns, kawakawa, supplejack and low parataniwha can be seen. King fern is present but is not obvious from the track. Native pigeon and other bush birds are common. This broadleaf-podocarp vegetation continues to the upper forest margin, where there is a wonderful view west to a narrow ridge dominated by kauri rickers, tanekaha, hard beech, tawa, rewarewa and occasional rimu and miro.

The track continues over pasture up to the trig or down 300 m over pasture to the kauri ridge to continue the loop back to McMillan Rd. On the ridge dense kauri, most less than 50 cm diameter, dominate with tanekaha and hard beech. The lack of an understorey gives the stand an unusual appearance, probably related to past stock browsing. A low ground cover of ponga, hangehange, pigeonwood, *Coprosma rhamnoides* and crown fern has established after excluding stock. Further down the ridge kanuka becomes frequent with tanekaha and the occasional beech and totara, finally returning back to broadleaf-podocarp forest near the starting point.

Four km east of Pukekohe along Pukekohe East Rd, near the junction with Runciman Rd. The crater is on privately owned farmland but can be viewed from both roads, or from the grounds of Pukekohe East Presbyterian Church in Runciman Rd.

This is the best-preserved explosion crater and tuff ring in the Franklin Volcanic Field. It was produced about 700,000 years ago when a series of explosive eruptions blasted through existing basalt lava flows forming a 1-km-diameter, 80-m-deep, steep-sided crater. A mixture of volcanic ash and rock ripped from the walls of the volcano's neck was thrown out and accumulated around the edge of the crater as a tuff ring. Both Runciman and Pukekohe East Rds run along the crest of this tuff ring where they overlook the crater.

The historic Pukekohe East Presbyterian Church provides an excellent vantage point from which to view the crater. This simple, pitsawn kauri structure was constructed in 1863 during turbulent times. Less than a year after it was consecrated the church had been fortified by the construction of a heavily timbered stockade around its perimeter and was the focal point of a major battle.

On 14 September 1863, a Maori force of 200 attacked the incomplete stockade manned by 17 local settlers. They held the position without losses until they were assisted by two British Regiments, whose casualties numbered three killed and seven wounded. Approximately 40 Maori were killed during the battle. The mass grave of six Maori is marked by a large stone near the church.

The church features several bullet holes in the ceiling and above the pulpit. In the graveyard a bullet mark can be seen on the rear of the tombstone of one Betsy Hodge.

Pukekohe East Crater from the south-east.

Anzac Rd, off Kitchener Rd, provides access to the Massey Memorial Lookout and carpark at the top of Pukekohe Hill. Pukekohe Pioneer Cottage is in Roulston Park, Stadium Drive; toilets.

Pukekohe Hill (213 m) is one of the largest volcanoes in the Franklin field and also the youngest. It erupted 500,000 years ago and is a gently sloping shield volcano built up of numerous overlapping basalt lava flows. These flowed out in all directions to form an extensive apron of lava flows extending south to the Waikato River and north beneath Pukekohe. The upper flows are deeply weathered, forming rich red volcanic soils which are extensively used for horticulture.

Pukekohe Hill lies near the centre of the Franklin Volcanic Field (see pp. 18). From its top, visitors get excellent views over most of the field, which erupted 1.5–0.5 million years ago. A direction table locates points of interest in the surrounding landscape.

European settlement began in the Pukekohe area in 1855, although the main wave of English and South African settlers arrived 1864–65. They ran small cattle herds and grew cereals on land slowly cleared of its dense, puriri-dominated, forest cover. With the construction of the Auckland rail link in 1875, and the introduction of refrigeration in the 1880s, dairying became the predominant economic activity. The town of Pukekohe has been the administrative centre of the Franklin district since 1912.

In 1904 Pukekohe began supplying Auckland with potatoes, and soon became the nation's main source of early potatoes and onions. The warm, north-facing, volcanic soils of Pukekohe Hill are famed for being able to produce three crops every 14 months.

Pukekohe Pioneer Memorial Cottage was thought to have been the Martyn home stockaded by British troops in 1863, but recent research shows that it was a farm-worker's residence constructed by John Martyn, c.1859. Even so, it is an important example of a pioneer cottage. It was relocated and restored by the local historical society as a district museum, and displays china, silverware, colonial artefacts and memorabilia.

Pukekohe Hill is topped by a grove of mature totara, although its Maori name – 'the hill where the kohekohe tree grows' — indicates that it once had a different forest cover.

At the end of Alexandra Redoubt Rd, 1.5 km off Buckland Rd, 2 km south of Tuakau.

Alexandra Redoubt was built between 12 and 28 July 1863 by 300 men of the 65th Regiment commanded by Colonel Alfred Wyatt. The reboubt was sited on a bluff 90 m above the Waikato River, giving views upriver to Koheroa Ridge and downriver to Te Kohanga. A steep pathway with 365 steps gave access to the river. The fortification was not attacked, although the 65th Regiment were involved in a number of battles while based at the Redoubt. On one occasion the redoubt's 63-pounder guns were used to fire on Maori canoes travelling on the river below.

Alexandra Redoubt is today the best preserved of the many earthwork fortifications built in the region, 1862–63. The redoubt retains its parapets, ditches and flanking bastions or caponiers. The stone causeways that flanked the tent lines, and acted as artillery platforms, are still clearly visible, as is the site of the well. The redoubt is surrounded by an old cemetery.

A South African oxalis (*Oxalis purpurea*) having large rose-coloured flowers with yellow centres grows in profusion in the mown lawns around the redoubt. Snowflakes from Europe have become established in the redoubt ditches. Both these species are also commonly growing wild at Waikumete Cemetery (**67**).

The redoubt has regenerating forest on three sides. A short bush track loops down through it and includes a wide view of the river. Kanuka dominates the bush with fine round-headed canopy trees of tarata or lemonwood. Rewarewa, mahoe, mapou and ponga are frequent, with shrubs of kawakawa, akeake, hangehange, *Coprosma areolata* and tanekaha. The bamboo-like sedge, *Gahnia lacera*, and the native iris, *Libertia grandiflora*, are locally common ground-cover plants.

The north-eastern caponier of Alexandra Redoubt contains an obelisk bearing the names of all of the soldiers killed in the district during the New Zealand Wars.

Two km south-east of Patumahoe. Access off Glenbrook Rd via Kingseat, Mauku and Findlay Rds.

St Brides Church is one of the best preserved Selwyn-style timber churches in New Zealand. It was designed by Dr Purchas, then Vicar of Onehunga, and built between 1859 and 1861, under the direction of Bishop Selwyn. The church has an unusual side-entrance porch which is balanced by the vestry on the opposite side. St Brides retains its original furnishings, including its oil lamps. Its timber interior features locally sawn totara framing and a beautiful example of kauri scissor truss roof supports.

St Brides Church, consecrated in 1861.

The church was deliberately sited on the crest of a hill so that its spire would be a landmark for the isolated local settler community. When war appeared imminent between Maori and European in South Auckland only a year after the church had been opened, the Colonial Government decided to fortify St Brides because of its strategic position. A stockade consisting of earthworks and a wall of horizontally laid logs and vertical split slabs was constructed around the church in 1862. Rifle loopholes, 54 of which can still be identified, were cut into the church's outer walls. A major military camp accommodating 2000 troops was based around St Brides during 1863. It was probably for this reason that it was not attacked, unlike the Pukekohe East Church (**123**), which was manned by only a small group of local settlers.

Surrounding the church is a historic cemetery which contains the graves of many local pioneer settlers. Nearby in Pukekohe-Waiuku Rd is the Titi Hill Cairn, which commemorates a battle fought on the spot on 23 October 1863. In this engagement eight Europeans and an estimated 16 Maori died.

Wrights Watergardens (open November–April) are signposted off Mauku Rd, halfway between Mauku and Patumahoe. Here are dozens of ponds developed out of an old basalt quarry containing a vast rainbow of coloured waterlily and lotus flowers. The adjacent Mauku Falls tumble over the edge of a basalt lava flow from the 650,000-year-old Mauku shield volcano in the Franklin Volcanic Field.

Access from Glenbrook Station Rd, off the main road to Waiuku. Open Sundays and most public holidays from Labour Weekend to Queen's Birthday inclusive. Toilets, BBQs and picnic area.

Glenbrook Vintage Railway is an operating steam railway and living museum of New Zealand railway history founded in 1970. It is sited on part of the old New Zealand Railways Waiuku branch line which operated 1922–67. The facility is based around a beautifully restored, rural railway station of the 1920s, complete with station building and platform, refreshment room, signal box, water tank, and station-master's house. The station building was rebuilt by combining the old Glenbrook and Patumahoe Stations. It is manned by volunteer staff dressed in Edwardian NZR uniforms.

The Glenbrook Vintage Railway currently operates or is restoring seven historic steam locomotives, a variety of ex-NZR rolling stock and other railway equipment. It offers hand- and motor-jigger rides and 12-km-return steam-train rides to Fernleigh. A short stop is made at the Pukeoware workshops where restoration and maintenance work can be viewed. The current steam locomotive roster includes an ex-NZR WW engine, an ex-Taupo Totara Timber Co. Mallet engine, and an ex-NZR C Class engine.

The train ride is ultimately to be extended beyond Fernleigh to Tamakae Reserve, Waiuku (**128**). The route passes through grazed farmland developed on the rich red-brown volcanic soils of the weathered and eroded Mauku shield volcano. Just west of the station is the interactive Glenbrook Farm Park, which features displays of farm and exotic animals and birds.

Glenbrook Vintage Railway.

Waiuku Museum (open weekend afternoons); Hartmann House (open daily 10 am–4 pm); Jane Gifford *bookings at Waiuku Information Centre.*

Waiuku is a significant part of the ancestral domain of the Ngati Te Ata tribe, who still maintain Tahuna and Reretewhioi Marae nearby. They once occupied the fortified pa Pae o Kaiwaka near the present Methodist Church, Queen St. The pa protected the northern end of the important Awaroa portage between the Manukau Harbour and the Waikato River.

The present-day historical focal point of the town is the 'Waiuku Heritage Area' located in Tamakae Reserve. This spot is important in local tradition as it was associated with the ancestor Tamakae. He used 'uku' or a soft white clay soap taken from the riverside to enhance his appearance and thus win the hand of a Waikato chieftainess. This gave the tribe a union of great mana, and was the origin of the name Wai-uku.

Waiuku was visited by European traders and missionaries from the 1820s, although the township was not surveyed until 1851. It developed around Waiuku Landing, one of the busiest small ports in the region in the late 19th century (see p. 73). A reminder of the town's maritime past is the *Jane Gifford,* which is moored at the landing. This 20-m sailing scow, which was one of 32 vessels built by Davie Darroch at Omaha, is one of the last of the distinctive flat-bottomed scows which served the small ports of New Zealand under sail, 1875–c.1930. The *Jane Gifford* was restored, 1985–94, and now takes regular trips on the South Manukau, except during winter. White-faced herons hunt for food in the tidal creek by the landing, which is lined by mangroves and introduced cord grass (*Spartina*).

Tamakae Reserve is the location of Hartmann House, a restored pioneer cottage and crafts centre, and also of the Waiuku Museum. Its thematic displays portray the history of the district in remarkable detail. Near the reserve is the Kentish Arms Hotel (1852),

New Zealand's oldest continually licensed hotel. It is one of many pioneer buildings to be found in the town, which is the centre of a thriving pastoral farming district.

The Jane Gifford, *built by Davie Darroch at Omaha in 1908, with Tamakae Reserve beyond.*

Access via Constable and Karioitahi Rds, west of Waiuku. Sandy beach, surf patrol in summer, changing sheds.

The black sand of Karioitahi Beach is backed by flax-covered cliffs eroding into ancient sand-dune deposits.

Karioitahi Rd passes privately owned Lake Whatihua, one of a number of lakes and wetlands that fill hollows between the old sand dunes along the west coast.

The Manukau sand-dune barrier, which forms Awhitu Peninsula and all the high land along the coast south to the Waikato River mouth, was formed by the gradual build-up of a series of coastal sand dunes. Each set of dunes, stabilised by forest, was subsequently partly buried by a later dune advance and so the process has continued over the last 2 million years or so.

The eroding coastal slopes at Karioitahi expose cross-sections through several series of these ancient sand dunes. The steeply sloping layering within many of the sand beds (known as cross-bedding) records the wind-blown advance of the sand-dune front. Vegetation here is mostly flax, but houpara, tauhinu, coastal toetoe, wire vine, knobby sedge and sand coprosma are also present.

The coastline is currently eroding, but this is only a recent phase in its long history of alternating growth and erosion. Maori traditions document the presence of a large, forested sand flat, with dune lakes, wild fowl and eels, which extended westwards from the Peninsula out into the Tasman Sea, c. 250–300 years ago. It would have looked similar to the Whatipu sand flat today (**63**), only considerably larger. This 'Lost Land of Paorae' was eroded away during the 18th century.

The construction of hydro dams and the dredging of the Waikato River in the last 50 years has greatly reduced the supply of sand being fed to the coast. The current accelerated coastal erosion may be a result of this.

Karioitahi Beach has abundant black sand of the magnetic iron oxide mineral titanomagnetite, derived by erosion from the volcanic ash beds of Taranaki's volcanoes to the south. The richest deposits, in dunes south of Waiuku, are quarried as the iron feed stock for the Glenbrook Steel Mill.

Access from Brook Rd, off Awhitu Rd. Picnics, BBQs, toilets, safe swimming at high tide, walks.

Most of Awhitu Regional Park is grassland with numerous clumps of mature exotic conifers and recent plantings of Chinese poplars. Pohutukawa grow on the cliffs with varying degrees of native cover underneath. Young native plantings thrive in many places.

There are two long beaches each backed by a modified swamp that provides habitat for secretive fernbirds and banded rails.

The Brook homestead.

Kahikatea have been planted in the wetlands and the drains will be allowed to fill in, assisting swamp rehabilitation. Around their tidal mouths are areas of mangroves, salt marsh and salt meadow. A lake created in 1985 has patches of the emergent bright green sedge *Eleocharis sphacelata*, and swamp millet dominates the margins.

Commonly seen feeding on the tidal flats are oystercatchers, pied stilts, reef herons and in summer godwits. The small island and reefs on the outer tidal flats are favoured perching sites for gulls and shags. Kingfishers nest in the coastal cliffs, which are made of soft sandstone that accumulated 500,000 years ago as sand dunes when the Manukau Barrier was forming. Ridges in the park are capped by a series of three terraces at around 40 m, 20 m and 12 m above sea level. These were tidal flats eroded into the soft sandstones during warm periods when sea level was at around its present height. Uplift of the peninsula has gradually raised the terraces, so the highest is the oldest and they are progressively younger lower down.

In 1875 English immigrants John and Sarah Brook and their five children settled on this land and built the shanty that still stands on the headland between the two beaches. This was replaced about 1880 by the Brook homestead that was brought around from Orua Bay and erected near the shanty. The Brooks kept cattle and sheep, grew vegetables and supplemented their larder with fish. The central part of the property remained in Brook family ownership until sold to become a Regional Park in 1971. This area contains many old planted trees including a spectacular macrocarpa, some 3.5 m in diameter.

Signal station at end of Manukau Heads Rd (45 minutes drive from Waiuku); views.

Many places of historical interest may be observed en route to Manukau South Head from Waiuku. Tahuna Marae is a focal point of the Ngati Te Ata tribe, with its meeting house Te Uwira, c.1880. The Williams Family Museum in Marae-o-Rehia Rd houses a remarkable range of restored vintage tractors. Until 1863 Pehiakura, the largest Maori village in the district, stood on the ridge now followed by Douglas Rd. It was visited by Governor Hobson and numerous missionaries 1835–63. The hamlet of Pollok was settled by Scots from Pollok Shaws near Glasgow in 1865.

At the west end of Orua Bay is the site of the Maori settlement of Awhitu from which the peninsula takes its name. It was named because of the 'yearning' of Hoturoa, the commander of the Tainui canoe, on leaving the district. The bay was also the site of a mission station established by William Woon in 1834. The 'Red Gum' growing near the beach is claimed to have been planted by Rev. James Hamlin in 1836, making it the region's oldest exotic tree.

Manukau South Head Signal Station has guided vessels over the treacherous Manukau Bar since it was transferred from Paratutai on the Manukau North Head in c.1870. Its viewing platform offers magnificent views over the harbour entrance and the adjoining coastline. To the southwest is the old Awhitu Lighthouse, which replaced an earlier light tower in 1873.

Most of the original forest of Awhitu Peninsula has been cleared, including extensive kauri which was logged from 1835 on. A number of fine regenerating stands of native forest dominated by taraire, with large puriri, tawa, karaka, kohekohe and titoki, are still visible from the roads. Totara and kahikatea are frequently present and several dense stands of regenerating kauri exist (e.g. Kemp Rd). Some gullies contain king fern, pukatea and maire tawake. Native pigeon are common when the broadleaf trees are fruiting. Large and spectacular pohutukawa grow well away from the coast.

Awhitu Peninsula is a series of stabilised and now grassed sand dunes that have built up over the last 2 million years. Whatipu Beach at the south end of the Waitakere Ranges is visible in the distance.

Islands

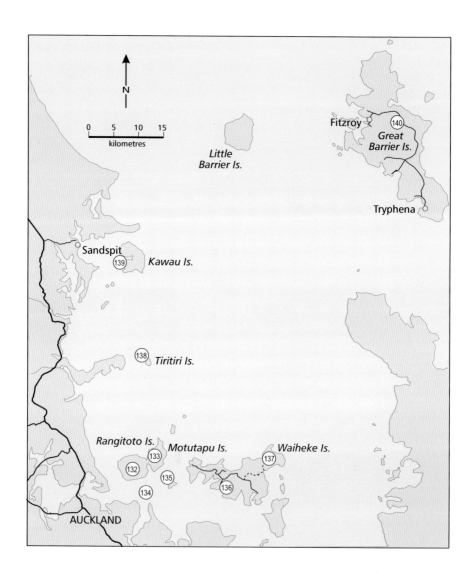

Islands

Rangitoto Island from Tiritiri Matangi Island.

Page 261: Great Barrier Island.

Access by ferry from downtown ferry steps. Toilets, drinking water, rocky paths; walk to top of island (2 hrs return from wharf); can be very hot in summer. Tractor train rides to top.

An old bach near Rangitoto Wharf is surrounded by introduced wild succulent plants.

Rangitoto is the largest and youngest of Auckland's 48 volcanoes. Its eruption, about 600 years ago, was witnessed by Maori inhabitants on Motutapu Island (**133**). Rangitoto erupted in the sea in the entrance to the Waitemata Harbour and was formed during eruptions probably lasting one to several years.

Fire fountaining of frothy lava from the vent threw up a series of scoria cones, while voluminous lava poured out in all directions to build up a gently sloping, circular shield volcano of overlapping lava flows. The steep-sided scoria cones are restricted to the upper, central part of the island with the last cone and its 60-m-deep crater forming the peak. On either side are the remains of several older scoria cones. They form the distinctive 'bumps' on Rangitoto's profile when seen from Auckland.

Most of the lava flows were of the aa variety, in which their molten lava slowly moved along inside a thick carapace of broken-up chilled crust. Near the centre of the island are a number of lava caves that are worth a visit, especially if you have a torch. These formed when hot lava drained out from inside the solidified outer crust of the flows leaving hollow tubes. Access is gained where the roof has collapsed.

Botanically, Rangitoto is unique in New Zealand, with trees growing directly out of basaltic lava which is still in the process of being colonised by pohutukawa. The amount of vegetation cover is related to substrate. The friable scoria cones have already developed a near-continuous forest cover and in places a thin soil layer. In contrast some of the lava flows are still bare, supporting only hardy lichens — crustose forms looking like splashes of paint on the rocks, and low stubbly *Stereocaulon*. Elsewhere lava flows are well forested by pohutukawa, creating a mosaic of forest and open areas over the island.

Pohutukawa are the primary pioneering trees forming growing islands of shade, leaf litter and moisture in which other vegetation can become established. Most of the 'pohutukawa' trees are hybrids with northern tree rata, which occurs on the island's higher slopes. Also unusual are the many plants that live on the branches of trees (epiphytes) elsewhere grow directly on the lava, e.g. puka (**82**), northern tree rata, Kirk's tree daisy, tank lilies, orchids and ferns. Mangroves also grow directly on basalt lava.

Nearly 230 native species of vascular plants grow on the island together with a similar number of wild exotic plants. Some of these are aggressive weeds such as rhamnus, pine trees, pampas grass and tuber sword-fern. Near old bach sites there is often an array of garden remnants, including colourful exotic succulents which are pre-adapted to Rangitoto's hot, dry summers. Rock wallabies and possums have grossly modified the vegetation and have only recently been eradicated.

The most common bush birds are insect feeders, such as fantail, grey warbler, silvereye and shining cuckoo (September–April), which lays its eggs in grey warbler nests. Tui are obvious in the summer when feeding on pohutukawa flowers. On the low, rocky coastal flats there are black-backed gull breeding colonies. People venturing too close to these colonies in the breeding season will be dive-bombed by protective parents.

Rangitoto literally means 'blood red sky'; however, the name is traditionally linked with a fight between Tamatekapua and Hoturoa, the commanders of the Arawa and Tainui canoes respectively. Tamatekapua was injured, hence the name Te Rangi i totongia a Tamatekapua, 'the day the blood of Tamatekapua was shed'.

The island's creation was associated in tradition with the creation of the North Shore volcanic field (see p. 138). Its distinctive peaks were known variously as the Nga Pona toru a Peretu ('the three knuckles of Peretu'), and as Nga Tuaitara a Taikehu ('the dorsal fins of Taikehu'). Rangitoto's link with these illustrious ancestors and its long use as a burial place confirm its great spiritual and symbolic importance to local iwi.

The island provided an early source of basalt for use in building construction (**79, 88**). It was designated a public domain in 1890 under the control of the Devonport Borough Council. Its management over the next 50 years had an impact on the island's naturalness yet created a remarkable assemblage of historic places.

Rangitoto Beacon (1887) was one of the first structures built from Wilson's Portland Cement (**11**). Initially lit by gas, it was electrified in 1929. Quarrying continued on the island and salt ponds were trialled unsuccessfully near McKenzie Bay, 1892–96. The island's well-formed roads and distinctive stone structures were constructed in the 1920s–40s by prisoners and army labour. In this period the north-east coast of the island was used as a graveyard for large sailing vessels and steamers. Many of them were stripped to build Rangitoto's distinctive and controversial baches, constructed when the Devonport Borough Council issued occupation licences to fund developments on the island.

Moisture-loving kidney ferns grow in profusion under pohutukawa.

During the Second World War a Fire Command Post on the summit was used to co-ordinate Auckland's coastal defences. A controlled mine base and other military facilities were constructed at Islington Bay.

Access by ferry from the ferry steps in downtown Auckland. Extensive farm walks, safe swimming at several beaches.

The entrances to the tunnels of an abandoned Second World War underground command post and ammunition store dot the hillside on Motutapu Island.

Motutapu is a low-lying island of 1508 ha. It is mostly composed of ancient greywacke (see p. 35) that can be seen in the coastal rocks around its eastern side. Tightly folded beds of red and green chert are present intertidally at Administration Bay.

The greywacke is overlain by Waitemata Sandstones on the western side of the island and these are exposed in the cliffs north and south of the Islington Bay causeway. A walk north-west from the causeway around the coast at low tide to Administration Bay is of geological interest. In several places, the tops of early Miocene greywacke stacks stick up through their basal Waitemata cover beds in the cliffs (see p. 26). The large plates of a deep-water barnacle are found fossilised in siltstone around the base of a stack on which they lived 20 million years ago.

Motutapu is mantled in volcanic ash from Rangitoto. It is thicker (2–3 m) on the northern parts of the island than the southern, suggesting predominant winds from the south-west during eruptions. The buried site of a prehistoric Maori village has been excavated beneath this ash behind a small beach on the north-west corner of Motutapu. Here dog and human footprints preserved in the fresh ash show that the inhabitants witnessed the eruptions (see p. 75).

Te Motu tapu a Taikehu ('the sacred island of Taikehu') was named by the Tainui tohunga Taikehu as a symbol of his mana and to commemorate a significant place in the Society Islands. The island has the Auckland region's most remarkable, intact and visible archaeological landscape, which reflects at least five centuries of human occupation. Its over 300 recorded archaeological sites include numerous pa, undefended village and garden sites, food-storage pits, cooking areas, middens, and several stone-working areas.

Superimposed on the pre-European archaeological landscape are sites that reflect over 150 years of European occupation. The island has been an extensive pastoral farm since the 1840s, with the main farm settlements being in Emu and Home Bays. During the Second World War the island was an important military base. Barracks (now an outdoor education camp) were constructed at Administration Bay, and coastal defence installations were built in prominent positions. They included a 6-inch gun battery and observation post, numerous pill boxes, and an underground command centre and ammunition store, whose tunnels are of great interest to visitors.

Today the island is a pastoral farm. A 50-year restoration programme was initiated by DoC in 1992. It aims to progressively replant extensive areas using appropriate indigenous species sourced from the island's bush remnants and adjoining islands. At the same time the archaeological landscape will be preserved and interpreted. Many aggressive weeds, such as rhamnus, smilax and pampas grasses, are present. They threaten the success of the programme if weeding is not attended to before areas of pasture are retired for revegetation.

Original native vegetation is limited to the extensive wetlands (some with bush fringes) and a few small patches of forest with no understorey. Both habitats are often grazed by stock. Wetlands along the narrow valley floors include artificial ponds, raupo stands, quaking swamps (mainly of native sedges) and grazed streams with wet grassy margins. Scattered pohutukawa are the main coastal trees with tawapou often present.

Away from the coast a mixture of broadleaf trees dominate the forest stands where mangeao is a common constituent along with puriri, taraire, kohekohe and rewarewa. The small number of large trees, large vines and epiphytes indicates that these trees are not direct remnants of an old forest. Native bush birds are low in numbers, the insect-eating species being the most common. Like other places with extensive wetlands and pastural areas (**9, 24**), paradise shelducks and pukeko are abundant. Pied stilts nest here and wild turkeys roam the hills. Many exotic trees have been planted as shelter belts and ornamentals.

Browsing by possums and rock wallabies has had a major impact, especially on the coastal vegetation. They have recently been eliminated from the island but rats, mice, feral cats, stoats and rabbits are still present on both Motutapu and Rangitoto.

The smooth, ash-draped hills of Motutapu contrast with the pohutukawa-clad slopes of Rangitoto beyond.

Access by private or charter boat, no scheduled ferries. Farm walks, swimming at northern beach.

Motukorea's old stone wharf provides a dry landing at high tide for visitors disembarking from the old trading schooner Te Aroha.

Motukorea is one of Auckland's youngest volcanoes. It erupted about 10,000 years ago when the Waitemata Harbour was still a forested river valley (see p. 20). Initial eruptions produced a large explosive crater surrounded by a relatively high tuff ring. The eroding remains of the north-east sector of the tuff ring form the high cliffs on that side of the island. The layers of bedded ash (tuff) contain rock fragments ripped from the walls of the volcano's throat, such as greywacke, Waitemata Sandstone, Parnell Grit and pieces of fossil shell. These include shells of the Sydney mud cockle, *Anadara,* which became extinct in New Zealand about 100,000 years ago.

Subsequent fire-fountaining produced scoria cones within the explosion crater. The last cone, which has a deep crater, forms the highest point of the island, with remains of earlier cones forming surrounding knolls. Extrusion of lava from around the base of the cones formed an apron of flows extending 2 km to the south and west. These flows probably overtopped and removed the tuff ring around this sector of the volcano.

Motukorea — 'island of the oystercatcher' — was cleared of forest, settled and cultivated in pre-European times. Stone heaps and retaining walls mark the sites of early gardens, and earthworks from three defended pa remain. The largest pa is on the rim of the main cone, with smaller pa on the eastern cliffs and the western scoria knoll.

The earliest recorded European visitors to Motukorea were Richard Cruise, Samuel Marsden and John Butler in 1820, when kumara and potato were being grown on the island by local Maori. William Brown and John Logan Campbell purchased the island from Ngai Tai chiefs (see p. 80) from both Maraetai and the Hauraki area. Campbell and Brown lived in a large raupo whare constructed for them by Ngai Tai on the western flats and used the island as a trading base for a few months before moving in to the newly established Auckland township. Brown sold the island in 1873 and it was subsequently farmed by the Featherstone (1879–1903) and Alison (1906–46) families.

The sites of their farm houses are marked by introduced trees, building foundations and a stone-lined well on the north-west flat near the stone wharf.

The Alisons were principal shareholders in the Devonport Steam Ferry Company, and Motukorea became a popular destination for ferry loads of picnickers between 1900 and 1940. The remnants of a wooden wharf used by these ferries can be seen beneath the cliffs at Davis Memorial Bay. A cairn behind this bay marks the gifting of the island to the people of Auckland by Sir Ernest Davis in 1955.

Five obsolete paddle steamers were abandoned on the west side of Motukorea by the Devonport Steam Ferry Company between 1908 and 1914. The remains of their hulks can still be seen near the old stone wharf at low tide. Small red lampshells attach by their stalks to the undersides of low-tide basalt boulders nearby — one of only a few places (including Rangitoto) where they can be seen intertidally.

Fauna and flora values are low for this grassy island. The coastal margin, however, is ideal habitat for small numbers of variable oystercatchers, reef herons and several pairs of New Zealand dotterels which nest there. Banded dotterel also visit the island. Motukorea is now thought to be free of all introduced animal pests.

The island has been grazed for over 150 years. The rank exotic pasture, dominated by Kikuyu grass, contains patches of bracken fern and the soft native meadow rice grass. The only significant bush is on the north-eastern tuff cliffs, where pohutukawa, houpara, ngaio, mahoe and whau are present. On the flats are individual specimens, groves and lines of planted native and exotic trees, especially pohutukawa and macrocarpa. Aggressive weeds such as rhamnus, smilax, bone-seed, pampas grass and privet species are present.

Motukorea is one of Auckland's youngest volcanoes. Lava flows form the flats and underlie the sea in the foreground (west side).

Access by ferry from the ferry steps in downtown Auckland. Farm walks, changing sheds, safe swimming beaches, kiosk, BBQs, picnic areas, camping.

Most of Motuihe is made of eroding Waitemata Sandstones and Parnell Grit (see p. 26–28) that overlie older greywacke. A 20-m-thick bed of Parnell Grit forms most of the high cliffs around the east side of the island. Basal Waitemata sequences that record the subsidence and formation of the deep-water Waitemata Basin, 20 million years ago, can be seen at the south-east end of Ocean Beach and around Limestone Point, on the south-west coast. At the latter locality there are fossilised lampshells, octocorals and giant barnacle plates.

Motuihe is a shortened version of Motu a Ihenga, 'the island of Ihenga'. The name commemorates the visit made to the island by Ihenga, an illustrious ancestor of the Arawa tribe, in the 14th century. In local tradition the human occupation of Motuihe extends back to the most ancient inhabitants of the region, the Turehu, renowned for their weaving and culinary skills (see p. 71).

Motuihe has a rich assemblage of pre-European archaeological sites including fortified pa, open settlements, karaka groves, cultivations and food-storage pits. Te Rae o Kahu, the pa at the south-east end of Ocean Beach, provides one of the finest examples of a headland pa in the region.

Motuihe came into European ownership in 1839. William Brown and John Logan Campbell farmed the island in conjunction with Motukorea (**134**) in the 1840s–50s. Many of the olive trees planted by Campbell around the farm settlement are still fruiting.

The headland at the north-west end of the island has terracing, areas of tarseal, gun emplacements, a water tower and exotic trees as reminders of its colourful European history. A human quarantine station operated on this headland, 1874–1929. A cemetery

contains the graves of many who died, in particular during the 1918 influenza epidemic.

During the First World War the station was used as a prisoner-of-war camp, best known for the escape of German Count Felix Von

The northern headland of Motuihe Island was the site of a quarantine station, prisoner-of-war camp, health camp and naval training establishment.

A 2-m-thick bed of flaggy limestone (basal Waitemata Group), made of fragmented shallow-water shells, forms artistic shapes on the south-west shore of Motuihe Island.

Luckner and his crew in 1917. From 1929 to 1940 the quarantine buildings were used as a children's health camp.

During the Second World War, the northern end of the island became the naval training establishment HMNZS *Tamaki*, which remained in use until 1962. The landmark brick and concrete water tower is the only substantial structure that remains from this phase of Motuihe's history.

The many exotic trees on this northern part of the island include Norfolk pines, several *Pinus* species, especially Aleppo pine (*P. halepensis*) and loblolly pine (*P. taeda*), Moreton Bay fig, gum trees, olive trees which now grow wild, Italian alders, holm oaks and a Queensland box. Rhamnus, a tall shrub of the Mediterranean, is probably the most aggressive weed on the island. It has been present for over 70 years.

Most of the island is farmed but two distinctly different patches of forest exist in the south. The smaller eastern patch is in two gullies and is dominated by taraire with areas of kohekohe and a few puriri and karaka. Because this area was only recently fenced from stock there is little understorey. The larger unfenced forest patch, facing west, contains many large pohutukawa with smaller trees of mahoe, karaka, kohekohe and kanuka underneath. Puriri are present at the southern end. Scattered pohutukawa grow right around the coast of Motuihe.

Forest birds are limited and include native pigeon, tui and fantail. The intertidal reefs provide ideal feeding grounds for New Zealand dotterel, variable oystercatcher, white-faced heron, kingfisher and ducks which are all best seen at South-east Beach. Cats and rats have had a heavy impact on the native fauna. DoC is currently attempting to remove these predators along with the rabbits.

Access from Gordons Rd, off O'Brien Rd, c. 5 km south of Ostend. Picnics, toilets, camping, safe swimming for children at high tide, walks, horse riding.

Whakanewha, meaning 'to shade the eyes from the setting sun', was occupied by Maori for many generations, as is reflected in numerous shell middens and the pa located above the eastern end of the bay. In the 1850s the Maori inhabitants of Whakanewha grew large quantities of fruit and vegetables for sale in the Auckland market, and received regular visits from Auckland-based missionaries.

Samuel Wood purchased part of the land and settled on it c.1855. His occupation was disputed by local Maori not consulted in the transaction and they burnt down his house as ritual plunder. The Crown confirmed Wood's title in 1858, but he sold it soon after. His house site is still identifiable near the wetland on the east edge of the park.

Whakanewha was purchased in 1994 for development as a regional park. It extends from the ridge line down to the coast, where three small streams enter Whakanewha (Rocky) Bay. The forested catchments of these streams are the strength of the park. Inland much of the vegetation is mature coastal forest dominated by broadleaf species (taraire, puriri, karaka, kohekohe, tawa) and podocarps (kahikatea, tanekaha). Some pohutukawa, rimu and kauri are also present. Native pigeon, tui and smaller bush birds are common. Regenerating kanuka and manuka shrublands cover most of the lower slopes and many of the ridges, all of which were in pasture 50 years ago.

A large wetland on the southern stream is dominated by raupo with bolboschoenus and swamp millet. Bittern, banded rail, spotless crake and fernbird are secretive birds all found in this swamp. On the tidal flats white-faced heron, pied stilt, Caspian tern, godwit, ducks, pied and variable oystercatchers and New Zealand dotterel feed.

Waiheke is without possums, which means that the usually possum-browsed mainland trees, such as kohekohe, pohutukawa, tree rata and totara, thrive, flower and set copious fruit.

Whakanewha Regional Park (270 ha) consists of a beautiful crescent-shaped sandy beach backed by hills covered in mature taraire and kohekohe coastal forest interspersed with areas of regenerating shrublands.

Walking access from the end of Man-O-War Bay Rd; entrance to Stony Batter Reserve 3 km; Stony Batter south to Opopo Bay 2.5 km; Stony Batter north to Hooks Bay 2 km. Walkway crosses private land, closed for lambing (August–September). Bring torch for exploring tunnels; panoramic views.

The walkway crosses farmland at the remote eastern end of Waiheke Island, giving magnificent 360-degree views over Waiheke Island and the Hauraki Gulf.

The boulders strewn over the hilltops are volcanic breccia. These are the only remains of two large andesite strato-volcanoes that erupted near the eastern end of Waiheke about 15 and 8 million years ago, at the same time as similar volcanoes were active on the adjacent Coromandel Peninsula. At that time the

Fluted boulders on the Stony Batter hilltops are the eroded remains of two large andesite volcanoes.

land was continuous across to Coromandel, as the Firth of Thames did not begin to subside until a few million years ago.

Beyond the Stony Batter trig station are the remains of a coastal gun battery constructed by the Government during the Second World War when a Japanese attack seemed imminent. The battery included three 9.2-inch guns, each weighing 128 tons with a range of 26,000 m. The gun emplacements were connected by tunnels to an underground complex which included barracks, a cook house, hospital, engine room, plotting rooms and magazines. The complex was never fully completed and the guns were fired only once, for practice in 1947. The guns and equipment were removed in 1958 leaving the emplacements, tunnels and underground complex, which are well worth exploring by torchlight.

The Hooks Bay track begins beyond the gun emplacements and proceeds through open farmland to a small gravel beach at the eastern end of the attractive main bay. The Opopo Bay track passes through farmland and native bush to a gravel beach.

Several small forest remnants, dominated by the plum-fruited taraire, are present near the tunnels. Native pigeon are common and their favoured perch sites are well marked on the ground by low mounds of pigeon-processed taraire kernels and seedlings.

Access by ferry from Gulf Harbour (Whangaparaoa Peninsula) or Auckland. A Nature Reserve administered by DoC. Wharf, toilets, information centre by lighthouse, bush walks.

Tiritiri Matangi, meaning 'buffeted by the wind', lies 4 km off the end of Whangaparaoa Peninsula. It is eroded out of ancient greywacke rocks, which can be seen around its shores. The island was occupied by the Kawerau subtribes and later Ngati Paoa, largely in conjunction with the seasonal use of the shark-fishing ground to the west. This occupation was concentrated on the west coast of the island where there was easy access to the sea. The focal points of pre-European settlement were Tiritiri Matangi Pa, located at the north end of Hobbs Bay, and the now-eroded Papakura Pa at the north-west end of the island.

Tiritiri was purchased by the Crown in 1841 although sporadic Maori occupation continued until 1856. Between 1863 and 1971 the island was leased, with the Hobbs family grazing it in conjunction with their Whangaparaoa property for 70 years. The island had been cleared of almost all of its original coastal forest by 1900.

Since 1865 the 20-m Tiritiri lighthouse has guided gulf shipping. It is the centrepiece of New Zealand's best-preserved historic lighthouse complex, which includes a signal station, several fog horns, and two lighthouse-keeper's cottages. The lighthouse was electrified in 1955 and has been automated since 1981.

In 1971 Tiritiri was added to the Hauraki Gulf Maritime Park. Since 1984, over

A young planted forest has replaced Tiritiri's rank pasture. Visitors are landed at the wharf by public transport.

Friendly takahe enjoy a water trough near the visitor centre on Tiritiri.

250,000 locally propagated native trees have been planted out on the island by thousands of volunteers of all ages. Initially pohutukawa was the main plant used, with lesser numbers of hardy shrubs such as karamu, karo, flax, whau, mahoe and cabbage tree to shade out the thick grass and provide shelter for later plantings of taraire, kohekohe, puriri and others. The revegetation programme is now virtually completed.

As the new plantings have grown up, many endangered native birds have been successfully introduced to the island including red-crowned parakeet, North Island saddleback, brown teal, whitehead, takahe, North Island robin, little spotted kiwi, stitchbird and kokako. Forest birds that survived on the island and are now thriving include native pigeon, tui, bellbird, kingfisher, fantail, silver-eye, grey warbler and a few morepork.

Other native birds breeding on the island include pukeko, harrier, little blue penguin, variable oystercatcher and grey-faced petrel. With the removal of the Polynesian rat (kiore) in 1993 both fauna and flora have benefited. Kiore were eating invertebrates, lizards, eggs and young birds as well as the fruit, seeds and bark of many plants. Today weeds are being controlled, with Japanese honeysuckle proving to be the most difficult.

The Supporters of Tiritiri Matangi group was formed in 1988. It has greatly assisted the restoration programme on the island through material contributions, donations, physical support, involvement in management and promotion of Tiritiri. The island is New Zealand's most successful restoration project involving the public. Its success has been instrumental in establishing the revegetation project on Motutapu Island (**133**). Nearly 20,000 people visit Tiritiri annually and it is the only place where the public can easily see such a range of threatened bird species in a natural setting.

Access by ferry from Sandspit (near Warkworth) or downtown Auckland. Mansion House Bay has kiosk, changing sheds, safe swimming, walking tracks (to old coppermine, 2 hrs return).

The old stone and brick chimney of the pumphouse built to dewater the shafts of the Kawau copper mine during the attempt to reopen it 1854–5.

The island was named Te Kawau tu maro ('the cormorant that stands sentinel') by the ancestor Toi te Huatahi. Kawau was occupied for generations by Ngati Tai and then the subtribes of the Kawerau confederation until the 1840s. One of the few surface archaeological features that reflects this long occupation is Momona Pa, located on the ridge south of Mansion House.

Copper and manganese were discovered on Kawau in the early 1840s and copper was mined 1844–51 and 1854–55, with an island community of over 300 people. Reminders of this colourful era can be visited at South Cove. These include several old shafts and adits and the prominent pumphouse chimney. The stabilised skeleton of the copper ore smelting house (1849) can be visited by ferry in Bon Accord Harbour.

The copper mine was sited on a 3-m-thick, ore-bearing lode that lay within the surrounding greywacke rocks. Small lava flows were extruded onto the deep ocean floor, 150–200 million years ago. Associated with these were submarine hydrothermal springs called 'black smokers'. Metal sulphides, oxides and silica, rich in iron, manganese and copper, precipitated from these plumes of hot mineral-rich water and collected around them on the sea floor.

These deposits were deeply buried, tilted to vertical and later uplifted and eroded to uncover the mineralised lode. Near the surface, weathering has oxidised the sulphides leaving rust-coloured iron oxide (limonite) and sporadic blue and green copper carbonates (azurite and malachite minerals), which stain the cliff above the mine entrance.

The ore was transported along tunnels in small hand-pushed railway trucks and hauled to the surface up shafts using horse-powered whims. Most of the mine was sunk below sea-level and water seepage was a major problem, requiring constant pumping.

Sir George Grey purchased Kawau in 1862 and proceeded to upgrade and enlarge Mansion House (originally built for the copper mine manager) as his private residence, guided by architect Frederick Thatcher. After Grey's retirement as Governor and later as Premier of New Zealand in 1877, he entertained many prominent visitors at Kawau. Grey sold the island in 1888 and it was subdivided in 1906. Mansion House saw a succession of owners who used it variously as a private home or boarding house. In 1977 it was purchased for the Hauraki Gulf Maritime Park. Mansion House has been restored to what it was like in the time of Sir George Grey and is open to the public. Mansion House Bay is the focal area of the DoC administered public reserve, which covers 10 percent of the island.

Plants in and around Mansion House Bay are a peculiar mixture of unusual exotic species introduced by Grey. Many, such as Mauritius hemp and brush bloodwood, have become wild. Fine specimen trees near Mansion House include Chilean wine palms (from S. America), bunya bunya (Queensland), hoop pine (Australia and New Guinea), Moreton Bay fig (E. Australia), camphor laurel (China, Japan), giant bird of paradise (South Africa) and a Himalayan bamboo (*Bambusa balcooa*). A holm oak (Europe) and an African coral tree kaffir boom (*Erythrina caffra*) on the beachfront are still recovering after storm damage. Several of these trees are scarce in New Zealand.

Kookaburra and four species of wallaby, also introduced by Grey, still thrive on the island. Browsing by wallabies is preventing native forest regeneration and they are considered as much a pest as the possums that have devastated the pohutukawa. Wallabies are now being fenced out from conservation land around Mansion House Bay, except for an enclosure where they are kept for visitors to see.

Peacocks and introduced North Island weka are often seen on the lawns around Mansion House. Further afield in the tall tea tree and pine plantations you may hear and see fantail, silver-eye, tui, shining cuckoo, native pigeon, grey warbler, bellbird and kaka. Morepork are heard at night. The numerous brown kiwi that are present on the island are thought to be descendants of birds released by Grey. Their shrill calls and cries are heard at night when they hunt for earthworms and other invertebrates.

Mansion House, former home of Sir George Grey, on Kawau Island.

Access via scheduled ferry services from downtown Auckland and scheduled air services from North Shore and Mangere Airports. Buses and tours are available on the island. Information on the island's heritage and 100 km of walking tracks available from DoC.

The imposing pinnacles and bluffs around Mt Hobson (Hirakimata) in the centre of Great Barrier Island are the eroding remnants of a violent rhyolite volcano that was active 8–9 million years ago.

Great Barrier (Aotea) is a natural paradise providing a memorable day visit or longer stay. Lying 100 km north-east of Auckland, it is the largest island off the North Island coast. It has a rugged landscape dominated by spectacular rocky bluffs rising to the high point of Mt Hobson (Hirakimata, 621 m). The west coast includes five harbours — the most spectacular of which is the drowned river system of Port Fitzroy. The east coast features beautiful sandy beaches ideal for swimming and surfing. Sixty per cent of the island is reserve land administered by DoC.

The island is predominantly of volcanic origin. Andesite stratovolcanoes, rather like modern Mt Ruapehu, erupted here at the north end of the Coromandel volcanic chain 10–18 million years ago. Their rubbly breccias and dark grey flows form the coastline around most of the island, except in the north and at Harataonga, where the underlying greywacke rocks (see p. 35) rise above sea level.

Domes of viscous rhyolite lava were intruded, and superheated ignimbrite flows were erupted from three centres 5–10 million years ago. These are the lighter-coloured rocks that form Rakitu Island and the Te Ahumata and Mt Hobson highlands in the centre of Great Barrier. Bush tracks lead to the Kaitoke hot springs — a tame reminder of the violent volcanic eruptions that once formed the island.

Great Barrier has been linked by land to the North Island for most of the last 18 million years. During the Ice Ages of the last 2 million years, sea level has yo-yo'd up and down, periodically flooding the Colville Channel and making Great Barrier an island. The most recent occurrence was just 12,000 years ago when sea level rose at the end of the Last Ice Age (see p. 21).

Great Barrier possesses outstanding habitats harbouring threatened flora and fauna. The island is the largest area in the country free from possums, mustelids and hedgehogs.

Most of its forests are still recovering from logging and fire, which is reflected in the abundance of manuka and kanuka. The flora contains a rich diversity of over 500 species of vascular plants. The summit of Hirakimata is clothed in unique unmodified kauri, yellow-silver pine, manoao forest. Several plants are restricted to this area, such as yellow-silver pine, tawari, southern rata, *Metrosideros parkinsonii*, *Archeria racemosa* and *Epacris alpina*. Here too is the world's main nesting area of the endangered

Great Barrier is the stronghold for the threatened New Zealand endemic brown teal (pateke), which total c.1500 birds on the island. These small ducks are commonly seen resting in fields, on harbours, by creeks and estuaries during the day, and are most active at night.

endemic black petrel (c.800 pairs) and smaller numbers of Cook's petrel. There are two endemic plants present in the central shrublands — a shrubby thick-leaved daisy, *Olearia allomii,* and a prostrate kanuka, *Kunzea sinclairii.*

The island has high populations of North Island kaka and banded rail, and is one of the few offshore islands having spotless crake and fernbird. A wide variety of sea birds nest on and around the island, and its beaches are home to many shoreline birds including the New Zealand dotterel. Great Barrier has the only known island population of the endangered Hochstetter's frog and supports a remarkable 13 species of skinks and geckos.

Whangapoua Estuary is the only large estuarine habitat on the island. It is one of the least modified in New Zealand and contains the highest bird diversity of any area on the island. West of Claris is Kaitoke Swamp, the region's largest freshwater swamp (266 ha), which contains brown teal, bittern, spotless crake, banded rail, fernbird and a pink flowering swamp orchid, *Spiranthes sinensis.*

Great Barrier has a rich human history spanning the entire chronology of the region's human settlement. In local tradition the island is referred to as 'the scales of Maui's fish' (see p. 70) and is associated with many ancestral canoes including the Aotea whose visit provided the origin of the island's Maori name.

Aotea was occupied for generations by tribal groupings of Tainui and Arawa descent, and from the 17th century by Ngati Wai, who still maintain marae at Katherine Bay. The long Maori occupation is reflected in a remarkable range of pre-European gardening, food-processing, settlement, defensive and sacred sites. Clearly visible examples can be seen at Medland's Beach and at Putuwhera Pa at Pa Beach, Tryphena.

Aotea was named Great Barrier by Captain James Cook in 1769 as it sheltered the waters of the Hauraki Gulf. Its early European history concerned successive forms of resource exploitation beginning with New Zealand's first copper mine in the north in 1842. Firewood and kauri timber extraction began in this period and extended for a century. The Kauri Timber Co. Mill at Whangaparapara was the largest mill of its type in the southern hemisphere, 1909–16. Near Port Fitzroy are the spectacular remains of one of the largest kauri driving dams ever built (see p. 92).

An early industry of note was ship building. The barque *Sterlingshire*, built at Nagle Cove (1841), was the largest sailing ship to be built in Australasia. The island's rugged coast has been the site of numerous shipwrecks including that of SS *Wairarapa,* which struck near Miner's Head at full steam in heavy fog in 1894 with the loss of 121 lives.

The discovery of gold and silver at White Cliffs (Te Ahumata) in 1892 led to a major mining enterprise based around the town of Oreville (population 500). The remains of its stamper battery can still be seen beside the Whangaparapara Rd. The region's largest whaling station was located opposite Whangaparapara Wharf, 1959–61.

From the 1850s the island's isolated pioneer families developed farms that provided a wide diversity of produce — including livestock, wool, fruit and honey. The present-day community, noted for its self-reliance, individuality and conservation ethic, is reliant on farming, fishing, marine farming and increasingly tourism.

Bus tours on the main Port Fitzroy-Tryphena Rd give visitors spectacular views over the pristine Whangapoua Estuary and Arid Island (Rakitu). Stops are sometimes made to view awesome Windy Canyon eroded through massive ignimbrite. The route between Awana and Medland's offers beautiful vistas, and inspiring archaeological sites can be seen on the Kaitoke-Medland's coast. The road then climbs over a forested saddle before emerging at picturesque Tryphena Harbour.

Medland's Beach is one of a number of idyllic, white sand, surf beaches on the east coast of Great Barrier Island.